FOUNDATION PROGRAMME

250

SJTs

FOR FOUNDATION YEAR ENTRY

Olivier Picard, Gail Allsopp, Lydia Campbell

1st edition

Published by ISC Medical
97 Judd Street, London WC1H 9JG
www.iscmedical.co.uk - Tel: 0845 226 9487

1st edition: ISBN13: 978-1-905812-16-5 (September 2012)
Reprinted October 2012

A catalogue record for this book is available from the British Library.

Printed in the United Kingdom by:
Purbrooks Ltd, Gresham Way, Wimbledon Park, London SW19 8ED

The authors have, as far as possible, taken care to ensure that the
information given in this text is accurate and up to date. However,
readers are strongly advised to confirm that the information with re-
gards to specific patient management complies with current legislation
and guidelines.

The information within this text is intended as a study aid for the purpose of the Foundation Programme selection examinations. It is not
intended to be, nor should it be used as, a medical reference for the
direct management of patients or their conditions.

Contents

The SJT Exam

1.1 Format of the SJT exam

The exam consists of 70 scenarios, which need to be addressed in 2 hours 20 minutes (averaging 2 minutes per scenario).

- 60 of the scenarios are live scenarios, i.e. they are marked and used for selection purposes.

- 10 of the scenarios are test scenarios, i.e. they are not used for selection purposes but are simply used to validate new scenarios for future use.

In the exam, you will not know which scenarios are used for selection purposes and which scenarios are used for testing purposes.

The scenarios address situations that candidates could expect to encounter during their FY1 year and come in two possible formats:

Format 1: Ranking (representing 2/3 of the questions in the exam)
You are presented with a situation and given five possible responses to that situation. Your task is to rank those five responses in order from the most to the least appropriate.

Format 2: Multiple Choice (representing 1/3 of the questions in the exam)
You are presented with a situation and eight possible responses to that situation. Your task is to select the three responses which, when considered together, would constitute the most appropriate response to the scenario.

The variety of format reflects the fact that some situations can be answered by a single action or set of actions which can be considered in isolation from the other options available (Format 1: Ranking), whereas other situations warrant a response requiring multiple actions that can be taken together (Format 2: Multiple Choice).

1.2 What the SJT exam tests

The SJT exam is designed to assess candidates against a long list of specific criteria, which can be summarised as follows:

Commitment to professionalism

- Is reliable and punctual
- Takes responsibility for own work and actions
- Demonstrates commitment and enthusiasm for own role
- Takes responsibility for own health and well-being
- Understands own role as a doctor and is able to own up to mistakes
- Is honest and trustworthy towards patients and colleagues
- Deals effectively with unreasonable/unsafe behaviours
- Challenges others when necessary
- Has an appropriate understanding of ethical issues

Coping with pressure

- Remains calm and in control, and shows good judgement under pressure
- Can cope with stress and emotions, and seeks support appropriately
- Can deal with the consequences of mistakes and decisions
- Is flexible and resilient
- Can manage uncertainty and ambiguity
- Deals with conflict appropriately

Effective communication

- Is a good listener
- Ensures the communication setting is appropriate
- Understands and uses non-verbal communication effectively
- Communicates accurately, concisely and clearly
- Asks questions appropriately and is available to answer questions
- Adapts the amount, style and content of information to the needs of the situation and the audience
- Communicates sensitively and diplomatically, but is assertive when required
- Is able to negotiate
- Clarifies information to check own understanding
- Keeps colleagues and patients informed appropriately
- Is concise and clear, and has high standards of written communication

Patient focus

- Shows respect for patients and is able to gain their trust
- Is available to patients, but also maintains appropriate boundaries
- Respects patients' beliefs and values
- Places patients at the centre of their care and works with patients
- Shows interest, empathy and compassion towards patients
- Is willing to spend time with patients and relatives, and build a rapport
- Deals with patients courteously and provides reassurance
- Maintains patient safety at all times

Effective teamwork

- Understands the roles, skills and responsibilities of others, and utilises the most appropriate person for a task or situation
- Is aware of own role and responsibilities within the team
- Builds a rapport and is willing to provide support, assistance and advice
- Respects others and values their opinions and contributions
- Delegates and shares the workload effectively
- Is willing to take directions from others and ask for advice

1.3 How the SJT exam is marked

The two types of scenario are marked slightly differently.

Format 1: Ranking

In this format, you are asked to rank five possible responses to a scenario, from the most appropriate to the least appropriate. The examiners will have decided on an "ideal" answer and you will be marked according to how much your own answer deviates from that ideal answer. The maximum mark you can get from a question is 20.

For example: let's assume that the ideal ranking for the options is ACEBD, where Option A is the most appropriate, and Option D is the least appropriate. Your score will be calculated according to a matrix which may look like this:

Correct ranking	If you ranked it 1st	If you ranked it 2nd	If you ranked it 3rd	If you ranked it 4th	If you ranked it 5th
A	4	3	2	1	0
C	3	4	3	2	1
E	2	3	4	3	2
B	1	2	3	4	3
D	0	1	2	3	4

If you ranked the options correctly you would score 5 x 4 = 20.

However, if you ranked the options EACBD instead, your score would be calculated as follows:

- For ranking option E 1st: 2 points
- For ranking option A 2nd: 3 points
- For ranking option C 3rd: 3points
- For ranking option B 4th: 4points
- For ranking option D 5th: 4points
- **Total: 16 points**

Note: Different questions may be scored according to different matrices.

Format 2: Multiple Choice

In this format, you are asked to select the three most suitable options out of a list of eight. The marking is simple: you will score 4 points for each option that you select correctly. The maximum score is therefore 12 points.

If the ideal answer is 'ABC', those who have selected all three correct options will score $3 \times 4 = 12$ points. Those who have selected only two of the three correct options will score $2 \times 4 = 8$ points.

1.4 How the "ideal" answer is determined

Before finding its way into the exam, each question is reviewed by a panel of experts. If the experts reach a consensus regarding the answer then that will be the taken as the "ideal" answer. This is the answer against which you will be scored. If the experts cannot agree on what the ideal answer should be then the question is reworked or rejected.

This implies that the ideal answer is the one that most people on the expert panel deem to be reasonable. That does not mean that everyone agreed with it, but simply that there was enough agreement to justify its inclusion in the examination paper.

In practice, there could be rankings which would be seen as suitable by many candidates but would not score the top mark simply because they do not conform to the ideal answer agreed by the experts. If high-performing candidates consistently came up with a ranking that was slightly different to the expert panel's ideal answer, there is provision within the rules of the exam for the scoring matrix to be reviewed accordingly.

2 Key Facts and Knowledge

The SJT exam essentially tests whether you are likely to make a good junior doctor. The vast majority of the criteria against which you are being assessed therefore originates from the GMC's *Good Medical Practice* document.

You will also need to demonstrate an ability to deal with several important ethical issues commonly encountered in medicine, such as confidentiality and consent.

In this section, we set out some of the most important facts that you will need to take into consideration when answering SJT questions.

2.1 The GMC's Good Medical Practice

The GMC's *Good Medical Practice* is a document setting out the responsibilities of all doctors towards society, their patients and their colleagues. It can be found on the GMC's website:

http://www.gmc-uk.org/guidance/good_medical_practice/contents.asp

It is crucial that you spend 30 minutes reading *Good Medical Practice* attentively on the GMC's website or in the booklet that you should have received from the GMC since, in the exam, you will be expected to demonstrate your understanding of its principles.

When doctors talk about *Good Medical Practice*, they often limit their thoughts to the "duties of a doctor", as reproduced in Table 1 on the next page. The "duties of a doctor" are only one part of *Good Medical Practice* and are essentially a high-level summary of some of the important concepts. *Good Medical Practice* in fact contains much more than that and attempts to flesh out some of the concepts described in the duties of a doctor. For example, paragraphs such as 43, 44 and 45 deal with the behaviour that you should adopt when confronted with a colleague who is behaving improperly. These paragraphs will play a pivotal role in helping you answer questions relating to difficult situations such as a drunken consultant or a colleague is who is underperforming.

Table 1 – Duties of a doctor registered with the General Medical Council

Patients must be able to trust doctors with their lives and health. To justify that trust, you must show respect for human life and you must:

Make the care of your patient your first concern

Protect and promote the health of patients and the public

Provide a good standard of practice and care
- Keep your professional knowledge and skills up to date
- Recognise and work within the limits of your competence
- Work with colleagues in the ways that best serve patients' interests

Treat patients as individuals and respect their dignity
- Treat patients politely and considerately
- Respect patients' right to confidentiality

Work in partnership with patients
- Listen to patients and respond to their concerns and preferences
- Give patients the information they want or need in a way they can understand
- Respect patients' right to reach decisions with you about their treatment and care
- Support patients in caring for themselves to improve and maintain their health

Be honest and open and act with integrity
- Act without delay if you have good reason to believe that you or a colleague may be putting patients at risk
- Never discriminate unfairly against patients or colleagues
- Never abuse your patients' trust in you or the public's trust in the profession

You are personally accountable for your professional practice and must always be prepared to justify your decisions and actions.

Source: www.gmc-uk.org

2.2 | Confidentiality

The patient's right to confidentiality

The right to confidentiality is central to the doctor-patient relationship. It creates trust which makes patients feel safe to share information, without fear of that information being used inappropriately. There are a number of simple measures that you can implement to ensure that patient confidentiality is protected. These include:

- Not leaving computers with patient records unattended
- Not leaving patient details showing on screen where they can be viewed by others
- Not letting patient notes lie around and not taking notes home with you unless they have been anonymised
- Not leaving handover sheets where they can be seen by patients and families
- Ensuring you check the identity of patients, particularly if you are discussing matters over the phone
- If the patient comes accompanied, asking the patient if they are comfortable with a third person sitting in on the consultation
- Avoiding using the public as translators, even if they offer (e.g. unaccompanied, non-English speaker in the Emergency Department). There are a number of commercial interpreters available via telephone (e.g. LanguageLine)
- Carefully considering your reactions to questions asked by relatives or outside organisations (police, social services, etc.) when directed towards you.

Breaching patient confidentiality

Although patient confidentiality should be protected, there may be instances where it needs to be breached, some of which may be relevant to your daily practice. The situations where breaching confidentiality is appropriate include:

- ***Sharing information with other healthcare professionals or others involved in the care of the patient***
  As a doctor, you constantly breach patient confidentiality by passing on information to other healthcare professionals. This may include sending a discharge summary to the patient's GP, or sending a referral letter to an-

other doctor. It is accepted that such breaches are a routine aspect of patient management, providing the information is restricted to essential information. The patient is deemed to have provided implied consent. However, you must make sure that the patient understands that such disclosure of information is being made and, if the patient objects to the disclosure, you must take every possible step to comply with their wishes.

- ***Using information for the purpose of clinical audit***
  In order for the results of clinical audits to be meaningful, they include a representative sample of the patient cohort. It is therefore in the interest of good quality healthcare for patient data to be used for clinical audit. Providing patients have been informed that their data may be used internally for the purpose of audit and healthcare improvement, and providing they have not objected to its use, then you may use their data for the purpose of audit. This is a form of implied consent since you are not actually asking the patient to agree; you are simply informing them and allowing them to disagree, which rarely happens. If data is being given to external organisations for audit purposes, then the data must be anonymised. The Data Protection Act also governs the way data is stored. Patients need to be informed which personal details are being held for audit or research purposes.

- ***Disclosures required by law***
  There are a number of statutory requirements such as notifying a communicable disease, in accordance with the Public Health (Infectious Diseases) Regulations 1988. This includes measles, meningitis, mumps, tetanus and many others. The full list is available from the Health Protection Agency's website at www.hpa.org.uk. As always, you should make every effort to inform the patient, but their refusal cannot discharge you from your legal obligations.

- ***Court order***
  You must disclose any information requested through a court order.

- ***Disclosures to a statutory regulatory body***
  When investigating the fitness to practise of a health professional, regulatory bodies may require information about specific patient cases. Whenever possible you should discuss the disclosure of the information with the patients concerned. If discussing consent is not practical, or the patient refuses to give consent, then you need to discuss the situation with the regulatory body in question (e.g. GMC). They may judge that the disclosure is justified even without patient consent.

- ***Disclosure in the public interest and to protect the patient or others from risk of serious harm or death***

  There may be cases where the benefit to society far outweighs the harm to the patient caused by the release of information:

  - In extreme cases of HIV patients knowingly infecting others
  - An epileptic driver who continues to drive, despite advice from the DVLA
  - Any case of very serious abuse where the victim is at serious risk of harm or death, even if they are a competent adult
  - Notifying the presence of a sex offender
  - A patient who is a doctor placing patients at risk through a medical condition (e.g. a surgeon with Hepatitis C).

- ***Treatment of children or incompetent adults***

  This may happen when a child comes to see you, is not competent enough to make a decision, but is asking you to keep their visit confidential (the same would apply to any incompetent adult). In the first instance, you will need to negotiate with the patient to convince them to involve an appropriate person. If they refuse, then you may need to involve a third party anyway but only if you consider that the treatment is essential and in the patient's best interest. The patient should be aware of your intentions at all times.

- ***Abuse or neglect of an incompetent person***

  The most common cases would be child or elderly abuse, or abuse of a patient with a mental illness. If disclosure is in the best interest of the patient then you should do so promptly. If you decide not to report, you should be able to justify your decision. In fact, with child abuse, there is a duty to share information with other agencies, such as social care and the police. Therefore, if you suspect a child is about to make a disclosure, you should inform them that you will keep information confidential, unless they tell you something that you would need to share in order to protect their best interests.

Involving the patient

Whenever you need to breach confidentiality, you should always discuss it with the patient beforehand, obtain their consent and inform them of your plan. Although potentially a difficult conversation, it would certainly be easier than having to explain the breach afterwards. Being open and honest is generally appreciated by patients, even in challenging situations.

General dealings with relatives

As a doctor, you will be confronted by many situations where relatives will want to know how a patient is doing. In such situations, the GMC's guidance is that "unless they indicate otherwise, it is reasonable to assume that patients would want those closest to them to be kept informed of their general condition and prognosis."

(Source: http://www.gmc-uk.org/guidance/ethical_guidance/confidentiality.asp)

2.3 Competence and capacity

The difference between competence and capacity

Consent can only be taken from patients who are deemed to be "competent", i.e. who understand the information and are capable of making a rational decision by themselves. Competence is a legal judgement.

Doctors also frequently talk about "capacity to consent" or "mental capacity". This is a medical judgement. Capacity is formally assessed by doctors and nurses who must be sure that a patient is able to understand the proposed management, to comprehend the risks and benefits, and to retain that information long enough to make balanced choices.

Because "competence" and "capacity" have similar meanings (in effect, a judge would rule as "competent" someone who has the capacity to make medical decisions), most doctors use them interchangeably.

Both competence and capacity are situation and time specific, i.e. they are determined at a particular point in time, in relation to a given treatment or procedure. So, for example, a patient may be competent enough to decide whether they agree to have their blood pressure taken, but not whether they should go ahead with a limb amputation.

Determining if someone has capacity to consent/is competent

Before you can obtain consent from a patient, you must ensure that they are competent, i.e. that they have the capacity to make the decision to go ahead with the proposed treatment or procedure.

The assessment of mental capacity should be made in accordance with the Mental Capacity Act 2005 (or the Adults with Incapacity Act 2000 in Scotland).

Essentially, a patient is considered to have capacity if he:

- Understands the information provided in relation to the decision that needs to be made
- Is able to retain the information
- Is able to use and weigh up the information
- Can communicate his decision, by whatever means possible.

Every adult is presumed to have capacity

English law dictates that every adult should be assumed to have capacity to consent unless proven otherwise. Essentially, this means that the patient retains full control of decisions affecting his care (i.e. his autonomy) unless someone challenges this assumption and conclusively proves otherwise.

A seemingly irrational decision does not imply lack of capacity

If a patient makes a decision that you consider irrational (such as refuses life-saving treatment), it does not mean that they lack capacity. Similarly, you should not presume that someone is incompetent because they have a mental illness, are too young, can't communicate easily, have beliefs that go against yours or make decisions with which you disagree.

If you are unsure about your assessment

There may be situations where you are unsure as to whether a patient should be considered to have capacity to consent or not. In such cases, you should:

- Ask the nursing staff who know the patient about the patient's ability to make decisions

- Involve colleagues with more specialist knowledge such as a psychiatrist or a neurologist.

Some hospitals have a clinical ethics team who can consider the particulars of the case and advise. If you are still unsure, you should seek legal advice as a court may need to make that decision.

2.4 Seeking consent from a competent patient

Definition of informed consent

Informed consent is the agreement, granted by a patient, to receive a given treatment, or have a specified procedure performed on them, in full consideration of the facts and implications. The following sections summarise the key issues that you need to be aware of for your interview.

Basic model to obtain informed consent from competent patients

When the patient is competent, seeking informed consent is a relatively straightforward process, as follows:

Step 1:   The patient and the doctor discuss the presenting complaint. During the consultation, the doctor gauges the level of understanding of the patient, takes account of their views and values, and presents a range of possible management options.

Step 2:   The doctor describes the available options, including:

- Diagnosis and prognosis, including degree of certainty and further investigations required
- Different management options available to the patient, including the outcome of receiving no treatment. It is likely that the doctor will recommend a preferred course of action, but he should in no circumstances coerce the patient
- Details of any necessary investigations/treatments and/or procedures, including their purpose, their nature and which professionals will be involved
- Details of the risks, benefits, side-effects and likelihood of success. The doctor should inform the patient of any serious possi-

ble risks (e.g. death, paralysis, etc.) even if the likelihood of occurrence is very small. He should also inform the patient about less serious side-effects or complications if they occur frequently
- Whether the procedure or treatment is part of a research programme or innovative treatment, as well as their right to refuse to participate in research or teaching projects
- Their right to a second opinion
- Any treatment that you or your Trust cannot provide, but which may be of greater benefit to the patient. This may include procedures for which no one has been trained in your hospital, or treatments not provided by your Trust on grounds of cost, but which may be provided elsewhere.

The information should be provided using terms that the patient can understand and the doctor should check the understanding of the patient, answering the patient's questions as appropriate. When asked questions, the doctor should endeavour to respond in the most informative manner, avoiding coercion. If necessary, the doctor should use all necessary means of communication, including visual aids, leaflets and models.

Step 3: The patient weighs up the benefits and risks and determines whether to accept or refuse the proposed options. If the patient refuses, then the doctor should explore their reasons and continue the discussion as long as the patient wants to. There may be concerns that were not identified or addressed previously. The doctor should inform the patient that they have the right to a second opinion and the opportunity to change their mind later on, if they so wish.

There are circumstances when further procedures may be necessary during the primary planned procedure (e.g. blood transfusion, or doing a different surgical procedure). You need to explain these anticipated risks to the patient clearly and obtain consent for these potential procedures (otherwise you will need to wake the patient up to seek further consent).

Who should seek consent from the patient?

The responsibility to seek consent from the patient rests with the doctor who is proposing the treatment or will be carrying out the procedure. It is possible to delegate the task to someone else, but only if the person seeking the consent is suitably trained and qualified and they have appropriate knowledge of the treatment/procedure and the associated risks. Although the task of consenting is delegated, the responsibility still rests with the doctor who is proposing the treatment or doing the procedure.

Verbal vs written consent

The importance of recording consent is to demonstrate that the process took place with due care and diligence and that both parties had a shared vision of the proposed procedure and any key complications.

In many cases, implied or verbal consent is sufficient. For example, if a patient undresses so that you can examine them, their compliance constitutes consent.

For simple or routine procedures, investigations or treatment, verbal consent may be sufficient. However, you must make sure that the patient has properly understood the information provided and has taken an informed decision. You should also ensure that their consent is duly recorded in their notes, together with the information on which it was based.

You should get written consent:
- For complex or more involved procedures
- If there are serious risks involved
- If there are potential consequences for the patient's employment, social or personal life
- When providing clinical care is not the primary purpose of the investigation or procedure
- When the treatment is part of a research or innovative programme
- For procedures where written consent is required by law (such as organ donation or fertility treatment).

2.5 Dealing with a patient who lacks capacity

When a patient lacks capacity, the doctor must provide care which is in the patient's best interest. It is preferable for the patient to be as involved as they can be in any discussion about their care.

Whatever decisions are being taken by the doctor, the patient should be treated with respect, dignity and should not be discriminated against. In making decisions on behalf of the patient, the doctor should take account of a wide range of issues, including:

- Whether the patient has signed an advance directive stating how he wants to be treated in situations when he can't give informed consent
- The views of any individuals who are legally representing the patient or whom the patient has said they wanted to involve

- The views of any individuals who are close to the patient and may be able to comment on their beliefs, values and feelings (e.g. their relatives)

- Whether the lack of capacity is temporary (e.g. the patient may be temporarily unconscious) or permanent.

Unless the patient has signed an advance directive, the management decisions will rest with the doctor. Legally, relatives and others only have an advisory role. In practice, the doctor should try to seek a consensus around the care of the patient by involving all relevant parties in the discussions.

Sometimes there are disagreements, either between the doctor and the rest of their team, or between the medical team and those close to the patient. In situations such as these, it is important to seek conflict resolution through negotiation.

Useful resources could include consulting more experienced colleagues, using mediation services or independent advocates. In cases of more severe disagreements then legal advice should be sought and a court decision may be needed.

2.6 Competence/capacity in children

Can children give informed consent?

All children aged 16 or above can be assumed to be competent, i.e. essentially they can be treated in exactly the same way as an adult. Children under the age of 16 can give consent to a treatment, procedure or investigation if they are deemed to be Gillick competent, in reference to a famous House of Lords ruling on the ability of children under 16 to consent.

A child is deemed Gillick competent if they can understand, retain, use and weigh the information given and their understanding of benefits, risks and consequences.

Involving the parents

Even if a child is competent enough to make a decision to consent to a given procedure or treatment, you should make every effort to encourage the child to involve their parents. Whatever their involvement, parents cannot override consent given by a competent child.

Can children refuse treatment?

In Scotland, the situation is simple. Children can refuse treatment and the child's decision cannot be overridden by the parents.

In England, Wales and Northern Ireland, no minor can refuse consent to treatment when consent has been given by someone with parental responsibility or by the court. This applies even if the child is competent and specifically refuses treatment that is considered to be in their best interest. This is a rare event and you should seek legal advice through your Trust and your defence union. Enforcing treatment on a child against their will poses risks which need to be weighed up against the benefits of the procedure or treatment. You will also undoubtedly need to involve other members of the multidisciplinary team and an independent advocate for the child.

The above is the essential information that you will be required to know for the exam. If you feel you need to know more or are simply interested in the topic and want further detail on children's consent, you can consult the GMC booklet *0-18 years: guidance for all doctors* online at www.gmc-uk.org.

2.7 Dealing with emergencies in the clinical setting

If you are dealing with emergencies in the clinical setting, then all the rules described in previous sections apply.

If a patient is competent at that time and needs a procedure, you should seek consent, even if only verbal.

If the patient is not competent and you cannot determine the patient's wishes through the relatives or other sources, then you can treat them without their consent, on the condition that the treatment that you administer is limited to what is immediately necessary to save their life or prevent a serious deterioration of their condition. The guidelines also specify that the treatment you provide must be the least restrictive of the patient's future choices. If the patient regains capacity, you should explain what was done. For any other treatment beyond the strict minimum, you should seek consent from the patient.

For children, the same applies. The guidance issued by the GMC in *0-18 years: guidance for all doctors* (see www.gmc-uk.org) states that "you can provide emergency treatment without consent to save the life of, or prevent serious deterioration in the health of, a child or young person". Of course, this does not preclude you from involving the parents. If the parents disagreed with your emergency treatment, then you would be entitled to proceed with what you perceived to be in the best interest of the child.

2.8 Dealing with emergencies outside the clinical setting

Occasionally questions are asked about the behaviour you should adopt if an emergency takes place outside the clinical setting (e.g. you are on a plane or on holiday).

Do you have to get involved?

To answer this question, there are two principles to consider:

The law
In the UK, unlike the US, there is no specific "Good Samaritan" law. In fact, under UK law, there is no obligation for anyone (including a doctor) to assist another human who needs resuscitation or emergency assistance, unless that person has caused the problem in the first place.

Therefore, from a legal perspective you can choose to ignore an emergency if you wish, BUT from a medical perspective the GMC will require you to get involved as set out in the previous paragraph. If you refuse to get involved or choose to ignore the matter, you won't be sued, but you would be in breach of the GMC's duties of a doctor and may be reported to the GMC if this is discovered.

GMC guideline (Good Medical Practice)

This describes your medical responsibility as a doctor as: "In an emergency, wherever it arises, you must offer assistance, taking account of your own safety, your competence, and the availability of other options for care."

Essentially this means that, provided you are safe (e.g. not in the middle of a busy motorway) and provided you will not make things worse, then you are obliged to help.

Situations where a doctor may not be competent to help would include someone who has been out of clinical practice for a long time and may actually harm the patient by intervening directly. In that situation they should ensure that the right people are called. In an emergency in a completely different specialty, the patient may be better off being sent to hospital straight away, rather than being treated on site.

You need to make a judgement based on the circumstances. If you are in the middle of the jungle, there is no way the patient will ever get to a hospital and the only alternative is death, their best bet may be you, even if you feel shaky in your knowledge. Essentially you must weigh up the different options and ensure that you choose the alternative which is best for the patient.

3 Important Tips

As you go through the 250 practice questions in this book, you will start spotting the repetition of some of the themes and will become more confident in approaching a wide range of scenarios.

In this section, we have set out a number of tips which will help you prioritise and rank the various options more systematically.

1. **Select your answer according to what you <u>SHOULD</u> do and not what you <u>WOULD</u> do.**

    The exam is designed to test your understanding of your duties as a doctor. If you are confronted by a scenario, you should therefore choose the answer that conforms the most to what would be expected of you rather than the answer that corresponds to what you are likely to do.

    For example, let's assume that you were supposed to order some tests for a patient but had forgotten to do so because you were busy doing other things:

    *   In real life, when the registrar asks you whether the test results are back, you might simply tell him that you don't know but that you will check (i.e. basically tell him a small lie to avoid any embarrassment). That might be what you <u>would</u> do.

    *   However, in the exam, you would be expected to demonstrate honesty and to tell the registrar that you forgot to order the tests but will order them as soon as you can.

2. **Do not make assumptions about the scenario. Use the information provided.**

    Some scenarios may not contain all the information that you would like to have. Do not make assumptions to fill in the gaps; all the information you need is contained within each question.

3. **If a colleague is causing problems, you should always discuss the matter with them first unless the question states that you have already done so many times or you feel it may be unsafe.**

You will come across many scenarios that deal with colleagues making mistakes, behaving inappropriately or underperforming. In those scenarios, there will usually be an option which involves discussing the matter with your colleague. If that option is present, it will almost always rank at the top. There are, however, some exceptions, including:

- Situations where the question states that you have already talked to the colleague in question many times
- Situations where it may not be safe (e.g. if someone is violent or aggressive towards you).

Essentially, when there is a problem, you need to ensure that you give the person in question a chance to put things right. If you have concerns about patient safety then you should escalate the matter to a senior colleague.

4. **When ranking "bad" options, think of the consequences they may have on patients, you and your colleagues. If in doubt, remember that patient safety will always be more important than anything else.**

You will encounter scenarios where you may struggle to determine whether one option is better than another because both are actually inappropriate. In such cases, consider the impact your behaviour has on others and rank the options in accordance to the damage you are likely to cause. The more duties you breach and the more damage you cause, the lower the option will rank.

5. **Beware of questions where completing a critical incident form is an option.**

Many questions will deal with situations where mistakes are made. Though it may not always happen in practice, you should complete a critical incident form every time a mistake is made, even if that mistake has had no consequences at all. The point of a critical incident form is to report mistakes or near-misses (i.e. mistakes that nearly happened) so that lessons can be learnt.

However, before you select the "critical incident form" option, you must check that there are no other options which would have a more immediate impact and therefore would be more appropriate.

For example, let's assume that you are dealing with a Multiple Choice situation where the patient was prescribed the wrong drug but did not suffer any adverse effect. In such situation, you would be expected to:

- Inform the patient and apologise
- Inform a senior colleague
- Give the correct drug
- Complete a critical incident form.

If all those options appeared in the list then the first 3 options would be those you need to select because they are all essential immediate options. Though completing a critical incident form would be appropriate, it is less urgent and important than the other three options and therefore would need to be dropped.

If, however, the list of options did not contain "Inform a senior colleague" then the "critical incident form" option would form part of the answer.

6. **Make sure you understand the reason for informing colleagues.**

Several questions will contain options of the type "Inform your consultant" or "Tell the ward sister at the first opportunity". Those options are usually some of the most appropriate but it does not mean that you have to select them systematically.

Rank those options high whenever the person you seek to inform either has direct responsibility over the situation (e.g. contacting a consultant if a mistake has been made in the care of a patient) or if you require that person's help (e.g. contacting a registrar because you cannot deal with a situation by yourself).

In other situations, think twice before you contact someone about a problem in which they have no interest or for which they can't help.

4 160 Practice Scenarios Ranking Format

Scenario 1

You overhear a senior nurse telling a patient that the doctor looking after him is lazy. The conversation between the nurse and the patient has now moved on to other matters.

Rank in order the following actions in response to this situation (1= Most appropriate; 5= Least appropriate):

A. Immediately interrupt the nurse and tell her that she is being inappropriate.

B. Wait for the nurse to leave the bedside. Reassure the patient that the nurse was lying and that there is nothing to be concerned about.

C. Take the nurse to one side as soon as possible and ask her to explain her comments.

D. Leave the ward and inform your consultant.

E. Find the ward sister and inform her.

Scenario 2

You have received a message from biochemistry stating that the blood sample you took earlier that day on a patient was mislabelled. This patient is due to go to theatre tomorrow morning.

Rank in order the following actions in response to this situation
(1= Most appropriate; 5= Least appropriate):

A. Fill in a blood form and place it in the phlebotomist's slot for tomorrow morning.

B. Fill in a blood form and hand it to the ward sister.

C. Add to your "to-do list" a repeat blood sample on the patient, ensuring it is taken today.

D. Immediately go and retake the blood from the patient.

E. Write in the patient notes that the blood bottle was mislabelled.

Scenario 3

It is snowing and you are on call today for General Medicine. You are not a confident driver in snowy conditions and do not feel safe to drive to work.

Rank in order the following actions in response to this situation (1= Most appropriate; 5= Least appropriate):

A. Inform your registrar (ST3) that you may be late and try to get to work by public transport.

B. Attempt to drive to work, at a slow pace.

C. Call your registrar (ST3), and explain that you are not a confident driver and will wait for the conditions to clear before setting off.

D. Call your registrar (ST3) and explain that you are not confident driving in snowy conditions and will not be able to come in today.

E. Call your registrar (ST3) and inform him that you will not be coming in as you are not feeling well.

Scenario 4

One of your FY1 colleagues is away on annual leave which was booked 6 weeks ago. The department has not organised a locum to cover their leave and you have been asked to stay late to cover this evening's 5pm to 9pm on call.

Your contract states that you are expected to provide cover if a staffing emergency arises.

Rank in order the following actions in response to this situation
(1= Most appropriate; 5= Least appropriate):

A. Offer to cover the shift "on this occasion" stating that you would like the lack of cover investigated to prevent it occurring again.

B. Ask one of your colleagues to cover the shift as you have other obligations which cannot be cancelled.

C. Say no and leave at 5pm.

D. Cover the shift as you are contractually obliged to do so.

E. Ask to speak to medical personnel to ascertain why no locum was organised. This was an expected absence and they had ample time to organise a locum.

Scenario 5

You are the FY1 on call during the day and have been working a busy 9am – 9pm shift.

During the Hospital at Night handover, at the end of your shift, the site managers mention that the night medical registrar has called in sick with diarrhoea and vomiting, leaving only two ST2s and another FY1 at night to clerk in waiting patients and cover the wards.

There are currently six people waiting in A&E who still need to be clerked in.

Rank in order the following actions in response to this situation (1= Most appropriate; 5= Least appropriate):

A. Ask the Night Nurse Practitioners (NNPs) to clerk patients during the night's take.

B. Stay and clerk patients until the workload is more manageable for the rest of the team.

C. Call the on-call consultant to discuss the situation.

D. Ask an ST2 to phone the night registrar who was supposed to come in, and to ask him politely to come in for a few hours until the workload is more manageable.

E. Complete a critical incident form.

Scenario 6

You are an FY1 doctor covering the Paediatric ward as first on call. Your registrar (ST3) is busy in A&E with a very sick patient. He has asked you to attend the ward because the nurses want a sick baby reviewed.

You arrive on the ward and the nurse in charge tells you that the child should be seen as soon as possible as she is concerned that he may be deteriorating. She then tells you to go away because "You are too junior to see this complicated patient".

Rank in order the following actions in response to this situation (1= Most appropriate; 5= Least appropriate):

A. Explain to the nurse that the registrar (ST3) has asked you to attend in their absence and that this means that he trusts you with the task in hand. Reassure the nurse that, should you meet any difficulties, you will contact the registrar (ST3). Proceed to see the patient.

B. Thank the nurse for her input and tell her that, as a doctor, the patient is your responsibility and so you should proceed to see him. Reassure her that you are safe and ask her to deal with the registrar if she has any objections.

C. Tell her that, since the registrar (ST3) is busy and she doesn't want you to see the patient, she will need to find someone who is free and competent to review the patient.

D. Reassure the nurse that you won't take her comments personally and move on to your next patient on your to-do list.

E. Leave the ward and go straight back to A&E to seek further advice from your registrar, with a plan to return to the ward shortly thereafter once you have been advised.

Scenario 7

You are on night cover for a Geriatric ward. As you are re-cannulating an 82-year-old female patient, she tells you that she wants to die. She asks you to help.

Rank in order the following actions in response to this situation
(1 = Most appropriate; 5 = Least appropriate):

A. Tell her that she will need to discuss this with the team in charge of her care because, strictly speaking, she is not your patient.

B. Sit and talk to her; ask why she feels that way and try to ascertain if she has any signs of depression.

C. Sit and talk to her; ask why she feels that way and try to ascertain if she has capacity.

D. Ask her if there is anyone whom you can call for her, so that she can say goodbye.

E. Finish the cannulation, leave the bedside and relate the content of your conversation straight away to the nurse who is looking after her.

Scenario 8

Mrs Smith has recently undergone a CT scan, which has revealed that she has brain metastasis from a known colon cancer. She has been informed of the findings.

Her son approaches you and asks you what the scan revealed.

Rank in order the following actions in response to this situation
(1 = Most appropriate; 5 = Least appropriate):

A. Explain the results to the son, making sure that your explanations are without jargon and that he understands what you are saying.

B. Take the son into a quiet area, ask him to sit down and explain that his mother's cancer has spread and that she will need support from him.

C. Explain to the son that you are unable to talk to him about his mother's care without her permission.

D. Tell the son that his mother knows the results and he will need to ask her.

E. Tell her son that the results are not back yet.

Scenario 9

One of your colleagues told you about a very good course that he recently attended and which he recommended you should attend too. The admission process to that course is competitive and relies on an application form which takes some time to complete.

This course is essential for your portfolio as it will significantly enhance your chances of success when you apply for specialty training next year. The deadline for the application is tomorrow noon. That is the last opportunity you will have to apply as it is the last time it will run this year and it is only open to FY1 doctors.

You have just finished a 12-hour shift on the wards and are feeling washed out. You realise far too late that it will take a good 5 hours to complete the application form. It is already midnight and you have a busy shift tomorrow which starts at 8am.

Rank in order the following actions in response to this situation (1 = Most appropriate; 5 = Least appropriate):

A. Forget the application form; there is nothing that you can do about it.

B. Call your ST3 first thing in the morning to see if you can get some time off to finish the form. You can then go to work in the afternoon.

C. Contact the course organisers first thing in the morning and ask if you can get an extension to the deadline.

D. Copy the answers from a form that your friend did last year and which got him through.

E. Call in sick the next morning and do the form properly.

Scenario 10

A patient has complained to you that a small amount of cash has disappeared from his bedside table.

Rank in order the following actions in response to this situation (1= Most appropriate; 5= Least appropriate):

A. Request a team meeting to ask the culprit to replace the money.

B. Call the police.

C. Ask the patient for details about the alleged theft, reassure him that you will do what you can to deal with the issue, and notify a senior nurse of the problem.

D. Send an email to all your colleagues notifying them of the incident and asking them to warn their patients to be careful about personal possessions.

E. Remind the patient that he should be more careful about his possessions and tell him that you will see what you can do.

Scenario 11

After a long day, the FY1 who was meant to take over from you has called in sick, 10 minutes before the end of your shift, just as you were supposed to hand over to him.

You had arranged to go out with friends that evening and they are expecting you in 2 hours' time.

Rank in order the following actions in response to this situation (1= Most appropriate; 5= Least appropriate):

A. Do your colleague's shift for him and tell him that he can take on one of your shifts when he gets back.

B. Stay for two hours and then hand over to the registrar (ST3) on call.

C. Contact the registrar (ST3) on call to hand over to him and go home to get ready for your evening.

D. Contact the registrar (ST3) on call to hand over to him, offer to stay behind for a couple of hours and join your friends later.

E. Explain to your colleague that this places you in a difficult position, offer to stay for an hour and ask him to come in an hour's time to take over as you cannot stay any longer.

Scenario 12

After a 13-hour day, you are waiting for the arrival of your colleague so that you can hand over to her. You are exhausted because you have just switched over from a week of nights and you are starting to feel sleepy.

Your colleague is already 15 minutes late and has not called to say that she is ill.

Rank in order the following actions in response to this situation (1= Most appropriate; 5= Least appropriate):

A. Inform your registrar (ST3) that you are too tired to stay and that you need to leave immediately because you cannot function effectively.

B. Go and see your consultant and let him know that, because you are in breach of the 13-hour limit imposed by the European Working Time Directive, you will hand over to him before leaving.

C. Patiently wait for your colleague and cover her shift until she arrives.

D. Hand over to a nurse and go home.

E. Contact your colleague to see what the matter is and how long the delay is likely to last. If she is likely to be substantially delayed, then hand over to the registrar (ST3) and leave.

Scenario 13

You have arranged to go out for dinner with your partner tonight.

Just before leaving your shift you have been informed that a mandatory FY1 teaching session that was meant to take place tomorrow morning has now been brought forward and starts in 10 minutes.

Rank in order the following actions in response to this situation (1= Most appropriate; 5= Least appropriate):

A. Tell another FY1 to apologise to the group for your absence.

B. Find out what the meeting is about and discuss with the person running the meeting whether your attendance is strictly necessary. Attend if required.

C. Slip away unnoticed.

D. Tell a nurse to let the organiser know that you cannot make it.

E. Call your partner and inform him/her that you cannot make the dinner as you must attend an important teaching session.

Scenario 14

One of your friends, who is asthmatic and works as an engineer, is going on holiday to Europe tomorrow. He has forgotten to order a repeat prescription for his inhaler.

Rank in order the following actions in response to this situation (1= Most appropriate; 5= Least appropriate):

A. Tell him to go to his nearest A&E.

B. Get an inhaler from A&E yourself.

C. Get an inhaler from the ward.

D. Ask him to contact his GP.

E. Ask one of your more senior colleagues (ST1) if he could write a prescription for him.

Scenario 15

One of your colleagues arrives consistently late for his shifts.

Rank in order the following actions in response to this situation (1= Most appropriate; 5= Least appropriate):

A. Tell his senior about the delays.

B. Discuss the problem with other junior doctors.

C. Approach your colleague, tell him that his lateness is causing problems and that he must be on time.

D. Ask your colleague if there is a reason for his being late and whether there is anything you can do to help.

E. Make a record of the lateness, then watch and wait.

Scenario 16

A colleague asks you to review one of her patients as she is busy on the ward.

This means that you will have to stay late but it is already 5pm and you are about to go out with your family, who have come to collect you.

Rank in order the following actions in response to this situation (1= Most appropriate; 5= Least appropriate):

A. Agree to see the patient and tell your family to go home.

B. Ask your family to wait for you in the hospital restaurant whilst you see the patient quickly.

C. Ask your colleague to hand over the job to the FY1 on call.

D. Contact the FY1 on call yourself and hand over the job.

E. Tell your consultant to see the patient.

Scenario 17

You are about to give a case presentation to your department when a nurse bleeps you for an emergency on the ward.

Rank in order the following actions in response to this situation
(1= Most appropriate; 5= Least appropriate):

A. Go straight away without telling anybody.

B. Tell the nurse that you cannot attend the patient immediately but that you will go after the meeting.

C. Ask a colleague if he wouldn't mind attending the ward.

D. Cancel the teaching session and attend the emergency.

E. Apologise to the team at the meeting and ask a colleague to fill in while you find out more information and see if you need to attend at once.

Scenario 18

One of your colleagues confides in you that he has a cocaine addiction problem.

He is asking you to keep the information to yourself as he needs your support and no aggravation.

Rank in order the following actions in response to this situation (1= Most appropriate; 5= Least appropriate):

A. Tell your colleague that you have no option but to report the matter to a senior straight away.

B. Reassure your colleague that you will support him but tell him that he needs to address the matter with his seniors; otherwise you will have no option but to tell them yourself.

C. Report the matter to a consultant without telling your colleague that you have done so.

D. Agree with your colleague and keep quiet about it.

E. Investigate whether your colleague has performance problems and report the matter to the consultant if he has any.

Scenario 19

A patient, whom you have been treating on your ward for the first time, offers you a £100 book voucher to thank you for your help in his recovery on your ward.

During his short admission your only contact with the patient was with the team during ward rounds. You do not expect the patient to come back for another stay on your ward.

Rank in order the following actions in response to this situation (1= Most appropriate; 5= Least appropriate):

A. Tell the patient that you cannot accept the gift because it would not be ethical.

B. Accept the gift and give it to your partner.

C. Accept the gift and put it towards ward funds.

D. Politely refuse the gift but thank them for the thought.

E. Accept the gift but tell the patient not to let any of the team know as you do not want any trouble.

Scenario 20

You are dealing with a ward patient whose wife's best friend works on your ward as a nurse.

The patient has asked you specifically to ensure that no information about his health should be given to the nurse in question so that his wife cannot gain information about his health.

Rank in order the following actions in response to this situation (1= Most appropriate; 5= Least appropriate):

A. Inform the patient that there is nothing that you can do about it and that he will need to accept the situation as it stands.

B. Have a word with the rest of the team to ensure that the patient's confidentiality is maintained.

C. Tell the nurse that she must take some time off whilst the patient is on the ward so as not to compromise his right to confidentiality.

D. Have a word with the patient to understand the reasons behind his request and see if a possible compromise can be reached.

E. Transfer the patient to another part of the ward where the nurse does not work.

Scenario 21

You are a female FY1 based on the AMU (Acute Medical Unit).

A male patient from your base ward has just complained of some testicular pains. When you see him, he is embarrassed and says that he wants to see a male doctor only as he doesn't want to be examined by a woman.

Your male AMU colleagues are all busy with sick patients.

Rank in order the following actions in response to this situation (1= Most appropriate; 5= Least appropriate):

A. Refer the patient to the urology team so that they can examine the patient tomorrow.

B. Ask the male AMU SHO to examine the patient when he is free.

C. Ask a male nurse to examine the patient and describe the findings to you once he has finished.

D. Inform the patient that, as a doctor, you will preserve all patient confidentiality. Proceed to examine the patient with a male nurse as chaperone.

E. Hand over to the on-call team to examine the patient.

Scenario 22

You have just returned home after finishing a busy shift on the Acute Medical Unit (AMU). You realise that you have forgotten to check the results of a blood test that you requested earlier.

You live 40 minutes away from the hospital. You attempt to contact the FY1 on call, but he is not responding.

Rank in order the following actions in response to this situation (1= Most appropriate; 5= Least appropriate):

A. Telephone the on-call medical registrar and ask him to check the results for you.

B. Telephone another FY1 whom you know and is currently working on another ward. Ask him to check the test results on the computer.

C. Go back to the hospital and check the results yourself.

D. Call the ward and ask the sister to write a note for the FY1 on call.

E. Call the ward and ask the sister to bleep the FY1 on call to check the results.

Scenario 23

One of your patients wants to know the results of a pleural tap that was carried out earlier that week.

The system shows that the cytological results are "in progress". You telephone the histopathology laboratory, and are told that they have not received any samples with a cytology request form from you or your team.

Rank in order the following actions in response to this situation (1= Most appropriate; 5= Least appropriate):

A. Tell the patient that the sample has been lost, apologise and ask if they would mind having a second sample taken.

B. Tell the patient that the results are not back yet.

C. Tell the patient that you are going to check and that you will get back to them. Then tell the consultant that the sample has not been received by the laboratory yet and ask for his advice.

D. Tell the patient that more tests need to be done for which another pleural fluid sample is required. Then take the new sample to the lab yourself so that it doesn't get lost; ask the lab to perform the original test using the new sample.

E. Tell the patient that you will get back to them shortly and ask the lab technician to search through all the histopathology samples received.

Scenario 24

You are an FY1 doctor on the Acute Medical Unit (AMU). An unstable patient, Mrs Smith, is about to be transferred to the Intensive Care Unit (ICU) for urgent haemodialysis for intractable hyperkalaemia, escorted by you and two porters. The ICU is on the other side of the hospital.

You have developed a good relationship with Mrs Smith during her stay, and she confides in you that she is worried about her haemodialysis.

Just as you are about to leave, an AMU nurse runs after you and says that another patient has fallen and hurt her hip.

Rank in order the following actions in response to this situation
(1= Most appropriate; 5= Least appropriate):

A. Ask another AMU doctor to take Mrs Smith down to ICU, and go to AMU to assess the patient who has fallen.

B. Tell the nurse to wait with Mrs Smith in the corridor whilst you go and assess the fallen patient on the ward.

C. Ask the nurse to tell the registrar on the AMU about the fallen patient whilst you escort the patient to ICU.

D. Escort Mrs Smith to ICU then come back to AMU to assess the fallen patient.

E. Ask the two porters to take Mrs Smith to ICU without you, whilst you assess the patient who has fallen.

Scenario 25

You are an FY1 in Obstetrics and Gynaecology at a District General Hospital. Earlier that day, whilst you were in the office faxing a referral form, an FY2 colleague prescribed atorvastatin for a pregnant patient.

You know that atorvastatin is contraindicated in pregnancy. The patient has not yet been given the medication and the FY2 doctor is nowhere to be found.

Rank in order the following actions in response to this situation
(1= Most appropriate; 5= Least appropriate):

A. Change atorvastatin to a suitable alternative.

B. Find your FY2 colleague and query with him why he prescribed atorvastatin

C. Write in the patient's medical notes that atorvastatin is contraindicated in pregnancy and discuss with the team at the next ward round.

D. Take the drug chart with you and ask the ward pharmacist for advice. Change the prescription if required.

E. Cancel the atorvastatin prescription on the drug chart and ask your registrar (ST3) for advice.

Scenario 26

You are the FY1 in the Acute Stroke Unit. You notice that your fellow FY1's tie is swinging loose.

You bring this to his attention and he tucks his tie inside his shirt, but later on during the day you notice that his tie is swinging loose again.

Rank in order the following actions in response to this situation (1= Most appropriate; 5= Least appropriate):

A. Tell the FY1 to tuck his tie in again and leave it at that.

B. Tell the FY1 to tuck his tie in again and report the incident to the infection control nurse.

C. Inform the ward sister of the infection control hazard and ask her to have a word with your colleague.

D. Inform your educational supervisor.

E. Email his consultant regarding the incident.

Scenario 27

During the ward round, your consultant tells you to request a CT Chest-Abdomen-Pelvis for a patient.

Later on, the consultant radiologist refuses to grant the test, stating that there is insufficient information on the request form.

You know that the consultant radiologist is usually very pedantic and nearly always queries the paperwork.

Rank in order the following actions in response to this situation (1= Most appropriate; 5= Least appropriate):

A. Ask your consultant to talk to the consultant radiologist to persuade him to grant the test.

B. Document in the patient's notes that the consultant radiologist refused to grant the test.

C. Ask the consultant radiologist to contact your consultant to sort out the matter.

D. Visit the radiology department in person, explain to the consultant radiologist why you need the investigation and ask what information was missing from the request form.

E. Explain to the consultant radiologist that it is your consultant who requested the test and that therefore it will need to get done as otherwise patient safety may be compromised.

Scenario 28

During a ward round, your consultant asks you to prescribe trimethoprim as a course of antibiotics for a patient's urinary tract infection.

However, the microbiology registrar later assesses the patient and bleeps you to say that a different course of antibiotics should be prescribed in line with the Trust's antibiotics guidelines.

Rank in order the following actions in response to this situation (1= Most appropriate; 5= Least appropriate):

A. Discuss the microbiology advice with your consultant straight away.

B. Ignore the microbiology advice, and continue the antibiotics that your consultant has decided.

C. Document in the medical notes the microbiology advice but follow your consultant's antibiotic choice.

D. Change the consultant's antibiotic prescription to the antibiotic that microbiology recommended.

E. Prescribe the antibiotic suggested by microbiology in addition to the trimethoprim that your consultant had originally advised.

Scenario 29

You are an FY1 in Gastroenterology. The ward clerk tells you that the police are on the phone, asking about a patient who was discharged 2 weeks ago.

The police detective tells you that the patient is being investigated for benefit fraud. He wants to know details about the inpatient stay, including contact details and summary of treatment received.

He requests that you cooperate with his investigation.

Rank in order the following actions in response to this situation (1= Most appropriate; 5= Least appropriate):

A. Cooperate with the police and give the information that they request.

B. Disclose the patient's contact details only, but not any health details.

C. Refer the police to a senior colleague.

D. Ask the police to proceed with a court order for the information request.

E. Refuse to give the police the information on grounds of confidentiality and put the phone down.

Scenario 30

It is the day after the hospital mess party. Your FY1 colleague calls in sick and you are the only FY1 left in a Cardiology firm.

Later that evening, you notice that your colleague has posted photographs of himself on a social networking site, where he is shown drinking heavily and vomiting from the night before. To your knowledge, this is the first time this has happened.

Rank in order the following actions in response to this situation (1= Most appropriate; 5= Least appropriate):

A. Tell your colleague to take the pictures down and inform the consultant this has happened.

B. Tell your colleague to take the pictures down and explain to him that his behaviour is not professional and that he ought to be careful as he may be compromising his career.

C. Ignore the matter.

D. Tell the consultant what has happened.

E. Keep a copy of the internet page and wait for the next time it happens to report it.

Scenario 31

It is 9am on a weekday. A patient has asked to be discharged as soon as possible so that he can get back to work that morning to attend an important meeting.

The previous day, the registrar made it clear to you that he wanted to discuss some important matters with the patient before he was discharged. However, the registrar is running late and will not be at the hospital for some time.

Rank in order the following actions in response to this situation (1= Most appropriate; 5= Least appropriate):

A. Discharge the patient yourself and send a text message to the registrar.

B. Explain to the patient that the registrar is running late and that it is important that he waits until the registrar's return. Tell him that he is free to go if he wishes and that, if he gives his phone number, the registrar will contact him when he arrives.

C. Telephone the registrar and ask if there was any particular reason why he wanted to see the patient before discharge. Agree with the registrar whether the patient can be discharged or not.

D. Allow the patient to go to work, but take his telephone number so he can be contacted later by the registrar.

E. Tell the patient that he cannot be discharged until the registrar arrives. Inform members of staff that they should stop the patient from leaving the ward if he tries to.

Scenario 32

You have been informed by a nurse that your post-thyroidectomy patient is struggling to breathe on the ward. Your ENT consultant is currently busy dealing with a critically ill patient in theatre.

In the bay next to you, the Critical Care Outreach Team (CCOT) is reviewing another patient who has recently being stepped down from ITU. On the ward, a registrar from another surgical team is seeing patients.

Rank in order the following actions in response to this situation (1= Most appropriate; 5= Least appropriate):

A. Ask for advice from the Critical Care Outreach Team (CCOT) which is in the bay next to you.

B. Call the resuscitation team.

C. Go to the theatre and ask the consultant to come back to see this patient immediately.

D. Ask for help from the surgical registrar who is seeing his patients on the ward.

E. Wait until the consultant has finished dealing with his critically ill patient in theatre.

Scenario 33

You are the Respiratory FY1 and need to give a mixture of intravenous antibiotics to a patient diagnosed with Hospital-Acquired Pneumonia (HAP).

Unfortunately, the protocols which are normally available on the Intranet cannot be accessed as the Intranet is down. You are also unable to locate a protocol folder on the wards despite an extensive search by everyone.

Rank in order the following actions in response to this situation (1= Most appropriate; 5= Least appropriate):

A. Tell your registrar that the protocol is unavailable and ask him what drugs are normally given.

B. Prescribe what you think the right drugs are.

C. Telephone the on-call microbiologist and ask for advice.

D. Ask your other FY1 colleagues for advice so that, between all of you, you are able to remember most of the antibiotics.

E. Look on the internet and find a similar HAP antibiotic dosing protocol for another hospital.

Scenario 34

You are attending to an 80-year-old patient who was admitted to the Acute Medical Unit (AMU) last night.

He has not had his morning dose of medication because the on-call team which clerked the patient in overnight did not write the dosages of the medications down. Though he can remember the names of the medications, he is unable to remember the dosages.

From what he is telling you, one of the medications he is taking slows the heart rate down; however, you notice that his heart rate is slightly elevated.

Rank in order the following actions in response to this situation (1= Most appropriate; 5= Least appropriate):

A. Ask permission from the patient to phone his next of kin so that he/she can bring the medications that the patient normally takes.

B. Look at the last discharge summary, which was written last time he was in hospital 2 years ago, and prescribe the same dose of medications.

C. Phone the GP to get a medication history.

D. Prescribe a stat dose of a different heart-slowing drug to quickly slow the heart down.

E. Start the patient's medications on the lowest safe doses according to the BNF. Write in the patient's clinical notes that the on-call medical team should titrate up the medications if required.

Scenario 35

It is a Saturday night and there is a 2-hour wait in the Medical Admission Unit. An intoxicated patient begins shouting and threatening staff because he wants to be seen immediately.

Rank in order the following actions in response to this situation (1= Most appropriate; 5= Least appropriate):

A. Refuse to treat the patient and tell him to leave.

B. Call security.

C. Tell the patient to keep quiet and advise that he will be seen as soon as possible.

D. See the patient straight away.

E. Advise the patient that there is a zero-tolerance policy towards staff violence. Inform him that, if he continues, he will be asked to leave.

Scenario 36

A colonoscopy was requested for a 72-year-old patient who presented with fresh red blood mixed in his stools and a history of weight loss. After the colonoscopy, a diagnosis of colonic adenocarcinoma was made.

The patient does not yet know the diagnosis and needs to be informed. You are the Gastroenterology FY1 and have established a good rapport with the patient.

Rank in order the following actions in response to this situation
(1= Most appropriate; 5= Least appropriate):

A. Ask the consultant to inform the patient.

B. Ask the doctor who performed the colonoscopy to inform the patient.

C. Notify the next of kin first, so that he can inform the patient himself.

D. Inform the patient yourself.

E. Write in the discharge summary that the GP should notify the patient.

Scenario 37

You are an FY1 for a Vascular team at a District General Hospital (DGH). You suspect that a certain nurse is making up patient observations, and you feel that she may be compromising patient care.

Your suspicion was confirmed when a patient under your care was transferred to another hospital and you found that the patient's observations were still being recorded on the patient's notes within the DGH.

You have previously approached the nurse to raise your concerns but she always denied it and explained that someone else must have made the entries under her name.

Rank in order the following actions in response to this situation (1= Most appropriate; 5= Least appropriate):

A. Inform the consultant.

B. Ignore it as this is a nursing issue.

C. Inform the ward sister.

D. Speak to the nurse again and reiterate your concerns.

E. Keep the matter to yourself but make sure that your patients are safe by conducting your own observations for your patients under the care of that nurse.

Scenario 38

You are an FY1 for the Intensive Care Unit (ICU). One of your patients is a 34-year-old woman who was admitted with an intracranial haemorrhage. She is on a ventilator for respiratory support.

You are asked by the nurse in charge to review the patient; the nurse feels that the patient has deteriorated. You perform tests of brain-stem function and confirm brain-stem death. The patient did not leave any specific wishes for her care.

Rank in order the following actions in response to this situation (1= Most appropriate; 5= Least appropriate):

A. Request that the ventilator be switched off.

B. Inform the next of kin of the brain-stem death.

C. Ask the ICU consultant to review the patient and to break the news to the next of kin.

D. Call the next of kin to inform them of this development and ask for permission for organ donation.

E. Request EEG testing to confirm brain-stem death.

Scenario 39

You are an FY1 on the Medical Admissions Unit (MAU). One of your patients, Mr Jay, is a 56-year-old cleaner who works in your hospital and has been admitted with a chest infection. He is now stable.

The head cleaner has been informed by the HR department that Mr Jay would be off sick for a while but was told nothing more. He meets you in the corridor and says "I have heard that Mr Jay was admitted yesterday. How is he doing?"

Rank in order the following actions in response to this situation (1= Most appropriate; 5= Least appropriate):

A. Tell the head cleaner that you haven't reviewed Mr Jay since he was admitted.

B. Tell the head cleaner that you need Mr Jay's permission before you can divulge anything.

C. Just tell the head cleaner that Mr Jay is getting better but do not reveal any more information.

D. Tell the head cleaner that you can't tell him anything, but that if he wants to know more he will need to talk to Mr Jay himself on the respiratory ward.

E. Tell the head cleaner that the best source of information on Mr Jay's health status would be the HR department.

Scenario 40

You are an FY1 on call at night for General Surgery at a small District General Hospital (DGH).

It is 3am. A nurse bleeps to let you know that one of your patients, who has recently undergone an emergency Hartman's procedure for large bowel obstruction, is hypotensive at 78/54 mmHg, tachycardic at 120 and is in a lot of pain.

When you assess the patient, you notice that the small bowel has herniated through the stoma site.

You phone the on-call surgical SHO but the theatre nurse who picks up the phone says that he is currently in theatre performing an emergency appendicectomy.

Rank in order the following actions in response to this situation (1= Most appropriate; 5= Least appropriate):

A. Bleep the surgical registrar to come and review the patient.

B. Leave a message with the theatre nurse for the surgical SHO to come and review the patient after his emergency operation is done.

C. Contact the medical registrar to review the patient.

D. Go through switchboard to call the surgical consultant.

E. Bleep the on-call anaesthetist to prep the patient for emergency surgery.

Scenario 41

You are a surgical FY1 covering the wards during a weekend on call.

Twenty minutes from the end of your shift, you receive a call from the SHO, asking you to come urgently to help clerk in a patient with suspected pancreatitis in A&E. The SHO can't clerk them in because she is currently busy with another patient.

As you are about to leave your ward to go down to A&E, a nurse tells you that one of your surgical patients is experiencing haematemesis and another patient on the same ward has spiked a fever despite being on metronidazole.

Rank in order the following actions in response to this situation
(1= Most appropriate; 5= Least appropriate):

A. Tell the surgical SHO that you are no longer able to assist her, and bleep the surgical registrar to come and help you assess the ward patients.

B. Tell the nurse that you are busy with another patient. Hand over the ward patients to the night team and go to A&E. Clerk in the patient with suspected pancreatitis.

C. Tell the surgical SHO that you are no longer able to assist her and take blood cultures from the patient spiking a fever. Then assess the patient with haematemesis.

D. Tell the surgical SHO that you are no longer able to assist her and assess the patient that presents with haematemesis. Then deal with the patient with fever.

E. Hand over all the ward patients to the night team for review, and tell the surgical SHO that you cannot see the patient with suspected pancreatitis as you need to make the handover list for the night team.

Scenario 42

You are an FY1 in Psychiatry at a District General Hospital (DGH). You are running a clinic in parallel with your consultant.

You see a 43-year-old female patient who has a history of paranoid schizophrenia. She tells you that she plans to stab her employer tomorrow, and she has bought a knife.

Having talked it through with her, you believe her intentions are serious.

Rank in order the following actions in response to this situation (1= Most appropriate; 5= Least appropriate):

A. Inform the patient's employer as well as the police about the patient's intentions.

B. Inform the patient's employer about the patient's intentions.

C. Inform the police about the patient's plans for the employer, without asking the patient for her consent.

D. Respect the patient's confidentiality but attempt to discourage the patient from taking action.

E. Ask for consent from the patient first before disclosing to the police.

Scenario 43

You are an FY1 in Vascular Surgery. One of your patients has recently come back from theatre. You note that she is very drowsy.

After performing an arterial blood gas (ABG), you note that the patient has Type 2 respiratory failure and is acidotic, which you feel warrants a course of non–invasive ventilation (NIV).

You phone the local CCOT (Critical Care Outreach Team) to review the history and the ABG result, but the CCOT nurse refuses to set up the NIV as he feels that the ABG result does not justify NIV.

He asks you to review the patient in 30 minutes' time and get back to him with the new ABG results.

Rank in order the following actions in response to this situation (1= Most appropriate; 5= Least appropriate):

A.   Phone the CCOT nurse again 30 minutes later. Exaggerate the ABG results to persuade him to set up the NIV machine.

B.   Contact the consultant for advice.

C.   Contact the Respiratory registrar for advice.

D.   Re-assess the patient in 30 minutes' time with a new ABG. Discuss this new assessment with the CCOT nurse.

E.   Set up the NIV equipment for the patient yourself.

Scenario 44

You are an FY1 in Gastroenterology. You are currently looking after a patient with terminal metastatic pancreatic cancer.

The patient is elderly and frail, but alert and awake. The family is closely involved with his care and asks that you do not reveal the result of the latest CT scan to him. They feel the prognosis would make his remaining days miserable.

Rank in order the following actions in response to this situation
(1= Most appropriate; 5= Least appropriate):

A. Follow the family's wishes and withhold the results from the patient.

B. Tell the family that the patient is entitled to know the results of the scan.

C. Tell the family you can follow their wishes as long as they put in writing.

D. Agree that you will not say anything. Then ask your SHO to break the news to the patient instead.

E. Write to the GP, asking him to communicate the results of the CT scan to the patient.

Scenario 45

You are an FY1 in Cardiology. You have just presented the results of your audit on heart failure medication use at a National Conference. You conducted with your consultant.

A drug company representative is impressed with the results and wishes to have a copy of the patient data that you collected for the audit.

Rank in order the following actions in response to this situation (1= Most appropriate; 5= Least appropriate):

A. Give the rep all the patient data.

B. Give the rep the patient data but in anonymised form.

C. Tell the rep it would not be ethical for you to provide the data.

D. Ask the rep to give you a formal request in writing.

E. Ask the rep to email your consultant with the request.

Scenario 46

You are a Gastroenterology FY1. A 90-year-old female patient has been admitted to hospital following a gastrointestinal bleed. The bleeding stopped after treatment by a proton pump inhibitor. She lives with her daughter and son-in-law.

You notice that she is underweight and has several bruises on her limbs. She confides to you that her son-in-law (who is her carer) occasionally hits her when he is drunk. She tells you that, because it doesn't happen that often and she wishes her son-in-law to remain her carer, she does not want to take the issue further or even raise it with anyone.

Assume that the patient is competent.

Rank in order the following actions in response to this situation (1= Most appropriate; 5= Least appropriate):

A. Ask her if you could talk to her daughter about her son-in-law's drinking problems.

B. Contact social services to make a safeguarding referral.

C. Report the assault to the police.

D. Advise the patient that she should be admitted to a nursing home.

E. Give the patient contact details of relevant support groups.

Scenario 47

You are the General Surgical FY1 on call. A 20-year-old girl has been admitted with abdominal pains. Her observations are stable, and she was last seen in the TV room watching her favourite series with enjoyment.

She refuses to have blood taken as she claims to have a phobia of needles and doesn't like the "prickly feeling you get".

Rank in order the following actions in response to this situation (1= Most appropriate; 5= Least appropriate):

A. Explain to the patient the importance of having blood tests. Then attempt to take blood straight away.

B. Ask a nurse to hold her down whilst you take blood.

C. Discharge the patient as she is refusing blood tests.

D. Observe her overnight.

E. Offer to put some local anaesthetic cream on her arm before attempting to take blood again 30 minutes later.

Scenario 48

You are an FY1 in Endocrinology & Diabetes. You have been invited to a dinner given by a pharmaceutical company in the context of a conference on diabetes.

In addition to the free dinner, there is a lecture given on the latest drugs currently in development for diabetes, as well as a complimentary "goody bag" containing £50 in book vouchers.

Rank in order the following actions in response to this situation (1= Most appropriate; 5= Least appropriate):

A. Refuse the invitation to attend.

B. Attend the lecture component only.

C. Do not accept the book voucher; accept only the dinner and lecture.

D. Accept the book voucher, dinner and lecture.

E. Accept the dinner and book voucher only.

Scenario 49

You are an FY1 in Geriatrics. You have been looking after a patient with multiple co-morbidities. The patient is due to be discharged to a physio-therapy rehabilitation unit once you have completed his referral form.

The patient is extremely grateful for the care he has received and his family brings in a home-cooked meal, a cake and a bunch of flowers for you.

Rank in order the following actions in response to this situation (1= Most appropriate; 5= Least appropriate):

A. Refuse all the gifts.

B. Accept the gifts with gratitude and take them home.

C. Accept the home-cooked meal but refuse the rest.

D. Accept the gifts and tell the patient that you are sure the team will appreciate the gesture.

E. Refuse the gifts for now, but say that you will accept it when you have completed the patient's rehabilitation referral form.

Scenario 50

You are the Respiratory FY1. An 86-year-old patient hands you an envelope and says that this is for you, and only you, as you have looked after him so well.

You open the envelope and find that it contains £500 in cash.

Rank in order the following actions in response to this situation (1= Most appropriate; 5= Least appropriate):

A. Refuse the money entirely.

B. Accept the money with gratitude.

C. Accept the money and donate it to charity.

D. Accept the money and buy chocolates for all the staff on the ward.

E. Tell the patient you will be able to accept only half of the money as £500 is rather a lot.

Scenario 51

You are an FY1 in Orthopaedics. A 16-year-old girl has been admitted following a road traffic accident. She has a fractured left femur and has lost a lot of blood.

She and her family are practising Jehovah's Witnesses. Her haemoglobin level is 5.8 g/dl (11.5-16g/dl), and she has made the conscious and informed decision to accept a blood transfusion as this is life-threatening.

Her mother and father intervene and tell you that they refuse to consent to the blood transfusion.

Rank in order the following actions in response to this situation (1= Most appropriate; 5= Least appropriate):

A. Explain to the parents that, since the girl has consented, you will now need to proceed. Apologise for any hurt this may cause and transfuse the girl.

B. Respect parental wishes and do not transfuse.

C. Withhold the transfusion until the parents have had time to seek advice from the Jehovah's Witness society.

D. Advise the parents that they have to get a High Court injunction to stop the transfusion. Give the blood transfusion.

E. Call the hospital lawyers. Withhold the transfusion until the lawyers have given their advice regarding transfusion.

Scenario 52

You are an FY1 in Paediatrics. A 5-year-old boy has been admitted four times previously this year with several episodes of trauma that did not seem related.

Today, the child is brought in with a large burn on his leg. The explanation given is that he has "slipped into a hot bathtub".

Rank in order the following actions in response to this situation (1= Most appropriate; 5= Least appropriate):

A. Admit the child to remove him from the possibly dangerous environment.

B. Call the police.

C. Ask the parent whether there has been any abuse.

D. Report the family to social services.

E. Discharge the child from hospital without further investigations.

Scenario 53

You are doing an FY1 taster week in a GP practice, and you have your own GP list. A 16-year-old girl comes in complaining of nausea. She is accompanied by her mother.

Her mother has to step outside to answer her phone. Whilst alone with you, the girl tells you that she has taken a pregnancy test and it was positive.

The girl wishes to continue with the pregnancy under your care. She is adamant that you should not tell her parents about the pregnancy.

Rank in order the following actions in response to this situation (1= Most appropriate; 5= Least appropriate):

A. Provide prenatal care. Do not tell the mother that she is pregnant.

B. Provide prenatal care. If the mother asks about pregnancy, tell the truth.

C. Refuse prenatal care. Inform the mother that she is pregnant.

D. Provide prenatal care. Inform the mother that she is pregnant.

E. Provide prenatal care. Speak with the girl in private and encourage her to tell her mother about the pregnancy.

Scenario 54

You are an FY1 doing a taster week in a GP practice, and you have your own GP list.

One of your patients is a pregnant woman who is Rhesus sensitised due to a previous history of pregnancy terminations which occurred before she met her current husband. Her current husband, who is Rhesus negative, is also one of your patients and is not aware of his wife's previous pregnancy terminations.

During an earlier prenatal visit attended by this woman and her husband, the doctor had mentioned in passing that the woman was Rhesus sensitised. It didn't mean much to the husband at the time; but he has come back today to ask what made his wife Rhesus sensitised.

Rank in order the following actions in response to this situation
(1= Most appropriate; 5= Least appropriate):

A. Tell the husband that you cannot tell him anything as you are bound by your duty of confidentiality. Apologise for not being able to be more specific.

B. Tell the husband that you have a duty of care towards him as he is also a patient and that he is therefore entitled to know about his wife's history of previous abortions.

C. Tell the husband that his wife is better placed to answer his question.

D. Tell the husband that Rhesus sensitisation is due to her catching a cold.

E. Tell the husband that you can't speak specifically about his wife's situation because of your duty of confidentiality, but that Rhesus sensitisation could be due to a wide range of factors including previous blood transfusions.

Scenario 55

You are an FY1 in Psychiatry and are looking after a 30-year-old schizophrenic patient on the ward. She has an abscess in her lung, but she is refusing antibiotic treatment for it. She has also refused to take her medication for schizophrenia for the past 2 weeks.

She is thought to be fully competent regarding her understanding of this abscess, including the effects and consequences of not being treated.

She does feel, however, that the security guards are poisoning her antipsychotics; hence she is refusing to take them.

Rank in order the following actions in response to this situation
(1= Most appropriate; 5= Least appropriate):

A. Detain her for treatment of both her abscess and her schizophrenia.

B. Detain her for treatment of her schizophrenia only.

C. Detain her for treatment of her abscess only.

D. Discharge the patient as she is competent.

E. Discharge her and follow up with a home visit in 3 days' time.

Scenario 56

You are an FY1 in the Medical Admission Unit, and you are clerking in a 21-year-old woman with an 8-year history of anorexia nervosa. She has severe hypoglycaemia and deranged electrolytes, and is physically quite unwell.

She has not eaten anything for a week and is refusing treatment in hospital because she says she couldn't bear putting on any weight. She understands the consequences of her actions.

Rank in order the following actions in response to this situation (1= Most appropriate; 5= Least appropriate):

A. Refer her to the psychiatric team for treatment by the team for her anorexia nervosa.

B. Admit her to the hospital under the Mental Health Act.

C. Restrain her in order to place a nasogastric tube and force-feed her.

D. Get an immediate urgent psychiatric review.

E. Discharge her.

Scenario 57

You are an FY1 currently working in A&E.

A 24-year-old intravenous drug user asks you whether you could give him some sterile needles and syringes.

Rank in order the following actions in response to this situation (1= Most appropriate; 5= Least appropriate):

A. Do not give the man needles and syringes.

B. Give the man needles and syringes.

C. Refer the man to a specialist centre to exchange needles.

D. Do not give the man needles and refer him to a drug cessation programme.

E. Call the police to search the man for possession of drugs.

Scenario 58

You are an FY1 and are currently at home. Your neighbour calls you and tells you that his 10-year-old daughter, whom you sometimes babysit and know quite well, has a throat infection. He would like you to examine her.

Rank in order the following actions in response to this situation (1= Most appropriate; 5= Least appropriate):

A. Examine and assess the child. Prescribe analgesia and antibiotics if appropriate.

B. Tell the neighbour that you are not meant to examine or treat friends or family. Ask him to take the child to the local out-of-hours service.

C. Tell him to take the child to A&E if he is worried.

D. Tell him that it is probably nothing.

E. Examine and assess the child. Give your suspected diagnosis to the father but do not prescribe medications.

Scenario 59

During a clinic run by your consultant, you walk into the room and find him with his arms around a patient's shoulder.

Rank in order the following actions in response to this situation (1= Most appropriate; 5= Least appropriate):

A. Assume that there must be a reasonable explanation for the situation and ignore the issue.

B. Ask the patient to leave the room so that you can have a word with the consultant.

C. Report the matter to the Clinical Director.

D. Have a word with the consultant after the patient has left and ask him about the circumstances.

E. Seek advice from the ST5 who is running the clinic next door.

Scenario 60

A patient discovers it is your birthday, and presents you with a relatively inexpensive bottle of your favourite drink.

Rank in order the following actions in response to this situation (1= Most appropriate; 5= Least appropriate):

A. Refuse the gift because it is against regulations.

B. Graciously accept the gift, telling the patient that it is kind of her.

C. Accept the gift but make sure you inform your seniors.

D. Accept the gift but tell the patient that it is not necessary; you will continue to care for her in the same way.

E. Refuse the gift but double-check your hospital protocol on gifts afterwards.

Scenario 61

Whilst you are conducting a clinic, a female patient mentions that, during her previous consultation, one of your colleagues examined her breasts. This seems odd to you because there is nothing mentioned in the notes.

Rank in order the following actions in response to this situation (1= Most appropriate; 5= Least appropriate):

A. Ask the patient about the circumstances surrounding the examination and, after the consultation, ask the colleague involved for further details on the issue.

B. Tell the patient that this might constitute an assault and explain the complaint procedure to her.

C. Say nothing to the patient and report the incident to the Clinical Director.

D. Seek advice from a trusted senior colleague.

E. Contact the GMC.

Scenario 62

You are a surgical FY1 on call during a weekend when there are poor staffing levels. On the ward an elderly patient is deteriorating rapidly despite the team's best efforts, to the point that you are starting to feel that a Do Not Resuscitate order may be appropriate.

The patient's wife pulls you aside and tells you in no uncertain terms that she has talked to their sons and daughters and the family is in agreement that everything is to be done for the patient, whatever his condition and prognosis.

Rank in order the following actions in response to this situation (1= Most appropriate; 5= Least appropriate):

A. Seek advice from the on-site on-call registrar.

B. Call the on-call consultant at home.

C. Discuss with the patient and summarise your conversation with him in the notes.

D. Write in the notes that the patient should be resuscitated if needed.

E. Tell the relative that DNR orders are ultimately a doctor's decision and that their and the patient's stance does not actually matter in this instance.

Scenario 63

You are a medical FY1. You have been asked to see a patient who is very muscular, has many tattoos and has been to prison for violence in the past. The room where you are meant to see the patient is some distance away from your department and is a bit isolated.

Rank in order the following actions in response to this situation (1= Most appropriate; 5= Least appropriate):

A.   Refuse to see the patient.

B.   Ask a receptionist to organise a room closer to your department.

C.   Ask one of the nurses to accompany you.

D.   Go and see the patient on your own, being as careful as you can.

E.   Ask one of the nurses to go and see the patient to determine whether there is an urgent clinical need to see the patient straight away.

Scenario 64

One Friday morning, a colleague of yours calls the ward from home, saying that she will not be coming in because she is feeling unwell.

Subsequently, you find out that she in fact spent a long weekend abroad with her family and was never actually unwell.

Rank in order the following actions in response to this situation (1= Most appropriate; 5= Least appropriate):

A. Do nothing.

B. Tell your consultant as soon as you find out about the lie.

C. Ask this colleague about the situation and warn her that you will have no option but to mention something to the consultant if this recurs.

D. Discuss the matter with your fellow junior doctors.

E. Ask this colleague about the situation at the next team meeting.

Scenario 65

You walk into the doctors' mess and catch one of your ST3s watching child pornography on his laptop. He is not aware of your presence.

Rank in order the following actions in response to this situation (1= Most appropriate; 5= Least appropriate):

A. Nothing. He is watching the images on his private computer and therefore it is his own business.

B. Inform the police.

C. Send an anonymous note to your colleague saying that you spotted him watching the images and that the consultant will be warned next time it happens.

D. Approach a senior colleague whom you can trust and let him handle the matter.

E. Notify the medical personnel department.

Scenario 66

A nurse with whom you used to work on another ward tells you that one of her colleagues was very drunk during the Christmas party and was flirting heavily with one of the paramedics. Her seniors were not present at the party.

Rank in order the following actions in response to this situation (1= Most appropriate; 5= Least appropriate):

A. Do nothing.

B. Approach the nurse and tell her that, by making a fool of herself, she acted unprofessionally.

C. Have a word with one of her seniors.

D. Ask your consultant to have a word with one of her seniors.

E. Contact the Director of Nursing about the issue.

Scenario 67

You leave the hospital and see a homeless person on a bus stop bench just outside A&E. He is holding an empty bottle of wine and is vomiting on the pavement.

Rank in order the following actions in response to this situation (1= Most appropriate; 5= Least appropriate):

A. Walk past him and ignore him.

B. Go up to him and see if he is okay.

C. Take him to A&E.

D. Go to A&E yourself and ask a member of the team to take charge of him.

E. Call 999.

Scenario 68

Whilst on a ward round with your consultant (your ST3 is away today), a patient goes into cardiac arrest. The arrest call has been put out and the team has yet to arrive.

Having completed your ALS course a month ago and led several arrests since, you are best placed to assume the role of team leader. Your consultant has not recertified his ALS for many years but is now giving orders that you know are inappropriate.

Rank in order the following actions in response to this situation (1= Most appropriate; 5= Least appropriate):

A. Ensure that only basic life support is being given while you are waiting for the arrest team to arrive.

B. Let the consultant take over the handling of the arrest and discuss with him later how it may be better to let colleagues more experienced with cardiac arrest lead such situations in future.

C. Let the consultant give orders but signal to the nurses to do differently when you feel his orders are not appropriate.

D. Reassure the consultant that you are the most experienced and up-to-date person on the team. Then take over the leadership of the team.

E. Ask a nurse to call another consultant with cardiac arrest experience from the adjacent ward. Let your consultant lead the arrest while waiting for the other consultant to arrive.

Scenario 69

You walk into the mess and find one of your colleagues taking a gulp from a bottle of whisky, while you know that his shift does not end for another three hours.

Rank in order the following actions in response to this situation (1= Most appropriate; 5= Least appropriate):

A. Let your colleague know that his behaviour makes him unsafe towards patients and that, as a result, you will need to inform his educational supervisor.

B. As your colleague does not appear to be drunk, let the matter drop for the time being.

C. As your colleague does not appear to be drunk, let the matter drop but let him know that you will need to talk to senior colleagues if you catch him again.

D. Discuss the situation with your colleague to determine the reasons for his drinking and offer to help him out. Encourage your colleague to discuss the situation with his seniors.

E. At the end of your colleague's shift, organise a meeting with other junior doctors to discuss how you can best proceed.

Scenario 70

A 17-year-old female patient presents in MAU covered with very severe bruises. She explains that she lives with a criminal who sometimes beats her up when he is high on drugs.

When you offer to help her out, she refuses to allow you to tell anyone about it.

Rank in order the following actions in response to this situation (1= Most appropriate; 5= Least appropriate):

A. Maintain your patient's confidentiality and do nothing.

B. Tell the patient that, whether she gives consent or not, you have a duty to contact social services or the police.

C. Seek advice from one of your senior colleagues about how you should proceed.

D. Ask the girl if she would be prepared to discuss the issue with someone from social services. If she refuses, do it anyway but without her knowledge.

E. Contact her partner to discuss the situation with him.

Scenario 71

You have arrived home at the end of a very busy 12-hour on-call shift.

You suddenly realise that you forgot to hand over to the night FY1 that an urgent FBC result needed to be chased on a patient who might need a transfusion following a post-operative bleed.

Rank in order the following actions in response to this situation (1= Most appropriate; 5= Least appropriate):

A. Call the ward where the patient is staying and ask the nurses to bleep the FY1 to ensure he chases the blood result urgently.

B. Call the ward where the patient is staying and ask the nurses to ensure the blood test result is found. Ask them to add it to the on-call doctor's ward list of jobs to review.

C. Call the lab from home and chase the result. If it is abnormal, call the FY1 covering the ward to ensure the patient gets treatment.

D. Call the registrar (ST4) and ask him to ensure he reviews the patient.

E. Call the FY1 on call and hand over the patient ensuring they get the result as soon as they can.

Scenario 72

You are expected to complete an audit by a specific deadline. You have left it late and now only have 24 hours left to collate 50 sets of patient notes, identify and collect the data required for analysis and then write it up for submission.

You are currently working busy shifts.

Rank in order the following actions in response to this situation (1= Most appropriate; 5= Least appropriate):

A. Ask your supervising consultant if he will approve cover for you to ensure that you complete the audit by the deadline.

B. Ask one of your fellow FY1s to cover your bleep for the rest of the day to enable you to complete the audit by the deadline.

C. Arrange to collate 10 sets of notes, acquire the data and multiply the results by 5, giving you 50 sets of data.

D. Talk to your supervising consultant and explain that you have not completed the audit and ask for an extension on the deadline.

E. Work overnight at the hospital on the audit project to ensure that you complete the task. If the next day you are too tired, you always have the option not to go to work.

Scenario 73

The hospital prescribing policy states that Augmentin (co-amoxiclav) should not be prescribed without approval from the microbiology team.

Your consultant asks you to prescribe Augmentin at 1.2g tds intravenously for a patient.

Rank in order the following actions in response to this situation (1= Most appropriate; 5= Least appropriate):

A. Say nothing but contact the microbiologist for advice once your consultant has left.

B. Approach your consultant and quote the ward prescribing policy.

C. Refuse to prescribe the drug.

D. Say nothing and ask your ST3 at the end of the ward round for advice.

E. Prescribe the Augmentin but document in the notes that you are prescribing the drug against your best judgement.

Scenario 74

You have received a voicemail message on your mobile phone to ask you to call your bank's fraud department urgently.

They have contacted you three times already and you failed to call back because you were too busy. The message informs you that, if you do not call back urgently, your bank account will be frozen. The message explains that the bank simply wants to check a few transactions with you and states that the call is expected to last no more than 5 minutes.

You are due in theatre to assist your consultant. He has asked you to get there as soon as you can because the ST2, who is currently assisting, has to leave to attend a course.

Rank in order the following actions in response to this situation
(1= Most appropriate; 5= Least appropriate):

A. Ask a fellow FY1 from another team to go to theatre to cover for you so that you can make the phone call.

B. Go to theatre straight away and leave the call until later.

C. Go to theatre and inform the theatre nurse that you will be delayed by 10 minutes due to an emergency. Call the bank and then go to theatre.

D. Call the theatre team to tell them you are on your way, make the call to the bank, and then go to theatre.

E. Call the theatre nurse and tell her that you are too busy to replace the ST2 and they will need to find someone else to assist. Then call the bank.

Scenario 75

You are running a pre-admission clinic alongside a nurse practitioner.

You see a patient who was born with a congenital heart defect (transposition of the great arteries) and has been listed for a routine hernia repair. You are not entirely sure of the nature of the pre-operative investigations that you should be carrying out.

**Rank in order the following actions in response to this situation
(1= Most appropriate; 5= Least appropriate):**

A. Call your ST3 and ask for advice regarding what investigations to do pre-operatively.

B. Do the routine pre-operative investigations; there is no indication to do anything else in the notes.

C. Call the anaesthetist and ask for advice regarding what investigations need to be done pre-operatively.

D. Ask the nurse practitioner for advice regarding pre-operative investigations.

E. Call your consultant and ask for advice regarding what investigations need to be done pre-operatively.

Scenario 76

The FY1 taking over from you at 9pm for the night shift is running late.

His car has broken down and he is waiting for the emergency services to recover him and his car. He has no idea how long this will take. You have already worked a 13-hour shift and are exhausted. You need to go home and sleep as you are due to work a 12-hour shift tomorrow.

Rank in order the following actions in response to this situation (1= Most appropriate; 5= Least appropriate):

A. Wait until 10pm and then leave. You need a good night's sleep before your shift the following day.

B. Leave at 9pm. Your shift is over.

C. Call the bleep holder for the hospital and explain the problem, informing him that you have to leave at 9pm due to fatigue.

D. Talk to the ST3 on the night shift and explain that you need to leave due to fatigue.

E. Stay until the FY1 arrives, no matter how late this is.

Scenario 77

A fellow FY1 tells you that his supervising ST5 on call has made six clinical mistakes so far during the shift. One of them endangered a patient's life.

Rank in order the following actions in response to this situation (1= Most appropriate; 5= Least appropriate):

A. Tell your colleague to complete a critical incident form.

B. Advise the FY1 to go straight to the consultant with his concerns.

C. Offer to go with the FY1 to the on-call consultant to explain his fears.

D. Have a look at the on-call rota to make sure you are not on shift with this particular ST5 in the near future.

E. Contact the ST5 and report what the FY1 is saying about him.

Scenario 78

A relative of a patient approaches you, mentioning that she is upset with the standard of care on the ward.

Rank in order the following actions in response to this situation (1= Most appropriate; 5= Least appropriate):

A. Sit the relative down and ask what her concerns are.

B. Gently inform the relative that you are not experienced enough to deal with such complaints and ask her to talk to one of the nurses.

C. Advise her you are not in a position to discuss any aspect of patient care because of confidentiality issues.

D. Explain to her what PALS (Patient Advice and Liaison Service) do and give her a telephone contact number that she can call.

E. Go straight to the patient and ask him whether he can tell you what the problem is.

Scenario 79

A patient refuses to allow you to cannulate him stating "You tried three times yesterday and I'm bruised; please go and get someone who knows what they are doing."

Rank in order the following actions in response to this situation (1= Most appropriate; 5= Least appropriate):

A. Call your ST3 so that he can do the cannulation.

B. Apologise to the patient. Gently explain to him that you are only an FY1 and need to learn. Proceed with a further attempt.

C. Sit and talk to the patient to try to understand why he is concerned and ask if he will let you try just one more time under the supervision of a senior colleague.

D. Ask a nurse to come and help hold the patient while you try again.

E. Apologise and offer to get another person to help.

Scenario 80

During a protected teaching session your bleep goes off. The administrator holding the bleeps interrupts your teaching session to let you know that the nurses on the ward need to have a patient reviewed.

Rank in order the following actions in response to this situation (1= Most appropriate; 5= Least appropriate):

A. Ignore the bleep.

B. Ask the administrator to tell the nurses that you are unavailable and that they should contact another member of the team.

C. Go quickly to the ward to ask the nurses why the patient needs reviewing. Deal with the patient if there is a sense of urgency. If it can wait, then return to the teaching session straight away.

D. Briefly excuse yourself from teaching. Call the ward and explain to the nurses that you are unavailable. Ask what the nature of the problem is. If it can wait, then tell the nurses they need to contact another member of the team. If it is urgent, only go there if there is no one else on the ward who can deal with it.

E. Go and review the patient. Return to teaching as soon as practically possible.

Scenario 81

Your consultant is due to give the FY1s (including you) some bedside teaching. Ten minutes before the start of the session, he tells you that he is unable to lead the teaching session because of a genuine emergency.

He wants you to ensure that the students still meet and that you lead the session yourself.

Rank in order the following actions in response to this situation (1= Most appropriate; 5= Least appropriate):

A. Tell the FY1s that the session is cancelled.

B. Explain to the consultant that you do not feel experienced enough to lead the FY1 teaching without senior support.

C. Try your best and make a complaint to the postgraduate tutor.

D. Ask the consultant to rearrange the teaching for another time.

E. Ask the consultant for a list of suitable patients.

Scenario 82

One of your ward patients tells you that her son, who is a doctor, has told her that the treatment she is getting on the ward is inferior to the treatment she would get if she were in her son's hospital.

The patient is worried but when you ask her what she is worried about she is not able to tell you and only says: "I don't know. My son did tell me, but it all sounds a bit complicated to me."

Rank in order the following actions in response to this situation (1= Most appropriate; 5= Least appropriate):

A. Ask her to talk to the consultant at the next ward round.

B. Give her the Patient Advice and Liaison Service (PALS) telephone contact so that they can formalise their complaint.

C. Inform the consultant as soon as you can.

D. Ask her for her son's contact number and her permission to discuss the issues with him.

E. Ask her whether her son is likely to visit soon. You can then arrange a meeting with the patient, the son and relevant members of your team.

Scenario 83

The FY1 with whom you share the ward always stays late and is usually on the ward before you arrive.

Rank in order the following actions in response to this situation (1= Most appropriate; 5= Least appropriate):

A. Do nothing but just keep an eye on your colleague to make sure he is okay.

B. The following morning, ask the FY1 if he needs any help when you come in. Take some of their work off him to help out.

C. Once you have finished your jobs for the day, offer to help the other FY1 with his own jobs.

D. Inform his FY2 that you have noticed the other FY1 works long hours and suggest he offers to help.

E. When you leave at 5pm, tell the other FY1 that he now needs to go home, insisting that he hands over to the on-call FY1.

Scenario 84

One of your ward patients speaks a language that you do not recognise and cannot speak a single word of English. There is usually a family member with her to interpret but today there is no one.

You need to take some blood from the patient today and your usual translation service is unable to ascertain what language the patient speaks.

Rank in order the following actions in response to this situation (1= Most appropriate; 5= Least appropriate):

A. Take the blood.

B. Approach the patient, show her the blood taking equipment and mimic the blood taking procedure. Then proceed to take the blood.

C. Approach the patient, and using very simple English explain that you are going to take some blood. Then take the blood.

D. Leave the form for the phlebotomist the next day.

E. Call a family member and ask if they can come in to help you out.

Scenario 85

One of the FY1s is not working well as a team member. Whenever you take a handover from him, there is always a huge list of jobs that need completing, which he has not been able to finish on time. This happens when you take over on both night and day shifts.

No other member of the FY1 team behaves in this way and everyone else appears to be able to complete their work on time.

Rank in order the following actions in response to this situation (1= Most appropriate; 5= Least appropriate):

A. Arrange a meeting with all the FY1s to discuss expectations for handovers.

B. Ask this particular FY1 for a chat and mention your concerns over the large number of patients he is handing over.

C. Whenever you are handing over to this particular FY1, ensure that you always leave a bigger list of jobs, so as to share the work evenly.

D. Try to change your shifts to ensure you do not take a hand over from this particular FY1.

E. The next time he hands you a list of jobs, ask him why there are so many. Ensure you do that every time he hands over to you.

Scenario 86

You are running late for work and have not had your morning coffee or breakfast. You are on call tonight; you know that you may not get a break for hours and that you need to eat something to ensure you function adequately.

You were due on the ward round 15 minutes ago and they have started without you. You have only just arrived inside the hospital building; there is a coffee shop on site but there are three people waiting in front of you in the queue.

Rank in order the following actions in response to this situation (1= Most appropriate; 5= Least appropriate):

A. Go to the front of the queue, explain that you are a doctor on call and ask to be served first.

B. Page the registrar (ST3) on your team explaining that you have just arrived and that you will be there in 10 minutes. Join the queue.

C. Wait for your turn and get your coffee.

D. Go to the ward and go back to the coffee shop after your ward round.

E. Go to the ward and give some money to a secretary so that she can buy you some food and a coffee in the next 20 minutes or so. Join the ward round in the meantime.

Scenario 87

You are an FY1 in General Surgery. You are conducting a pre-operative assessment clinic when you discover that a patient has been prescribed by his GP two medications that interact. You know that they should not be prescribed together.

He is due to collect his next supply of medication from the community pharmacy in 3 days' time.

His operation is due to take place in 2 weeks' time.

Rank in order the following actions in response to this situation (1= Most appropriate; 5= Least appropriate):

A. Write a critical incident form.

B. Ask for advice from the ward pharmacist and change the medication accordingly. Write to the GP to inform him of the change.

C. Call the GP, discuss the issue of drug interaction with him and ask him to change the prescription.

D. Call the GP and leave a message with the receptionist asking the GP to check for interactions and to change the prescription for that patient.

E. Ask the patient to raise the matter with his community pharmacy when he next picks up his medications.

Scenario 88

You are sitting with your team (ST1, ST5 and consultant) having a coffee following a very long ward round, discussing important issues regarding training opportunities in the department.

During the discussion, your bleep goes off. It is the ward asking you to come and resite a venflon for a lady who needs antibiotics.

You expect that the discussion will last for another 10 minutes.

Rank in order the following actions in response to this situation
(1= Most appropriate; 5= Least appropriate):

A. Tell the nurse that you will attend to the patient in due course. Add the venflon to your to-do list.

B. Inform the nurse that you are in a meeting and ask her to ask the nurse practitioner who is working on the ward today to resite it. Ask her to call you back if the nurse practitioner is not available.

C. Apologise to your colleagues, ask your ST5 if he wouldn't mind scheduling the meeting for a quieter time and attend the ward straight away.

D. Tell the nurse you are on a break.

E. Inform the nurse that you are in an important meeting and recommend that she finds someone who is free to do it.

Scenario 89

You have just admitted a patient who needs a cannula before he can be admitted for observation into the surgical unit for elective surgery.

Whilst cannulating the patient, you accidently prick your finger. You are worried about the patient's HIV status.

Looking at the patient's notes, you see that all other blood-borne viral serologies are negative.

Rank in order the following actions in response to this situation (1= Most appropriate; 5= Least appropriate):

A. Ask the lab to use the pre-operative bloods taken from the patient to carry out an additional test for HIV. Because the same blood is being used for the extra test, there is no need to seek additional patient consent.

B. Ask the ward sister to consent the patient for an HIV test and to perform the test if consent is given.

C. Ask the patient for consent and perform an HIV test on the patient if consent is given.

D. Perform an HIV test on the patient with consent, using a disposable hospital number, but do not document the results.

E. Call the HIV registrar or Occupational Health for advice.

Scenario 90

Your FY2 has prescribed penicillin to a patient during the ward round. You think the patient is allergic to penicillin.

The drug chart does not say whether the patient has a drug allergy; the relevant section has somehow been left completely blank.

Rank in order the following actions in response to this situation (1= Most appropriate; 5= Least appropriate):

A. Tell the patient that a mistake has happened, apologise and tell him you will try to get one of your seniors to sort the problem out.

B. Ask the nurse if she remembers whether the patient has an allergy to penicillin and re-prescribe the right antibiotic as required.

C. Ask the patient whether he has an allergy to penicillin and ensure an appropriate antibiotic is prescribed.

D. Ask the registrar if he remembers whether a penicillin allergy was mentioned at the ward round, and ensure an appropriate antibiotic is prescribed.

E. Delete the penicillin prescription from the drug chart until the allergy is confirmed then ensure an appropriate antibiotic is prescribed.

Scenario 91

You are a General Surgery FY1 in a large teaching hospital. An 18-year-old boy has been admitted following a road traffic accident in which his spleen has ruptured. He has lost a lot of blood.

Both he and his family are practising Jehovah's Witnesses. His haemoglobin is 6.2 g/dl (13.5-18g/dl), and he refuses a blood transfusion despite having been advised of the life-threatening consequences. The patient is competent.

Rank in order the following actions in response to this situation (1= Most appropriate; 5= Least appropriate):

A. Override the boy's wishes and give the boy a blood transfusion.

B. Respect the boy's wishes and do not give him a blood transfusion.

C. Ask for help from the Jehovah's Witnesses society.

D. Contact the Trust's legal advisers with the aim to seek a court order to enforce the transfusion.

E. Ask the parents to make the decision on behalf of their son and give a transfusion if they agree to it. Do not give a blood transfusion if they refuse.

Scenario 92

You are doing a taster week in a GP surgery, and you have your own GP list. A 14-week pregnant woman comes to your prenatal clinic at the practice. She has a history of previous STIs (Sexually Transmitted Infections) which were treated some time ago.

On checking her antenatal folder you notice that she declined the HIV test recommended as part of her booking test. You have explained to her the importance of performing the test for her baby's well-being but she refuses to be tested for HIV.

Rank in order the following actions in response to this situation
(1= Most appropriate; 5= Least appropriate):

A. Do not perform the HIV test and do not insist any further.

B. Request HIV serology to be added to the routine set of tests already taken. Tell the woman that you are doing so without her permission because consent is not needed since it is for the health of the baby.

C. Request HIV serology to be added to the routine set of tests already taken, without telling the mother.

D. Offer the patient an option to be referred to the local DGH for an appointment with the Obstetrics & Gynaecology consultant in order to discuss the issue further. In the letter, include the fact the woman has refused HIV testing, and whether the consultant can counsel the woman again.

E. Do not test the patient but ask her again at the next prenatal appointment.

Scenario 93

A 17-year-old girl has arrived to A&E with abdominal pains. On clinical examination, the surgical registrar suspects early appendicitis. He asks you to prepare the patient for surgery whilst he sees another patient.

The patient does not want to have surgery, and understands the implications of not having surgery. Her mother wants her to have the urgent surgery, but her father is unsure.

Rank in order the following actions in response to this situation (1= Most appropriate; 5= Least appropriate):

A. Admit the patient for observation, and try to persuade her in the morning to have the surgery again.

B. Discharge the patient, and tell her to come back to A&E if the pain does not resolve, or gets worse.

C. Give a stat dose of lorazepam and, when the patient is sedated, send her for surgery immediately.

D. Ask the mother to talk the child into having the surgical procedure tonight.

E. Ask the patient why she is worried about surgery, and try to address any issues or worries she may have.

Scenario 94

You are a medical FY1 and are caring for a patient who was admitted 4 days ago with suspected tuberculosis.

You consented the patient for an HIV test yesterday; the test has now come back positive. You have taken an extensive sexual history and you know that the patient is married and has unprotected sex with his wife most nights as they are trying for a child.

He is adamant that he does not want his wife to know; he feels that, if she knew about his HIV status, she would leave him.

The patient is likely to remain as an inpatient for a further 2 days before being discharged.

Rank in order the following actions in response to this situation (1= Most appropriate; 5= Least appropriate):

A. Inform his wife straight away without telling the patient.

B. Give the patient a few days whilst an inpatient to inform his wife. If he doesn't do so, inform him that you will have to inform his wife.

C. Keep his HIV status confidential but remind the patient before you discharge him that he should tell his wife of his positive status when he feels ready to do so.

D. Tell the patient that you will inform his wife of his HIV status that day.

E. Accept the patient's refusal for disclosure, document it in the clinical notes and do not approach his wife.

Scenario 95

You are an FY1 in the Acute Medical Unit (AMU). For a patient who originally had a serum potassium level of 3.0 (normal value 3.5mM – 5.5mM), the consultant prescribed 2 days of Sando-K potassium replacement tablets. However, no stop date was written for the Sando-K tablets and the patient has now had 5 days' worth of tablets.

You check the potassium level again and measure a potassium level of 5.5mM. The patient is asymptomatic.

Rank in order the following actions in response to this situation (1= Most appropriate; 5= Least appropriate):

A. Stop the medication and notify the patient.

B. Keep the patient on Sando-K as he is suffering no ill effects.

C. Stop the medication and complete a reflective entry in your e-portfolio.

D. Stop the medication, complete a yellow card and send to MHRA.

E. Stop the medication and complete a critical incident form.

Scenario 96

You are an FY1 in Gastroenterology and are currently working nights. One of your patients is a 56-year-old alcoholic who has tense ascites.

The medical registrar asks you to insert an urgent ascitic drain within the next hour. You are not comfortable doing the procedure alone as you have only done it once before under supervision.

The SHO and the registrar are about to go and see an emergency patient with bleeding oesophageal varices in Endoscopy. This is expected to take several hours.

Rank in order the following actions in response to this situation (1= Most appropriate; 5= Least appropriate):

A. Ask the on-call consultant to come in and supervise the procedure.

B. Delay the procedure until the registrar is available to supervise you.

C. Attempt the procedure by yourself.

D. Consult several reputable websites explaining the procedure and do the procedure yourself.

E. Ask the on-call surgical registrar to supervise the procedure.

Scenario 97

You are an FY1 on the Acute Medical Unit (AMU). You have just reviewed a patient who was admitted 3 hours ago with a head injury sustained after slipping on an icy pathway; he is otherwise well and desperately wants to go home to look after his children.

You inform him that he could probably go home after a few more hours as he is so well; you simply need to write the discharge summary.

The medical registrar reviews the patient later and informs him that he needs to stay overnight for neuro-observation. The patient is extremely angry and complains to the medical registrar that the FY1 (i.e. you) told him he could go home. He wishes to make a formal complaint and demands to see the consultant.

The medical registrar has just relayed that information to you.

Rank in order the following actions in response to this situation
(1= Most appropriate; 5= Least appropriate):

A. Inform the consultant of the incident, explain the situation and recommend that he talks to the patient.

B. Ask the medical registrar to apologise to the patient on your behalf.

C. Apologise personally to the patient for what has happened.

D. Try to avoid the patient in AMU in order not to aggravate the situation.

E. Speak to PALS (Patient Advise and Liaison Service) for advice.

Scenario 98

You are a Cardiology FY1 and you play for the local rounders club on a regular basis as a fielder. During a match, the pitcher throws a ball straight at the opponent batter's head, briefly knocking him unconscious.

The opponent is able to get up and seems fine. You escort him to the edge of the pitch, awaiting the arrival of an ambulance that you called.

Your rounders captain tells you to get back on the playing field.

Rank in order the following actions in response to this situation (1= Most appropriate; 5= Least appropriate):

A. Go back to fielding the match and ask a substitute player to keep an eye on the batter until the ambulance arrives.

B. Go back to fielding the match and check up on the batter regularly until the ambulance arrives.

C. Go back to fielding the match until the ambulance arrives and hand over to the paramedics.

D. Stay with the batter until the ambulance arrives.

E. Stay with the batter for a short while and hand over to a trained first aider volunteer to keep an eye on the batter until the ambulance arrives.

Scenario 99

You have been taken to a local football match by some of your non-medic friends. During the match, one of the players goes down during a tackle. The coach asks if there is a medic in the audience, and you volunteer to help. The player does not look very injured or distressed.

As you rush towards the player in question, the coach whispers to you for you to look busy and fuss around the downed player so that he can allow his team to have a rest.

Rank in order the following actions in response to this situation (1= Most appropriate; 5= Least appropriate):

A. Ignore the coach's request, make sure the player is safe and then leave the pitch.

B. Assess the patient, call an ambulance straight away and delay the match until the ambulance has arrived.

C. Assess the player and then stay on the pitch for longer than you think is necessary.

D. Tell the coach that you will not do what he says, assess the player, and leave when you feel the player is safe.

E. Leave the pitch straight away.

Scenario 100

You are an FY1, currently on call. You have just clerked in a patient who was admitted via A&E after suffering a witnessed grand mal seizure.

The patient discloses that he has suffered such fits before. Fearing that he might lose his driving licence, he refuses to give you his GP's contact details, or to stop driving. The patient then absconds from the hospital.

Rank in order the following actions in response to this situation (1= Most appropriate; 5= Least appropriate):

A. Contact the DVLA (Driver and Vehicle Licensing Agency) about the incident and notify the patient that you have done so.

B. Get the patient's details from the computer and write to the patient to remind him of the need to notify the DVLA.

C. Wait until the patient has given consent to report him to the DVLA.

D. Get the patient's details from the computer records and write to the patient's GP to arrange a meeting with the patient to persuade him to stop driving.

E. Contact the DVLA (Driver and Vehicle Licensing Agency) without notifying the patient.

Scenario 101

You are a Gastroenterology FY1. Your team has just admitted a 19-year-old male student who has taken an overdose of paracetamol.

He took the tablets following an argument with his mother over the "suitability" of his girlfriend. He is medically fit, has been reviewed by the psychiatric liaison service and is fit for discharge.

His mother has just visited, but he was asleep when she arrived. She hurries along to you and asks how her son is doing.

Rank in order the following actions in response to this situation (1= Most appropriate; 5= Least appropriate):

A. Refuse to speak to the mother outright.

B. Update the mother on the patient's medical condition but not the psychiatric status.

C. Ask the son whether you have consent to discuss any issues before discussing with the mother.

D. Answer the mother's questions accurately and document it in the notes.

E. Tell the mother to talk to her son when he wakes up, as you cannot tell her anything.

Scenario 102

You are an FY1 in Colorectal Surgery. Your educational supervisor for the attachment is also your consultant. He is with you in theatre and is about to operate on an anaesthetised woman with small bowel obstructions secondary to adhesions.

He asks you to perform a speculum PV (per vaginal) examination. That is the only DOPS (directly observed procedure) sign-off left for you to do and you have previously mentioned it to him that you had no idea how to do one. Your attachment will be finished in a few days; so this is pretty much your last chance to do one.

Rank in order the following actions in response to this situation (1= Most appropriate; 5= Least appropriate):

A. Ask the husband for permission before examining the patient.

B. Sign a Consent form 4 (consent form for patients unable to consent because they are unconscious) before proceeding with the PV examination.

C. Refuse to examine the patient.

D. Don't examine this patient but ask your consultant if he could sign you off for the DOPS anyway, as you know that you will be doing more PV examinations in the theatre list.

E. Examine the patient with the speculum and notify the patient afterwards.

Scenario 103

You are in the local shopping centre on a Sunday when you hear some-one greet you by your name.

You turn around and see Miss Smith, a patient you discharged, who was admitted with appendicitis 2 weeks ago. She calls you over and asks for an opinion on her acne, which has worsened since the operation.

Rank in order the following actions in response to this situation (1= Most appropriate; 5= Least appropriate):

A. Tell her to see the out-of-hours service for assessment.

B. Tell her to go to the local A&E department for assessment if she is worried.

C. Ignore the patient and pretend that you did not hear her.

D. Tell her that dermatology is not your specialty and she needs to see another doctor.

E. Tell her that she needs to go to her local GP for a routine appointment.

Scenario 104

You are a Paediatrics FY1. You have been asked to clerk in a 3-year-old child who is crying and has tummy pains.

You note that the mother has a bruise on her arm. She tells you that her husband got angry when her child vomited on the new dining room carpet, and that he hit her for not controlling the child.

She says that the husband has never harmed, or threatened to harm her child; this is the first time he has hit her and she does not want to escalate this any further.

Rank in order the following actions in response to this situation (1= Most appropriate; 5= Least appropriate):

A. Make a follow-up appointment for next week at the Paediatrics outpatient clinic.

B. Contact the police.

C. Give her contact details for a domestic violence group.

D. Talk to the husband in private and advise him not to hit his wife again.

E. Give her contact details for self-defence classes.

129

Scenario 105

You are in the hospital canteen, eating your lunch. You are on call and carry the "crash" bleep.

The bleep goes off for a cardiac arrest call.

Rank in order the following actions in response to this situation (1= Most appropriate; 5= Least appropriate):

A. Finish your lunch, buy a bottle of water and then head to the arrest.

B. Finish your lunch and then head to the arrest.

C. Drop everything and run to the arrest.

D. Package your lunch up, put it in your bag and take it to the arrest walking as quickly as you can.

E. Pick up your lunch and continue eating as you run to the arrest.

Scenario 106

You are an FY1 on the Acute Medical Unit (AMU). You are asked by the ward sister to sign a discharge summary and TTA (drugs to take away on discharge) that another FY1 has prepared; the sister could not get in touch with the other FY1.

You proofread the summary and the TTA, and discover that the other FY1 has noted "Penicillin allergy" in the discharge summary, but has prescribed Augmentin (which contains a penicillin) in the TTA as an oral antibiotic replacement for a non-penicillin IV antibiotic which has just finished today. You decide to keep your findings from the sister so as not to embarrass the other FY1.

Rank in order the following actions in response to this situation (1= Most appropriate; 5= Least appropriate):

A. Find the patient immediately to identify the nature of the allergy, change the antibiotic if required, notify the other FY1 and complete a critical incident form.

B. Find the patient immediately to identify the nature of the allergy, change the antibiotic if required, notify the other FY1 and complete an e-portfolio reflective piece.

C. Refuse to sign the TTA and discharge summary and tell the ward sister to bleep the other AMU FY1.

D. Change the antibiotic to another suitable antibiotic that does not contain penicillin and sign the amended TTA and discharge summary.

E. Change the antibiotic to another suitable antibiotic that does not contain penicillin, sign the amended TTA and discharge summary, and tell the other FY1 what has happened.

Scenario 107

You are an FY1 on a Respiratory ward. You have obtained a patient's consent for you to perform an arterial blood gas (ABG).

Just as you are about to start to take the ABG, a medical student takes you aside and tells you that he is keen to do it. He needs to get it signed off for his portfolio.

He has not done one before, but has read up about it in a clinical skills handbook.

Rank in order the following actions in response to this situation (1= Most appropriate; 5= Least appropriate):

A. Do the ABG yourself but sign the medical student off anyway, as you know that he will be doing many more of these during his attachment in respiratory medicine.

B. Do the ABG yourself, tell the medical student to watch you closely, and get the medical student to do the next one under supervision.

C. Ask permission from the patient to let the medical student do the ABG under close supervision and sign him off.

D. Let the medical student do the ABG by himself; and sign him off.

E. Let the medical student do the ABG under close supervision and sign him off. Do not tell the patient that it is the student's first time as it may make him nervous.

Scenario 108

Your hospital has recently been in the news because of a serious unto-ward incident. A journalist has just called and the call is being trans-ferred to you in the very busy MAU department where you work.

Rank in order the following actions in response to this situation (1= Most appropriate; 5= Least appropriate):

A. Tell the journalist that you are confident that the hospital is doing a very good job and that you know that everything is being done to remedy difficult situations quickly and efficiently.

B. Tell the journalist that you cannot speak with her and put the phone down.

C. Tell the journalist that, if she gives you her contact details, you will pass them on to the relevant person.

D. Tell the journalist to contact the Trust's Press Officer.

E. Tell the journalist that you will call her back at the end of your shift when you have more time to speak.

Scenario 109

In order to complete your FY1 assessment, you are required to carry out an audit. It is Friday lunchtime and you must present your preliminary results to your supervisor on Monday morning. To finish the current phase of the audit, you still need to enter data from the notes of twenty patients into a database on your own laptop.

In view of your workload, you may not be able to collate all the remaining data before the end of the day and you are unable to stay late. You have many personal commitments at the weekend which prevent you from coming back to the hospital to access the notes.

Rank in order the following actions in response to this situation
(1= Most appropriate; 5= Least appropriate):

A. Take the patients' notes home with you to continue the data input over the weekend.

B. Make photocopies of the relevant pages of the patient notes, removing any patient-identifiable information, and take these photocopies back home with you to work on over the weekend.

C. Draw a quick plan of the data required on a piece of paper and quickly collect the data needed before you leave for the weekend.

D. Look at the average profile of the patients that you have already entered into your database and create new patient data matching the average profile in order to reach the number of patients discussed with your supervisor.

E. Ask your supervisor to defer the meeting to another day, once you have had time to complete your input.

250 SJTs for Foundation Year Entry

Scenario 110

A 20-year-old girl was taken to A&E by her father after collapsing in the street. She subsequently developed abdominal pains and has now been accepted by your team on the general surgical ward where you are working as an FY1. She is now clinically stable and preliminary tests are unremarkable.

Her father is on the phone to you, asking for information about his daughter's admission.

Rank in order the following actions in response to this situation (1= Most appropriate; 5= Least appropriate):

A. Tell the father that you simply cannot communicate with him on any matter relating to his daughter as this would be breaching her confidentiality.

B. Reassure the father that his daughter is fine but that you cannot give any further details without talking to his daughter first.

C. Explain to the father that his daughter has developed abdominal pains but that you cannot give any further details without talking to his daughter first.

D. Explain to the father that you will need to determine whether his daughter is competent before deciding whether you are able to release any further details to him.

E. Hand the phone over to the ST5 and ask him to handle the call.

Scenario 111

You have been asked to provide a series of lectures to final year medical students on a range of topics with which you are very familiar.

One of the students, whom you know well, has somehow managed to get hold of a photocopy of the forthcoming exam papers and asks you to make sure that you address all the relevant issues at your teaching sessions.

Rank in order the following actions in response to this situation (1= Most appropriate; 5= Least appropriate):

A. Confiscate the papers and report the matter straight away to the deanery, naming the student involved.

B. Confiscate the papers and report the matter straight away to the deanery, withholding the student's name.

C. Advise him to throw away the papers without looking at them.

D. Ignore the matter.

E. Inform the student that, in order to maintain a fair process, he will need to make sure that all other students also have a copy of the exam papers.

Scenario 112

You are on call covering the general medical wards.

You already have a long list of things to do, and receive a call from CCU regarding a conscious hypotensive patient. The nurses insist that you attend immediately.

Rank in order the following actions in response to this situation (1= Most appropriate; 5= Least appropriate):

A. Drop everything and walk quickly to CCU to assess the patient.

B. Tell the nurses they will have to wait as you have a list of things to do.

C. Ask the nurses to call someone else as you are busy, giving them the bleep number of the doctor who will help them.

D. Ask for more information about the patient including their diagnosis and other vital signs. Prioritise accordingly.

E. Put out a crash call as you are unable to attend immediately.

Scenario 113

Judy, one of your outpatients, is 35 years old and has recently been diagnosed with an underactive thyroid. Her GP has started her on thyroxine.

At a clinic, she tells you that she is not taking the thyroxine as she uses homeopathic remedies for her hypothyroidism and is feeling much better as a result.

Rank in order the following actions in response to this situation (1= Most appropriate; 5= Least appropriate):

A. Ask her what she understands about her illness and request that she goes back to see her GP for a blood test in 3 months' time.

B. Tell her she should take the thyroxine and refer her back to the GP.

C. Tell her that she is being unreasonable, that there is no tangible evidence that homeopathy works and that she should take the thyroxine.

D. Do nothing. She has the right to make that decision.

E. Ask her if there were any problems with the thyroxine, if she understands why she should take it and what will happen if she doesn't take it. Explain anything she doesn't understand but offer her the choice of whether to continue to take the medication or not. Advise her to see her GP anyway.

Scenario 114

You are an FY1 in a Diabetes & Endocrinology firm. During an outpatients' clinic, you see an elderly foreign patient for her annual review. The patient cannot understand English.

She is accompanied by her 6-year-old granddaughter who tells you that she will interpret for her grandmother.

Rank in order the following actions in response to this situation
(1= Most appropriate; 5= Least appropriate):

A. Ask the receptionist to rebook their appointment along with an appropriate interpreter as soon as possible

B. See the patient but refuse to use the 6-year-old as an interpreter.

C. See the patient; ask what the problem is and if it is something simple that you feel a 6-year-old could explain to her grandmother then continue with the consultation, ensuring at the end of the consultation that the grandmother knows she should try not to use the child again.

D. See the patient but explain through the 6-year-old that it is not advisable to use a child as an interpreter. Ask if there is anyone else with her who could help.

E. See the patient and explain to her via the child that you will call Language Line (the telephone interpreting service) and use that instead of the child.

Scenario 115

Having just been present at a cardiac arrest situation where a patient did not survive, you have now been asked to inform the relatives of the patient's death. Your shift ends in 10 minutes.

**Rank in order the following actions in response to this situation
(1= Most appropriate; 5= Least appropriate):**

A. Ask the A&E sister to give the family a cup of tea and ask one of the nurses to get another doctor to break the news in 10 minutes' time.

B. Inform the family immediately of the patient's death.

C. Finish writing the notes from the arrest, compose yourself and arrange to meet the relatives in the relative room.

D. Hand over the job to another FY1 who needs the experience.

E. Hand over the job to the doctor who is taking over from you.

Scenario 116

A regular outpatient, whom you know very well, attends a clinic. She informs you that her ex-boyfriend is about to be released from prison and has called her, threatening to kill her.

You know that, in the past, she presented with severe bruising which she blamed on falls and car accidents.

She says she is too scared to go to the police.

Rank in order the following actions in response to this situation (1= Most appropriate; 5= Least appropriate):

A. Call the police and tell them about the threats.

B. Give her support, listen to her fears and then tell her that you will call the police to inform them of the threats made.

C. Give her support, listen to her fears and ask her if she will let you inform the police of the threats made.

D. Tell her there is nothing you can do as this does not fall within your remit.

E. Give her support, listen to her fears and wish her luck.

Scenario 117

You have been asked by your consultant to consent the next patient for theatre.

When you look at the list, the procedure listed is a Whipple's procedure (complicated surgery usually performed for pancreatic cancer) and you do not know what it is.

Rank in order the following actions in response to this situation
(1= Most appropriate; 5= Least appropriate):

A. Consent the patient.

B. Go onto the internet, find out what a Whipple's procedure is and return to your consultant to ask if he can help you.

C. Contact your ST5 and ask him to come and help you.

D. Go onto the internet, find out what a Whipple's procedure is and proceed with the consent.

E. Tell your consultant you cannot proceed with the consent.

Scenario 118

While attending a clinic, your 86-year-old patient, who is wheelchair-bound following a bilateral below-knee amputation, asks you to help him die.

Rank in order the following actions in response to this situation (1= Most appropriate; 5= Least appropriate):

A. Offer to help him die.

B. Refer him to a psychiatrist for depression.

C. Explain that you cannot help him die, but give him information about assisted suicide in Switzerland.

D. Assess his capacity and, if he has capacity, explain that you cannot help him die but give him information about assisted suicide in Switzerland.

E. Assess his capacity and, if he has capacity, assess him for depression.

Scenario 119

A fit and healthy 37-year-old woman attends A&E with a cold and the A&E doctors refer her to the medical team.

Her examination is normal and the medical consultant wishes her to be discharged as he thinks it is likely to be a viral infection. He has already explained to her that antibiotics will not help.

Before she leaves, the patient insists that you give her a prescription for antibiotics as her colds "always turn into chest infections" and it is really difficult to get an appointment with her own GP whenever things get worse.

Rank in order the following actions in response to this situation (1= Most appropriate; 5= Least appropriate):

A. Refuse to give her the antibiotics and explain why.

B. Explain that you won't prescribe the antibiotics right now. Advise her that if she wants the antibiotics she can go and see her GP today as he might prescribe them.

C. Explain the reason for your not giving antibiotics. Suggest she gets an appointment with her GP in 48 hours if she is not better.

D. Tell her to visit her GP whenever she can get an appointment. Give her a letter addressed to the GP advising him to prescribe the antibiotics.

E. Give her a prescription of antibiotics. Tell her to take them only if her condition deteriorates.

Scenario 120

You are working in the Acute Medical Unit (AMU). A 65-year-old smoker attends with a cough that has been present for 6 weeks; he has also had two episodes of haemoptysis. He is otherwise well.

He tells you that his GP has refused to give him antibiotics.

Rank in order the following actions in response to this situation (1= Most appropriate; 5= Least appropriate):

A. Admit the patient, suspecting a diagnosis of lung cancer.

B. Tell the patient that he has been mistreated by the GP. Send the patient back to the GP.

C. Organise immediate investigations including a chest X-ray and blood tests.

D. Prescribe antibiotics and refer the patient back to his GP.

E. Refer the patient to Oncology with a suspected diagnosis of lung cancer.

Scenario 121

You are an FY1 on call for General Medicine. The nurses on Ward H have called you as they want you to review an ECG that the nurse practitioner ordered for a patient with chest pain.

The patient is stable.

Rank in order the following actions in response to this situation (1= Most appropriate; 5= Least appropriate):

A. Advise them to call the nurse practitioner to review the ECG. Tell the ward nurses that, if the nurse practitioner needs help, she should call you and you will attend immediately.

B. Attend immediately as this may be a heart attack.

C. Ask for more information regarding the patient in order to assess how urgent this task is. Attend if it is urgent.

D. Add it to your list of things to do and attend when it reaches the top of the list.

E. Advise the nurses that they should only request investigations that they can interpret and that you cannot review the ECG as you did not perform it.

Scenario 122

At 9am, one of your outpatients referred for an in-growing toe nail states that he has severe toothache and a temperature.

Rank in order the following actions in response to this situation (1= Most appropriate; 5= Least appropriate):

A. Assess the patient for a dental abscess and treat it with antibiotics if required.

B. Tell him to go and see a dentist.

C. Explain to the patient that you are not trained in dental treatment. Advise him to seek help from a dentist.

D. Give him painkillers and advise him to see a dentist.

E. Assess the patient fully to determine why he has a temperature. If it is due to a dental cause, refer the patient to a dentist the same day.

Scenario 123

At the end of each outpatient clinic, you are supposed to meet with your ST5 to go over any problems that you may have encountered during the session.

Your ST5 always leaves before you have finished and is never available for your debrief.

Rank in order the following actions in response to this situation (1= Most appropriate; 5= Least appropriate):

A. Do nothing.

B. Ask another senior to meet with you at the end of each clinic.

C. Discuss the issue with the Clinical Director.

D. Arrange a meeting with your ST5 and tell her that you need to see her at the end of each session.

E. Arrange a meeting with your ST5 and ask her whether you could arrange a daily meeting to discuss problems.

Scenario 124

You are an FY1 in the Acute Medical Unit (AMU). A patient runs up to you, saying that a bee has got into the ward and has stung him.

He begins to show signs consistent with anaphylaxis following a bee sting.

Rank in order the following actions in response to this situation (1= Most appropriate; 5= Least appropriate):

A. Put out an arrest call.

B. Assess the patient's airway, breathing and circulation and give the appropriate dose of adrenaline.

C. Assess the patient's airway, breathing and circulation and reassure the patient that everything will be alright.

D. Start basic life support and commence good mouth-to-mouth contact if appropriate.

E. Assess the patient's airway, breathing and circulation and call a senior colleague.

Scenario 125

You are working as an FY1 in General Surgery. In an outpatient clinic, you see an 85-year-old man who has recently recovered from a UTI. He has an abdominal aortic aneurysm that has expanded over the last 3 months and now measures 8cm on ultrasound.

Your consultant has reviewed the patient and explained the procedure fully. The consultant also advised that he needed to come into hospital for an abdominal aortic aneurysm repair. The patient says that he needs 5 minutes to think about it first.

After the consultant has left the room, the man tells you he will not have the surgery. You have not seen the operation before and only have a sketchy theoretical understanding of the procedure involved.

Rank in order the following actions in response to this situation (1= Most appropriate; 5= Least appropriate):

A. Offer to talk to the patient to re-explain the advantages and disadvantages of surgery and ask if he is sure that he really does not want to consent. Document his decision and talk to the consultant.

B. Inform the patient that the surgery is important and that you will give him some time to think about the procedure. Document that the patient originally refused consent but is still thinking about whether to consent or not.

C. Tell the patient that the decision is his and document his refusal.

D. Inform your consultant.

E. Assess the patient's capacity and if he is competent then inform him that it is his choice if he does not want surgery. Document his refusal and inform the patient he can change his mind at any time.

Scenario 126

It is 2pm mid January in the Emergency Department. While reviewing a lady who is 36 weeks pregnant and has pneumonia, you notice that her three-year-old daughter, who has come with her, is wearing severely soiled clothes and has no shoes on.

Rank in order the following actions in response to this situation (1= Most appropriate; 5= Least appropriate):

A. Do nothing; the child is not your patient.

B. Immediately admit the child to Paediatrics.

C. Confront the mother and ask why the child looks so dirty.

D. Ask the patient to wait and then call her GP to ask if there are any concerns regarding the welfare of the child. Discuss your concerns with the mother if there are any issues.

E. Ensure you add a comment in her notes, asking the ward team who will take over the patient's care to review the child.

Scenario 127

You are working in Respiratory Medicine. Having trained you to perform pleural aspirations, your consultant now asks you to perform your first aspiration without supervision. You agree, feeling confident.

Everything goes well until you try to aspirate the fluid and get a dry tap. On review of the large pleural effusion on X-ray, you realise that you have tried to aspirate the wrong side of the chest.

Rank in order the following actions in response to this situation (1= Most appropriate; 5= Least appropriate):

A. Ensure the patient is stable, seek help from your consultant, explain what happened and then apologise to the patient.

B. Tell your consultant that it was a dry tap and organise for an ultrasound guided aspiration for another day.

C. Ensure the patient is stable and immediately inform your consultant.

D. Ensure the patient is stable and then proceed to aspirate the correct side.

E. Ensure the patient is stable, explain what has happened, apologise to the patient and then seek help from your consultant straight afterwards.

Scenario 128

You are working as an FY1 in General Medicine. At the beginning of the ward visiting time, the sister calls for your help.

A 70-year-old man visiting his wife had central crushing chest pain that lasted 45 minutes and was not relieved by sublingual GTN.

He had a heart attack 6 months earlier.

Rank in order the following actions in response to this situation (1= Most appropriate; 5= Least appropriate):

A. Tell the sister to send him straight to A&E.

B. Go and see the man straight away. Advise him that he may be having another heart attack and that it is important he is treated as soon as possible. Arrange to get him transported to A&E.

C. Go and see the man straight away. Refer him to the medical team on call.

D. Go and see him the man straight away. Tell him to take more sublingual GTN and you will call back in 30 minutes to see if he is any better.

E. Ask the nurse to tell the man that he should see his GP as soon as possible.

Scenario 129

You are on your way into work when you bump into a patient who you know was recently treated at your hospital. You remember her well as it was the first case of diabetic ketoacidosis that you had seen. She was newly diagnosed with type-1 diabetes one week ago and had to be started on insulin.

She is currently sitting down in a coffee shop, eating a bar of chocolate and drinking a can of sugary fizzy drink while chatting to friends.

Rank in order the following actions in response to this situation (1= Most appropriate; 5= Least appropriate):

A. Ignore the patient but write her a letter to remind her not to eat sweet things.

B. Approach the group and remind the patient that eating sweet things is not good for her diabetes.

C. Say hello, smile and make a mental note to look up her notes later and to call her GP to ask her to come in for a review.

D. Ensure the patient does not see you, as you don't want to embarrass her, but make a mental note to look up her notes later and to call her GP to ask her to come in for a review.

E. Call the on-call diabetic team and ask them to review the patient.

Scenario 130

You are an FY1 in Endocrinology & Diabetes. Your team has just taken over the care of a 64-year-old male who was recently diagnosed with Motor Neurone Disease.

He wishes to refuse all treatments and just "wants to die". He does not want his family to know that he has refused treatment.

Rank in order the following actions in response to this situation (1= Most appropriate; 5= Least appropriate):

A. Respect the patient's wishes and keep the information from family.

B. Tell the patient that you won't tell the family, but tell him that, if the family asks you directly, you will have to tell them all the information.

C. Tell the information to the family and ask them to try to convince the patient to continue treatment.

D. Discuss the patient's fears about the terminal phase and encourage him to speak to his family.

E. Tell the family that they should speak to the patient as he is feeling down.

Scenario 131

You are an FY1 doing a taster week in a GP practice. The next patient you see gives you a letter from a private Endocrinology clinic asking you to prescribe the weight loss drug Orlistat.

You know that the patient does not qualify for it because his BMI is 26. NICE suggests that Orlistat be prescribed only if BMI exceeds 30.

Rank in order the following actions in response to this situation
(1= Most appropriate; 5= Least appropriate):

A. Prescribe Orlistat.

B. Write to the private consultant asking for clarification on the reasons for prescribing Orlistat.

C. Refer the patient to an NHS Endocrinology consultant for a second opinion.

D. Reply to the consultant that you are not happy to prescribe Orlistat.

E. Write to the GMC regarding the inappropriate advice of the prescription of Orlistat from the private consultant.

Scenario 132

You are an FY1 in Cardiology. Your team admitted a 56-year-old man with endocarditis.

In accordance with your hospital's policy, the ward pharmacist automatically cancelled the IV antibiotic prescription after 7 days. You forgot to rewrite the antibiotic prescription and the patient has missed 2 days of antibiotics in what is supposed to be a 4-week-long course of IV antibiotics.

No harm has come to the patient and the IV antibiotics have now been rewritten.

Rank in order the following actions in response to this situation (1= Most appropriate; 5= Least appropriate):

A. Ask the nurse to inform the patient about the mistake.

B. Don't tell the patient anything as no harm occurred.

C. Inform the patient that, following an error by the pharmacist, the antibiotics were stopped with no consequence.

D. Inform the consultant but not the patient.

E. Explain the mistake to the patient and apologise. Tell him that you have forgotten to rewrite the antibiotics and reassure him that he will be fine.

Scenario 133

You are an FY1 in Vascular Surgery. You have "bleep-free" protected teaching time every Wednesday afternoon for 1 hour.

You are just settling into a lecture on glomerulonephritis when you get repeatedly bleeped from a ward in a short space of time. You have forgotten to give your bleep to the Education Centre.

Rank in order the following actions in response to this situation (1= Most appropriate; 5= Least appropriate):

A. Phone your team's SHO to let him answer the bleep on your behalf.

B. Switch the bleep off and ignore the bleep you received.

C. Go to the ward immediately without answering the bleep.

D. Tell the ward that you are on protected teaching time and so will only come when the teaching is finished.

E. Ignore the bleep that you have received until you get another one.

Scenario 134

You are an FY1 in Respiratory in a District General Hospital (DGH).

One of your patients, who was admitted for infective exacerbation of COPD, reveals to you that his GP refused to prescribe him salbutamol nebuliser unless he stopped smoking.

You feel that salbutamol nebuliser would really benefit the patient.

Rank in order the following actions in response to this situation (1= Most appropriate; 5= Least appropriate):

A. Explain to the patient that unless he stops smoking the nebuliser will not be an appropriate solution and will essentially be wasting NHS money, particularly as the illness is self-inflicted.

B. Add salbutamol nebuliser on the regular side but do not inform the GP.

C. Add salbutamol nebuliser on the regular side and inform the GP.

D. Tell the patient that you will only add salbutamol nebuliser when he has agreed to stop smoking.

E. Add salbutamol nebuliser and tell him that you will have to stop it if he doesn't stop smoking soon.

Scenario 135

You have prescribed a regular dose of codeine phosphate (analgesia) for one of your post-operative patients.

You are called to the ward to review the patient, who is still complaining of pain.

Rank in order the following actions in response to this situation (1= Most appropriate; 5= Least appropriate):

A. Prescribe oral morphine.

B. Review the drug chart.

C. Assess the patient for post-operative complications.

D. Write your findings in the notes.

E. Increase the dose of codeine.

Scenario 136

You work in Surgery on an 8am – 6pm shift, after which you are due to go home. Earlier, you admitted a patient who needed an appendicectomy. The patient was placed on the emergency theatre list and was due to have the operation an hour before the end of your shift. The patient is stable.

You were very keen to go and observe the procedure. You knew that, by that time, you would have finished all your jobs and be free to observe. You had agreed with one of your colleagues that he would take your bleep for that hour so that you could observe the surgery.

The theatre nurse calls you 3 hours before the end of your shift and tells you that, because one of the earlier patients took far longer than anticipated, your patient's appendicectomy will not get done before the end of your shift and will instead be done at some stage during the night.

Rank in order the following actions in response to this situation (1= Most appropriate; 5= Least appropriate):

A. Ask the nurse politely if she will juggle the list as a favour to you.

B. Accept that you won't be able to observe the case.

C. Ask the nurse to bleep you when the case goes to theatre so that you can consider coming back to observe.

D. Ask some of the patients who are due for surgery before your patient if they wouldn't mind swapping their theatre slot with your patient.

E. Tell the nurse that the patient is deteriorating and the surgery can't be delayed.

Scenario 137

You are working in A&E and you overhear a conversation between one of the other FY1s and a patient. Your colleague is asking if there is a possibility that the patient may be pregnant when the notes clearly say that she had a hysterectomy the year before.

You can hear that the patient has clearly become exasperated and tells your colleague to get "a doctor who knows what he is talking about".

You know that your colleague has had a succession of long shifts and is tired. The registrar seems busy dealing with a sick patient.

Rank in order the following actions in response to this situation
(1= Most appropriate; 5= Least appropriate):

A. Go to the cubicle. Apologise to the patient. Explain to the patient that your colleague is at the end of a very long shift and that you are new on shift. Ask your colleague if he would like you to assist.

B. Go to the cubicle. Tell the patient that you need to discuss something urgently with your colleague. Outside the cubicle, tell your colleague you will take over from him.

C. Go to the cubicle, apologise to the patient for the mistake and let her know that she can talk to you if she prefers.

D. Don't interfere and let your colleague deal with it.

E. Ask the registrar to intervene.

Scenario 138

You are at a discharge planning meeting on a Respiratory ward, discussing a patient who is due to go home later today. All elements of care are in place except for the provision of home oxygen, which you were meant to organise before the meeting.

You forgot to contact the GP but you are pretty sure that you can arrange the home oxygen in time for the patient's discharge.

Rank in order the following actions in response to this situation (1= Most appropriate; 5= Least appropriate):

A. Tell the team you had trouble organising the oxygen but you are very likely to get it sorted in time.

B. Tell the team it slipped your mind but you will get on to it as a priority.

C. Tell the team that the GP will get back to you but there may be a delay of a day.

D. Tell the team everything will be ready in time.

E. Tell the team you are waiting for the GP to confirm oxygen supply.

Scenario 139

You are an FY1 on an Elderly Care ward. The daughter of an elderly patient has arrived on the ward to take her father home.

His discharge is being delayed because the pharmacist has not yet processed his take-home heart failure medications.

The daughter has to leave soon because she is going out this evening.

**Rank in order the following actions in response to this situation
(1= Most appropriate; 5= Least appropriate):**

A. Advise the daughter to discuss the matter with the ward sister.

B. Delay the discharge by one day.

C. Call pharmacy to ask to expedite the dispensing.

D. Suggest that she takes her father home now and arrange for her to pick up the medications tomorrow afternoon.

E. Suggest that she takes her father home now. Arrange for a nurse who lives near her to drop off the medications later on that evening.

Scenario 140

You are an FY1 working a night shift covering medical wards. There is a locum doctor covering the surgical wards. He does not have a computer login to be able to order blood tests during the shift.

Rank in order the following actions in response to this situation (1= Most appropriate; 5= Least appropriate):

A. Give him your computer and blood-request login details. Allow him to use the system freely.

B. Ask him to wait until you need to access the system to order tests for your patients and you will bleep him so that he can order his at the same time.

C. Speak to the other doctors and nurses who are on shift and have computer access for blood test requesting. Ask them to request tests for the locum's patients whenever he needs it during the night; you will also do so yourself.

D. Ask him to bleep you whenever he needs tests requested, so you can come and order them for him whenever he needs.

E. Ask him to keep a list of the tests he needs to order. You will order them for him when you get the opportunity during the shift.

Scenario 141

You are an FY1 on a Stroke Unit in a large teaching hospital. A medical student was attached to the firm. Due to her poor attendance record, she was not signed off by the consultant.

She did her attachment again and you worked a lot with her. You found her clinical skills very basic and noted that she was rude to nursing staff. You remained supportive throughout because there were a few positive traits which were encouraging.

Having not heard from her since she left the firm, you receive an email out of the blue asking you to write a medical school application reference for her, as she is now transferring to a different medical school.

She tells you that it's okay if you don't want to do it as she can ask someone else instead.

Rank in order the following actions in response to this situation
(1= Most appropriate; 5= Least appropriate):

A. Refuse to write a reference.

B. Write a vague and non-committal reference.

C. Tell her that, if you write a reference, it will have to contain both the positive and the negative.

D. Ask her to write the reference and you will sign it.

E. Write a reference containing only the positive traits that she demonstrated.

Scenario 142

You are an FY1 in Orthopaedics, and are looking after an elderly patient who is recovering after a hip replacement. The procedure went according to plan and the patient is doing well.

The patient's daughter is a consultant in your hospital's radiology department. She knows her father had a hip operation done by your consultant. She catches you in the corridor and asks how her father is doing.

Rank in order the following actions in response to this situation (1= Most appropriate; 5= Least appropriate):

A. Tell her that her father is okay.

B. Tell her that you are unsure about how much you can reveal so she should talk to your consultant.

C. Tell her that you can't say anything to her without her father's permission.

D. Tell that that she should be able to get all the information she needs from the patient notes, which can be accessed via the Electronic Patient Record system.

E. Ask her to join the ward round the next day, but only for the part that concerns her father.

Scenario 143

You are an FY1 in Geriatrics working in a small District General Hospital.

You are doing some ward jobs when a relative of a patient (who was recently placed on the terminal Liverpool Care Pathway) comes out of the side room and asks to speak to you. The relative says that the patient is feeling nauseous and dry retching from the painkillers that he is currently taking.

You prescribe anti-nausea medication and ask the nurse to give it. The nurse replies that she is currently doing her food rounds for the ward and will give it afterwards.

Rank in order the following actions in response to this situation (1= Most appropriate; 5= Least appropriate):

A. Explain the situation to the ward sister so that she can ensure that the medication is dispensed.

B. Ask the nurse to give you the medication cupboard's key so that you can administer the medication.

C. Speak to the nurse again regarding the urgency of the situation for the medication to be dispensed.

D. Ask the nurse to make sure that she gives the medication as soon as she has completed her food round.

E. Ask the relatives to wait 5 minutes and to go and find the nurse if she hasn't given the medication by then.

Scenario 144

You are an FY1 on an AMU (Acute Medical Unit). You are attending to a patient who presented with urinary retention. A CT scan was requested, which showed prostatic cancer. The urinary retention resolved spontaneously.

The bad news is given to the patient, who replies that he doesn't believe in conventional medicine and wants to try homeopathy instead. You have already determined that the patient is competent and have explained that he has the right to make such decisions for himself.

Rank in order the following actions in response to this situation (1= Most appropriate; 5= Least appropriate):

A. Tell the patient that homeopathy will kill him.

B. Discharge the patient and take no further action.

C. Ask the patient to think about it and to contact his own GP if he wishes to discuss the matter further.

D. Ask the patient to think about it and to come back and see you whenever he wishes to discuss the matter further.

E. Book a follow-up appointment to review the patient in one week's time.

Scenario 145

You are an FY1 in Geriatrics and are currently carrying your ward bleep as well as the cardiac arrest bleep. You have just been asked to certify the death of an elderly patient. His family has not yet been informed.

You are in the doctors' room, documenting in the deceased patient's notes, when the nurse bleeps you to inform you that the deceased's family have just arrived.

Rank in order the following actions in response to this situation (1= Most appropriate; 5= Least appropriate):

A. Give both bleeps to the nurse to keep safe, whilst you speak to the family.

B. Leave the bleeps in the doctors' room.

C. Give the bleeps to a fellow FY1 to cross-cover.

D. Keep the bleeps but only respond to crash calls.

E. Keep the bleeps and respond to all calls.

Scenario 146

You are an FY1 in an Acute Stroke Unit.

You are working flat out and are barely managing to keep on top of your workload. You come to the hospital regularly at weekends for a few hours to finish writing discharge summaries that you struggled to complete during your normal hours.

On top of this, you are sleeping poorly, and have stopped enjoying the activities that you used to look forward to.

Rank in order the following actions in response to this situation (1= Most appropriate; 5= Least appropriate):

A. Take annual leave for a short break; get more sun, avoid coffee after lunch and do more exercise.

B. Speak to your consultant.

C. See your GP.

D. Ask a colleague to prescribe you a course of antidepressants.

E. Speak to your educational supervisor.

Scenario 147

You are an FY1 on the Acute Medical Unit (AMU).

Your FY2 failed to secure the CT1 post that he wanted and is planning to travel for the whole of next year. He asks you to prescribe some anti-malarial prophylaxis medication for him to take on his travels.

Rank in order the following actions in response to this situation (1= Most appropriate; 5= Least appropriate):

A. Tell the FY2 to "procure" some from the A&E medication cabinets.

B. Tell the FY2 to see Occupational Health.

C. Tell the FY2 to see his GP.

D. Take a full medical history from the FY2 and prescribe the medication.

E. Refuse his request.

Scenario 148

You are an FY1 on the Acute Medical Unit (AMU). Your consultant has asked you to perform a lumbar puncture (LP) on a patient who has suspected meningitis.

Although you have seen LPs being performed before, you are not comfortable doing one yourself; you ask your CT1 to do one whilst you watch.

Whilst watching the procedure, you notice that the CT1 is about to insert the LP needle in the wrong place. You immediately tell the CT1 that he is about to make a mistake but he replies that he thinks he is doing the right thing and that his registrar does it in exactly the same way.

Rank in order the following actions in response to this situation
(1= Most appropriate; 5= Least appropriate):

A. Tell the CT1 to hold the procedure and ask the registrar to come over straight away.

B. Tell the CT1 that it is his decision to go ahead with the procedure but that you will report the incident if something goes wrong.

C. Discuss your concerns about both the CT1 and the registrar with the consultant the next day.

D. Leave the bedside and complete a critical incident form.

E. Tell the patient that you disagree with your colleague and ask whether he wishes to withdraw his consent as a result of those differences of opinion.

Scenario 149

You are the FY1 on call for Elderly Care. An 80-year-old patient has just been admitted as he is experiencing musculoskeletal leg pains.

The patient was discharged from another hospital yesterday. The other hospital's discharge summary states that they added a 9-day course of amoxicillin, with the rest of his medications remaining unchanged.

The discharge summary does not explain why the amoxicillin was added.

Rank in order the following actions in response to this situation (1= Most appropriate; 5= Least appropriate):

A. Omit the amoxicillin.

B. Phone the team that discharged the patient from the previous hospital to ask why amoxicillin was prescribed.

C. Phone the GP and ask why amoxicillin was prescribed.

D. Ask the patient why he has to take the amoxicillin.

E. Prescribe the amoxicillin.

Scenario 150

You are an FY1 on call at night and are asked to insert a cannula for a patient who requires IV antibiotics.

You flush the line with what you think is normal saline; however, you soon realise that you have forgotten to prime the connector that you placed on the cannula with saline. As a result, 1ml of air is flushed through into the vein.

The patient suffers no adverse reaction.

Rank in order the following actions in response to this situation (1= Most appropriate; 5= Least appropriate):

A. Phone the consultant and inform the patient straight away.

B. Take no further action.

C. Complete a critical incident form.

D. Complete a reflective piece in your e-portfolio.

E. Inform the medical registrar and inform the patient later on during the night.

Scenario 151

You are an FY1 in General Surgery, working with a surgical registrar who is notorious throughout the hospital for being rather fierce.

The registrar constantly puts down your FY1 colleague in front of other people, including clinical staff. Last week, the registrar shouted at the FY1 for being slow in making a theatre list.

You don't seem to have the same problem with the registrar and you get on fairly well with him.

Rank in order the following actions in response to this situation (1= Most appropriate; 5= Least appropriate):

A. Advise the FY1 to speak to his educational supervisor about the matter.

B. Advise the FY1 to keep a note of each incident, including the context, what was said and who witnessed the incident.

C. Advise the FY1 to talk to his consultant about the matter.

D. Help the FY1 with the theatre lists.

E. Approach the registrar yourself to raise your concerns about his behaviour towards the FY1.

Scenario 152

You are the FY1 on call for nights. You have been asked by a nurse to insert a cannula for a patient requiring IV antibiotics since the old one has tissued and is therefore no longer working.

During handover, your medical registrar tells you that he doesn't want to be disturbed tonight as he has been on call for the last 12 hours and is also covering someone else's shift; so he wants to sleep.

You attempt to cannulate without success. You ask the SHO to try but he also fails, despite making two attempts.

Rank in order the following actions in response to this situation (1= Most appropriate; 5= Least appropriate):

A. Ask the SHO to attempt the cannulation again.

B. Bleep the anaesthetist to cannulate the patient.

C. Call the on-call consultant.

D. Wake up the medical registrar to attempt the cannulation.

E. Give oral antibiotics until the morning.

Scenario 153

You are an FY1 for the Respiratory firm. You see a patient who has poorly controlled asthma. He admits to you that he smokes copious amounts of cannabis.

Rank in order the following actions in response to this situation (1= Most appropriate; 5= Least appropriate):

A. Advise the patient regarding the harmful effects of smoking cannabis.

B. Search the patient's belongings for any cannabis and discard it.

C. Report the matter to the police.

D. Write to the GP regarding follow-up for cannabis smoking cessation after discharge.

E. Ignore the issue.

Scenario 154

You are an FY1 on the AMU (Acute Medical Unit). A patient recovering from pneumonia asks you to write a sick note.

Your best opinion is that the patient will require no more than 1 week's rest. The patient insists that he should get a sick note for at least 4 weeks.

Rank in order the following actions in response to this situation (1= Most appropriate; 5= Least appropriate):

A. Write a sick note for 1 week and ask the patient to go to his GP if he is still feeling unwell towards the end of the week.

B. Write the sick note for 1 week only and tell the patient that it would be against your best judgement to give more.

C. Write a sick note for 4 weeks.

D. Reconsider the facts to see if the sick leave duration needs to be extended.

E. Compromise by writing a sick note for 2 weeks.

Scenario 155

You are an FY1 on an AMU (Acute Medical Unit), and are currently hold-ing the AMU referral bleep.

The A&E SHO calls to inform you that a patient has come in with small bowel obstruction due to adhesions. This was diagnosed following a CT scan. She previously had an operation at a different hospital and was discharged 2 months ago.

The SHO tells you that he tried to get the surgical team to deal with the patient, but that they refused to accept the patient as they felt that she should be dealt with by the discharging hospital.

He asks you to accept the patient under the medical team instead.

Rank in order the following actions in response to this situation
(1= Most appropriate; 5= Least appropriate):

A. Accept the patient under the medical team and move the patient to AMU.

B. Go down to A&E and review the patient.

C. Refuse to accept the patient as they would be admitted under an inappro-priate team.

D. Discuss the case with the surgical SHO.

E. Ask your registrar to discuss the case with the surgical registrar.

Scenario 156

You are an FY1 doctor for the Cardiology firm. A 19-year-old student of the opposite gender has been admitted with chest pain.

During a ward review, the student says that you're such a cute doctor that they've made a special effort to dress up just for you today.

When you ask for a chaperone for the clinical examination, the patient says that you don't need a chaperone.

Rank in order the following actions in response to this situation (1= Most appropriate; 5= Least appropriate):

A. Insist on having a chaperone present whilst you do a full clinical examination.

B. Arrange for a doctor of the same gender as the patient to review the patient instead.

C. Discharge the patient from the hospital.

D. Phone the patient's parents to inform them of the situation.

E. Do only a brief clinical examination on your own.

Scenario 157

You are an FY1 on AMU (Acute Medical Unit) for a small District General Hospital. During the day you are bleeped by a nurse who asks you to review a patient who has fallen over.

You already have three cannulas to deal with and so you ask the nurse to bleep your other AMU FY1 colleague. The nurse responds that she already tried the other FY1 and he told her to let you know you that he was busy.

Having reviewed the patient and dealt with the cannulas, you go down to the mess and see your FY1 colleague sitting on a sofa, laughing with some other doctors whilst watching the TV. It is the first time this has happened but you are concerned that he may not be reliable.

Rank in order the following actions in response to this situation
(1= Most appropriate; 5= Least appropriate):

A. Speak to the AMU consultant.

B. Ask the nurse to bleep your colleague first whenever she requires assistance with a patient.

C. Take no action and pretend you didn't see the colleague in the mess.

D. Ask your FY1 colleague what happened.

E. Complete a critical incident form.

Scenario 158

For the past 2 months, you have worked as an FY1 in General Medicine. The registrar, who conducts all the ward rounds, tends to ignore you during the ward rounds. He only asks questions to the CT1 and ST3 doctors, and never to you.

Whenever you ask a question, the registrar just tells you to look the answer up. Whenever you volunteer to do simple procedures, the registrar always tells you that the other doctors need the practice more than you do.

Rank in order the following actions in response to this situation (1= Most appropriate; 5= Least appropriate):

A. Organise a meeting with the consultant.

B. At the next ward round, when the registrar refuses to allow you do a procedure, insist that you should do it since you are always left out.

C. Learn by watching the others.

D. Find an opportunity to discuss the matter with the registrar.

E. Arrange a meeting with the postgraduate tutor.

Scenario 159

An elderly patient from your ward is due for discharge later on today.

In the notes, you see a report by the Occupational Therapist (OT), which states that, following a thorough assessment carried out the day before, she found that the patient was fit for independent living.

This seems odd to you because, as recently as this morning, one of the nurses had reported to you that she had seen the patient looking unsteady on his feet, just about able to hold a mug full of hot water, and nearly spilling the hot water over himself.

Rank in order the following actions in response to this situation (1= Most appropriate; 5= Least appropriate):

A. Call the OT to discuss your concerns with her.

B. Request that the OT repeats her assessment.

C. Share your concerns with your consultant.

D. Share your concerns with social services.

E. Ask the relatives to purchase a safe cup holder and discharge the patient.

Scenario 160

You work as an FY1 on an Elderly Care ward. Following a request from your consultant, you ask a nurse to remove the urinary catheter from a patient.

The nurse tells you in a normal tone of voice that all nurses are very busy due to shortage of staff, that they don't have time to take patients to the toilet and therefore all catheters will need to remain in situ until the situation improves.

Rank in order the following actions in response to this situation (1= Most appropriate; 5= Least appropriate):

A. Inform the ward sister immediately of the impact that staffing is having on patient care and the need to remove straight away all catheters that are no longer required.

B. Kindly remind the nurse of the risk of infection and ask her to remove the patient's catheter as soon as she can.

C. Remove the catheter yourself.

D. Report the issue to your consultant.

E. Complete a critical incident form.

5 90 Practice Scenarios Multiple Choice Format

Scenario 161

You are an FY1 in Vascular Surgery in a District General Hospital (DGH).

The consultant has requested that a post-operative female patient has a catheter inserted in the morning for fluid balance measurements. The nurse was informed and she said that she would do it.

Later on in the afternoon, you find that the nurse has not yet done it. You ask the nurse why and she says that, being so busy, she had simply forgotten about it.

Choose the THREE most appropriate actions to take in this situation.

A. Notify the consultant and apologise to the patient.

B. Insert the catheter yourself.

C. Ask the nurse to insert the catheter and stand behind her to make sure she does it.

D. Complete a critical incident form.

E. Review the patient's fluid balance.

F. Ask the nurse to insert the catheter and stress why it is needed.

G. Complete a reflective e-portfolio form.

H. Speak to the ward sister about the incident.

Scenario 162

You are an FY1 in Diabetes & Endocrinology.

During the afternoon review, you note that a patient was given an insulin sliding scale that no one had prescribed. You also notice that another patient, who was prescribed an insulin sliding scale for her high blood glucose level, has not been given it. Both patients have similar names.

The patient with high blood glucose complains of having to go to the toilet frequently and of blurred vision. The other patient seems fine.

Choose the THREE most appropriate actions to take in this situation.

A. Notify the consultant.

B. Apologise to the patient who should have been receiving the insulin sliding scale.

C. Apologise to both patients.

D. Stop the insulin sliding scale for the patient who does not require it.

E. Review the patient who was placed on the sliding scale by mistake using the ABCDE approach.

F. Review the patient who needs to have the sliding scale using the ABCDE approach and start the insulin sliding scale as appropriate.

G. Complete a critical incident form.

H. Ask the nurses to place the patients on two different wards to avoid future confusion.

Scenario 163

You are an FY1 in Diabetes & Endocrinology. Your new locum registrar has just started in the firm. He seems to be making a lot of referrals to specialties and asks you to organise unconventional investigations. No harm has come to any patients to date.

Choose the THREE most appropriate actions to take in this situation.

A. Refuse to do any investigations or arrange any referrals that you feel are inappropriate.

B. Discuss your concerns with your consultant.

C. Do the investigations that you feel should have been ordered, instead of those requested by the registrar.

D. Raise your concerns directly with the registrar.

E. Write suitable comments in his 360-degree assessment form.

F. Do what the registrar asks but cover your back by documenting in the notes that you are doing so reluctantly and against your best judgement.

G. Wait until a patient has been harmed to act.

H. Refuse to work with this registrar.

Scenario 164

You are working busy and tiring shifts because your other FY1 colleague is on leave.

Your CT1 colleague is currently very stressed about her forthcoming MRCP exam. She left her revision until the last minute and revises late into the night. As a result, she is often tired and takes a 30-minute nap every lunchtime. You have also found some simple prescription errors on drug charts that she completed.

She leaves early most days to do some revision and hands you the bleep so that you can cover for her when she does. So far you have agreed to take the bleep reluctantly.

Choose the THREE most appropriate actions to take in this situation.

A. Tell the CT1 that patient care takes priority over the exam and she therefore needs to work her full shifts.

B. Discuss with the CT1 the issue of fairness of allocation of workload.

C. Discuss your concerns about patient safety with your consultant.

D. Ask the ward sister to let nurses know that, when both you and the CT1 are on shift, they should first call the CT1 so as to ensure a fair allocation of workload.

E. Ask the CT1 to talk to the rota coordinator and the managers about the possibility of getting locum cover.

F. Ask the nurses not to contact you too much as you are very busy as a result of taking on some of the CT1's work.

G. Tell your CT1 colleague that you cannot take her bleep.

H. Tell your CT1 colleague that she should ask for annual leave to finish her revision.

Scenario 165

You are an FY1 for the Cardiology firm. The relatives of one of your patients tell you that they are unhappy with Dr Smith, the cardiology registrar, because he took a long time to realise that the red marks on the patient's foot was athlete's foot.

Choose the THREE most appropriate actions to take in this situation.

A. Offer to re-examine the patient's foot.

B. Explain that, as the registrar is a cardiologist, athlete's foot is not part of his specialty and so he could be excused for not knowing everything.

C. Complete a critical incident form.

D. Advise the relatives to discuss the matter with Dr Smith.

E. Advise Dr Smith to discuss the matter with the relatives.

F. Explain to the relatives that you can only discuss the complaint with the patient.

G. Ask the relatives if they are otherwise happy with the care the patient has received.

H. Ask the relatives to raise the issue with the consultant.

Scenario 166

You are an FY1 for a medical firm. A patient has recently been admitted to the ward under your team's care. A newly qualified nurse comes to you and asks you to refresh her memory about the reasons for prescribing the drug Devmatizimab, which you have never heard of.

The drug was recently prescribed by the registrar; the patient has already started to take it and has been asking about it all day.

You have a sick patient to review and have no time to speak to the nurse right now. The registrar who prescribed the drug is in A&E reviewing patients.

Choose the THREE most appropriate actions to take in this situation.

A. Tell the nurse you don't know and need to rush off.

B. Ask the nurse to stop the medication until you have identified what the drug does.

C. Look the information up in the BNF once you have reviewed your other patient.

D. Ask the nurse to talk to the registrar if she can get hold of him.

E. Contact your registrar and ask for information.

F. Ask the nurse to check it out on the internet and inform the patient.

G. Tell the nurse that you don't know but that the registrar must have had good reason to prescribe it.

H. Tell the nurse to let the patient know that you will provide details about the drug when you have a moment.

Scenario 167

You are the FY1 on call for AAU (Acute Assessment Unit).

Just as he was about to be discharged, one of your patients fell on his left wrist. The wrist felt slightly tender on palpation, but an X-ray of the wrist taken after the fall did not reveal any obvious fracture.

You are now at the next day's X-ray review meeting and the radiologist identifies a small scaphoid fracture.

Choose the THREE most appropriate actions to take in this situation.

A. Tell the patient that the X-ray has shown something life-threatening and that he needs to get to A&E as soon as possible.

B. Apologise to the patient and ask him to come in because a scaphoid fracture was missed upon discharge.

C. Write a critical incident form.

D. Ask the patient whether he is symptomatic from the fracture; if he isn't, then do not call him in.

E. Tell the patient that one of the other doctors missed the scaphoid fracture and that he needs to come back in.

F. Speak to the consultant under which the patient was admitted whilst an inpatient.

G. Inform the patient about the missed scaphoid fracture and ask him to take painkillers.

H. Do not recall the patient.

Scenario 168

You are at the nursing station on a surgical ward. A nurse reminds your fellow FY1 that there are drug charts to be rewritten. He responds bluntly: "It's either drug charts or the theatre list and I know which one is more important." He then rushes off down the corridor.

A little later you overhear the nurse saying to her colleague, who was present during the incident: "I am going to get my own back and I'm going to say he's made a racist remark."

Choose the THREE most appropriate actions to take in this situation.

A. Suggest to your colleague that he apologises to the nurse.

B. Tell your colleague that the nurse was upset about his behaviour.

C. Tell your colleague that the nurse wants to report him for making racist remarks.

D. Speak to your consultant.

E. Go to Occupational Health and discuss your colleague anonymously.

F. Ask the other nurse to talk to her colleague and try to dissuade her from making her report.

G. Go to the sister and make a complaint against the nurse for bullying.

H. Talk to the sister and ask her to discuss the incident with the consultant.

Scenario 169

One of your patients is the first patient on the theatre list this afternoon for a hernia repair. He was duly placed on "Nil by mouth".

Just after the patient has left the ward to go to theatre, you notice an empty milkshake bottle at his bedside. You hurry to catch up with the patient on his way to theatre and he confirms that, since he was feeling thirsty, he organised for one of his relatives to buy him a milkshake from a coffee shop on the concourse, which he drank 10 minutes ago.

Choose the THREE most appropriate actions to take in this situation.

A. Call theatres immediately to see if the operation can be postponed to the end of the list.

B. Call your consultant immediately.

C. Take the patient back to the ward, and put the patient back on "Nil by mouth" straight away, explaining that this covers both solids and fluids.

D. Complete a critical incident form.

E. Ignore the intake of fluid as the amount is insignificant and it is only fluid.

F. Make a complaint to the catering manager.

G. Tell the nurses that they will need to be more observant in future.

H. Inform the patient apologetically that the operation will need to be cancelled.

Scenario 170

A nurse has called you to the ward to review a patient who had a nasogastric tube fitted earlier that day. She said it was signed off as safe to use; however, she found it difficult to aspirate and, upon giving a test bolus of water, the patient began to cough. The patient is stable.

You see in the notes that, at 3pm, another FY1 wrote an entry stating that he had checked the X-ray and confirmed that the tube was correctly positioned.

The radiology system shows that the radiograph was taken at 4pm but is not yet reported. You can see that the path of the tube is difficult to make out.

Choose the THREE most appropriate actions to take in this situation.

A. Complete a critical incident form.

B. Ask the nurse to place a new nasogastric tube.

C. Discuss with the FY1's supervisor your suspicion of a false entry.

D. Contact the hot seat radiologist to get an immediate report.

E. Discuss the matter with the other FY1.

F. Discuss the matter with your own consultant.

G. Report the nurse to her line manager.

H. Report the FY1 to the GMC.

Scenario 171

A patient on A&E with acute exacerbation of asthma requires an ABG for assessment.

As you approach the patient, the respiratory outreach nurse (trained for ABGs) tells you that he did the procedure himself and hands you the results slip. He tells you that the patient is hypoxic and requires immediate transfer to critical care for intubation.

The numbers on the results printout suggest that the nurse took a venous sample, not arterial. The bedside oxygen saturations are over 90%.

Choose the THREE most appropriate actions to take in this situation.

A. Accept the result based on the nurse's seniority.

B. Explain to the nurse why you think this is a venous sample.

C. Ask the nurse to repeat the sample.

D. Repeat the sample on your own.

E. Repeat the sample yourself with the nurse watching you.

F. Ask your registrar to review the results.

G. Complete a critical incident form.

H. Assist the nurse in transferring the patient to HDU.

Scenario 172

A 17-year-old girl presents to A&E accompanied by her father. She has an acute exacerbation of her asthma.

She seems reluctant to allow you to take blood from her arm. Having persuaded her of the importance of doing the blood tests, she turns her back on her father and rolls up her sleeve in such a way that he cannot see her arm. As she does so, you notice numerous slash cuts on her upper arm, consistent with self-harm.

As you glance at these cuts, she catches your eye, shakes her head, and gestures that her father (who is still in the room) does not know about the cuts.

Choose the THREE most appropriate actions to take in this situation.

A. Don't mention the marks to the girl at all.

B. Ask her about the marks before taking the blood.

C. Find an opportunity to have a casual chat with the father away from the patient, asking if he knows anything about the marks.

D. Find an opportunity to have a casual chat with the father away from the patient, enquiring about her general well-being.

E. Ask a psychiatrist to come and review the patient in A&E.

F. Make a social services referral today.

G. Seek advice from the registrar about possible safeguarding issues.

H. Find an opportunity to discuss the marks with the girl without her father being present.

Scenario 173

You have tried to take an arterial blood gas from a 28-year-old asthmatic patient and have already failed twice.

The patient is becoming distressed and this is causing deterioration in his breathing.

Choose the THREE most appropriate actions to take in this situation.

A. Try one more time since the arterial O_2 and CO_2 are of even more importance in a deteriorating patient.

B. Stop your attempt at arteriopuncture for now.

C. Ask for a nurse to come and help you reassure the patient while you try again.

D. Reassess the patient from an "ABC" point of view.

E. Ask a more experienced colleague to come and supervise you while you try again.

F. Ask a more experienced colleague to come and do the arteriopuncture.

G. Take a venous gas instead as it is easier.

H. Leave the room until the patient has calmed down. Come back to try again in 5 minutes.

Scenario 174

Your consultant has asked you to have a ward patient reviewed by the psychiatric team in order to assess his mental capacity. He wants this done today because the result of the assessment will help inform decisions for discharge planning.

You call the on-call psychiatric ST3, who tells you that he will see the patient the following morning on his ward round.

Your last job was a 4-month attachment in Psychiatry.

Choose the THREE most appropriate actions to take in this situation.

A. Call your consultant and seek advice on how to proceed.

B. Suggest that you assess the patient for capacity yourself.

C. Explain to your consultant the reasons behind the delay.

D. Demand that the psychiatric ST3 reviews the patient today as your consultant requested.

E. Call your previous psychiatric consultant to persuade him to get the ST3 to do the assessment.

F. Tell the psychiatric ST3 that the delay will result in important surgery for the patient being delayed.

G. Accept the ST3's decision to review the patient the following day.

H. Ask the nurses to try to speed up the review.

Scenario 175

A 26-year-old patient requires an urgent ultrasound scan pre-operatively.

She is due in theatre in 2 hours and you have just realised that you have forgotten to order the ultrasound.

Choose the THREE most appropriate actions to take in this situation.

A. Call your consultant immediately and explain your mistake.

B. Call the radiology department and ask for an urgent ultrasound to be done immediately.

C. Go to the radiology department and ask for an urgent ultrasound to be done immediately.

D. Go to the radiology department, talk to the on-call consultant, explain your mistake and ask if he is able to help.

E. Organise an intra-operative ultrasound scan.

F. Inform the theatre team that the patient's operation should be delayed.

G. Go to the radiology department with a paper request saying that you booked the scan early on the computer but it failed to register. Hence the delay.

H. Call the radiology department to find out who is covering ultrasounds today and ask what the list is like.

Scenario 176

You are told by an infection control nurse at a mandatory training session for all doctors that you must use alcohol gel before and after every patient examination or procedure.

You are given a small tube of alcohol gel to carry around the hospital. You know that the gel causes your eczema to flare up.

Choose the THREE most appropriate actions to take in this situation.

A. Talk to the lecturer after the training session to discuss your personal circumstances.

B. Use the alcohol gel as normal.

C. Do not use the alcohol gel.

D. Use the emollient that you normally use to wash your hands.

E. Arrange a meeting with Occupational Health.

F. Use soap and water at sinks instead of alcohol gel.

G. Use gloves at all times when dealing with patients.

H. Minimise your exposure to the gel by using it after each procedure but not before.

Scenario 177

You find one of your nursing colleagues in tears. She is upset because she has received some nasty remarks from some other nurses.

This is not the first time that you have caught her crying over this type of issue. She confides in you she is now keen to start looking for another job as she can no longer cope with the atmosphere in this unit.

Choose the THREE most appropriate actions to take in this situation.

A. Ask her how she is and how things are in general outside of work.

B. Reassure her that she is doing the right thing by leaving and offer her a reference.

C. Suggest that maybe she simply does not fit in the team and another job is a good idea.

D. Advise her she can go off sick if she is stressed and she can use this time to look for another job.

E. Advise her to try to arrange a meeting with her line manager and offer to go with her for support.

F. Suggest maybe she is being too sensitive and needs to get a thicker skin.

G. Offer her a shoulder to cry on whenever she needs it.

H. Try to help her find a nursing colleague for support during her remaining time on the ward.

Scenario 178

You are the FY1 on call for the night.

During the Hospital at Night handover, the site managers mention that the night medical registrar is currently dealing with a very sick patient in PCU (Progressive Care Unit), leaving only you to clerk in waiting patients and cover the wards. The FY2 on nights has called in sick due to diarrhoea and vomiting.

There are currently eight people waiting in A&E still needing to be clerked, and there are a further two sick patients in resus waiting to be assessed.

Choose the THREE most appropriate actions to take in this situation.

A. Ask the Night Nurse Practitioners (NNPs) to clerk in patients during the night's take.

B. Call the consultant on call to inform him of the situation.

C. Call the FY2 who is supposed to be on shift, tell him how many patients are waiting, and ask him kindly to come in for a few hours until the workload is more manageable.

D. Complete a critical incident form at the end of the shift.

E. Prioritise the sick patients in resus to be clerked in first and leave the other patients to be clerked in as time allows.

F. Clerk in the patients in the order in which they arrived to prevent any breach of the 4-hour rule.

G. Briefly clerk in the patients in the order they arrived and then identify the patients who would need reviewing later.

H. Email the FY2 a list of the patients you saw to keep him informed.

Scenario 179

You are a surgical FY1. One of your patients is a 34-year-old man who had an appendicectomy two days ago.

The patient has a surgical drain in-situ and the nurses are recording the output daily. Based on their record, you document that he drained 30ml of serosanguinous fluid yesterday.

However, last night, he spiked a fever and, on reviewing him again, you find that you had misread what the nursing staff had written. In fact he had drained 300ml of fluid. As a result, you have sent him for CT-guided percutaneous drainage of intra-abdominal fluid collection.

Choose the THREE most appropriate actions to take in this situation.

A. Write a new entry in the patient's notes with the current date and time.

B. Remove your original entry from the patient notes.

C. Write a new note, timing and dating it at the same time as the original note.

D. Write a critical incident form.

E. Use correction fluid to eliminate the original note.

F. Document the fact that the nurses failed to spot your mistake.

G. Inform the patient about your mistake.

H. Add another zero to the 30ml drained in the original patient notes and then countersign it.

Scenario 180

One morning at an X-ray meeting in General Surgery, the consultants are discussing the CT results of one of your patients: a 62-year-old married woman admitted with abdominal pain.

The radiologist comments on the size of your patient's uterus, suggesting she needs an MRI scan. However, you know from having talked to the patient recently that she had a hysterectomy 12 years ago.

Choose the THREE most appropriate actions to take in this situation.

A. Let the meeting finish and mention the hysterectomy to your consultant afterwards.

B. Let the meeting finish and mention the hysterectomy to the radiologist afterwards.

C. Go back to the patient later that day and ask her about her hysterectomy.

D. Interrupt the discussion to mention the conversation that you had with the patient in which the hysterectomy was mentioned.

E. Review the patient's notes to check whether she had a hysterectomy 12 years ago.

F. Tell the patient that there is a risk that her uterus may not have been removed.

G. Call the patient's husband to double-check the issue of the hysterectomy.

H. Complete a critical incident form.

Scenario 181

You are the FY1 for the Acute Stroke Unit at a DGH. A stroke patient has recently being transferred from a large teaching hospital for neuro-rehabilitation.

The patient asks to see you and tells you that he is not happy with the quality of the coffee he has been served and the number of speech and language therapy sessions he is receiving.

Choose the THREE most appropriate actions to take in this situation.

A. Buy a coffee from the local coffee shop for the patient.

B. Explain to the patient that, due to recent cutbacks in the NHS, there is a greater need for rationing.

C. Tell the patient you will see what can be done about the coffee and ask them to explain what they were expecting in relation to the speech and language therapy sessions.

D. Ask the Speech and Language Therapists to give the patient extra sessions.

E. Ask the patient to make a formal complaint in writing to the hospital.

F. Document the complaint and your actions in the notes.

G. Talk to the Speech and Language Therapy team about the patient's concerns and relay their explanations to the patient.

H. Explain to the patient that you will raise his concerns with the Speech and Language Therapy team. Ask the Speech and Language Therapy team to talk to the patient.

Scenario 182

You are the surgical FY1 working a weekend. There should be a phlebotomist ward round every day, including weekends.

It is now the second weekend in a row that the phlebotomist has failed to show up without a reason. You are left with a list of 18 patients to bleed and you still have many patients to review.

Choose the THREE most appropriate actions to take in this situation.

A. Inform the phlebotomist's manager on Monday that the phlebotomist has not turned up and failed to provide any warning or reason.

B. Write a critical incident form.

C. Deal with the most urgent blood samples and leave the non-urgent ones for Monday.

D. Ask the nursing staff to help you take the bloods.

E. Prioritise the bloods from urgent to less urgent and do as many as you can.

F. Stop reviewing your patients until all blood samples have been taken.

G. Send an email to the phlebotomy team asking them to take the bloods urgently on Monday morning.

H. Call the consultant on call.

Scenario 183

You are an FY1 working for the Renal team. One of your patients, who has just come back from a CT scan, calls you over to tell you that she can't find her purse. She thinks the nursing staff might have stolen it and wants to move to a different ward.

Choose the THREE most appropriate actions to take in this situation.

A. Tell the patient that it would be against the nurses' code of conduct to steal from patients.

B. Report the theft to the police.

C. Inform the ward sister of the missing purse.

D. Offer to help the patient search her bedside and her belongings again.

E. Search the nursing staff locker room.

F. Offer to move the patient to another ward.

G. Ask security to search the nursing staff on the ward to look for the purse.

H. Reassure the patient that you were not involved in the theft.

Scenario 184

You are an FY1 working for the Respiratory team.

Your fellow FY1 colleague has been making increasingly more mistakes. He has been charting patient blood results in the wrong patient's notes, and, on many occasions, has forgotten to leave out blood forms, despite having confirmed that he would do them.

Choose the THREE most appropriate actions to take in this situation.

A. Tell the registrar about your colleague's frequent mistakes.

B. Express your concerns to your colleague about the number of mistakes he is making and ask him to review all the patients he has seen that day and on previous days as far back as he can.

C. Inform your educational supervisor.

D. Email the other doctors on the ward to inform them of the situation and asking them to watch for potential mistakes.

E. Check all his jobs to ensure that no mistakes are made.

F. Ensure that a critical incident form is completed for each mistake that your colleague makes.

G. Let the ward sister know that your colleague makes frequent mistakes. Ask her to ensure that the nurses bleep you if they have any concerns about any patient.

H. Offer to help your colleague out with some of his jobs if you have some spare time.

Scenario 185

The current FY1 for Surgery tells you that the on call is unsafe. He is covering several busy wards single-handedly, with only one ST3 for backup. The ST3 is rarely there to offer support when there is a sick patient.

You find that slightly surprising because you were an FY1 in that same firm for the previous 4 months and you had no problem at all.

Choose the THREE most appropriate actions to take in this situation.

A. Reassure him that it will settle as he gets more comfortable with the post.

B. Offer to meet him with one of the night ward sisters to discuss his concerns.

C. Listen to the FY1's concerns and advise him to discuss it with the Medical Director.

D. Contact the FY1 course director informally and express your concerns that your colleague may not be coping.

E. Speak to the ST3 to find out more.

F. Listen to him and advise him to talk to his clinical supervisor.

G. Advise him to have an informal meeting with the ST3 in question to explain how they may benefit from additional support.

H. Listen to the FY1 and advise him to discuss the issue with his defence union.

Scenario 186

The rota for the surgical ward cover is written by the ST3.

It is the Christmas period and you are down on the rota to cover Christmas Eve, Christmas Day, New Year's Eve and New Year's Day nights from 8pm to 8am. You do not feel that this is fair.

Choose the THREE most appropriate actions to take in this situation.

A. Work the rota. Tell the nurses to bleep you only in extreme emergencies.

B. Accept the rota but call in sick on the last night.

C. Work the rota but have an arrangement with the medical FY1 to carry your bleep for half the time, whilst you do the same for him for the other half, so that you are both carrying two bleeps but for half the time each.

D. Arrange a meeting with the ST3 in charge of the rota, informing him that you feel it is unfair that you should have to cover all of the important holiday nights.

E. Spend some time looking at the rota and trying to rearrange the on call to make it fairer. Then approach the rota organiser with your ideas.

F. Arrange a meeting with all the FY1s to discuss sharing the on-call cover more equitably.

G. Tell your consultant that you think the rota is unfair and needs adjusting.

H. Tell your colleagues that you don't mind covering Christmas but you won't cover New Year.

Scenario 187

You are the FY1 working for the Endocrine & Diabetes team. You have just admitted a 19-year-old student. It is the seventh time she has been admitted for diabetic ketoacidosis (DKA) and you suspect it is mainly due to her non-compliance with medications (she is trying to lose weight).

From previous discharge summaries, you see that she normally self-discharges 24 hours after admission.

Choose the THREE most appropriate actions to take in this situation.

A. Call a family meeting with her parents. Inform them that their daughter is wasting NHS resources and is risking being barred from attending the hospital.

B. Arrange for the girl to meet a willing diabetic foot patient so that she visualises the impact of poor glycaemic control on her life.

C. Show the patient a resus situation where CPR is happening, explaining how valuable NHS resources could be better spent elsewhere.

D. Write in the patient's discharge summary that she is not to be admitted again because she is non-compliant with her medications.

E. Talk to the girl in private and ask her why she is experiencing DKA so frequently.

F. Explain to her that there is little you can do about her situation as she is competent and is entitled to make her own decisions.

G. Write to her GP, sharing your concerns about the girl's behaviour.

H. Arrange a follow-up appointment 1 week after discharge to check up on her progress.

Scenario 188

You are working on a general medical ward doing 9am to 5pm shifts. In addition you are on ward cover from 5pm to 9pm.

You have been experiencing lower leg pain for a while and your GP has recently prescribed codeine for it. You have assiduously been taking the medication over the past few days and have noticed that you are becoming increasingly tired around 4pm each day as a result.

Choose the THREE most appropriate actions to take in this situation.

A. Mention this to your consultant.

B. Stop the codeine and ask the nursing staff to give you some ibuprofen from the drugs trolley.

C. Try to swap your ward cover shifts with another doctor so that you can finish earlier whilst you are taking the codeine.

D. Do not mention the codeine or the tiredness to anyone.

E. Do sedentary paperwork until you complete your treatment to minimise the leg pain.

F. Ensure that you get sufficient sleep each night before your shifts.

G. Ask your GP to prescribe you an alternative for the pain.

H. Write a private prescription for tramadol and take that instead of codeine.

Scenario 189

You are the FY1 on call for night cover. Whilst walking down to the ward, you are stopped by a nurse who asks you to cannulate a patient for anti-biotics, mentioning that the last cannula tissued.

You explain to the nurse that, since you have two other patients to re-view, it would be appreciated if she could prepare the cannulation equipment to save time. The nurse snaps at you unexpectedly and says to you in front of another nurse: "Do it yourself; you're paid more than me so you should do some work for once."

It is the first time that this nurse has reacted so aggressively.

Choose the THREE most appropriate actions to take in this situation.

A. Discuss this event with your consultant.

B. Arrange for a meeting with the nurse to discuss the working relationship later on in the week.

C. Reply to the nurse that her behaviour is inappropriate.

D. Take the nurse to a private room. Inform her that you will only put the cannula in if she apologises to you.

E. Report the nurse to the ward sister.

F. File a complaint with the Human Resources department when you have time.

G. Prepare the cannula equipment yourself.

H. Ignore all future requests from this nurse until the situation is resolved.

Scenario 190

You are the FY1 on call for AAU (Acute Assessment Unit). You are working with a colleague who has recently told you that he has just being diagnosed as dyslexic. He has made a number of spelling mistakes and calculation errors of medications on drug charts.

Choose the THREE most appropriate actions to take in this situation.

A. Report your colleague to the GMC.

B. Ask the ward pharmacist to keep a close eye on his drug charts and correct his mistakes.

C. Ask the nursing staff to double-check all his signed prescriptions before administering them

D. Offer to check your colleague's prescriptions for him.

E. Ask the ward sister to keep a close eye on the drug charts that he has written and correct his mistakes.

F. Offer to help your colleague with his spelling and calculations, and offer to check his prescriptions if you have some spare time during your shifts.

G. Leave a note in all the drug charts for the FY1 to rewrite the incorrectly spelt medications.

H. Tell your AAU consultant.

Scenario 191

A 38-year-old man presents to the Emergency Department complaining of a testicular lump. He is convinced that he has testicular cancer.

Having examined it, you are certain that it is a benign epididymal cyst requiring no treatment.

Choose the THREE most appropriate actions to take in this situation.

A. Inform him of the benign diagnosis and provide reassurance.

B. Advise him to see his GP if he is still concerned.

C. Send him home.

D. Advise him that he should request an ultrasound from his GP.

E. Organise an urgent ultrasound to confirm the diagnosis.

F. Tell him that this is not an acute situation and that, in future, he would need to see his GP for benign issues.

G. Refer him to urology.

H. Refer him to Oncology.

Scenario 192

While you are working in the Emergency Department, a woman with a history of breast cancer presents with severe jaundice.

On examination, you feel a large mass in the right upper quadrant of her abdomen consistent with a hard craggy liver, highly suggestive of metastatic breast cancer.

She is insistently asking you what is wrong with her.

Choose the THREE most appropriate actions to take in this situation.

A. Refer the patient to the palliative care team.

B. Arrange for the community palliative care team to review the patient at home.

C. Arrange immediate admission.

D. Organise urgent tests to include liver function tests, liver MRI and mammogram.

E. Organise urgent blood tests to include liver function tests.

F. Tell the patient that there is something wrong with her liver and she needs more tests. If she asks, tell her that it may be related to the breast cancer.

G. Tell the patient that there is something wrong with her liver and that it is most likely that her cancer has spread.

H. Tell the patient that her cancer has spread, reassure her that everything will be done to help her and inform her that she requires admission.

Scenario 193

One of your patients has developed an acute onset headache just as you were about to discharge him from hospital. The patient has no neurological signs but you are convinced that this is a subarachnoid haemorrhage and requires urgent review.

You contact the medical ST5 on call who states that, since the patient has no neurological signs, she does not need to see the patient.

Choose the THREE most appropriate actions to take in this situation.

A. Discharge the patient and advise him to go to A&E if the headaches get worse.

B. Telephone the medical consultant on call and request the admission.

C. Try another specialty (e.g. neurosurgery) and see if they will review the patient for you for possible admission.

D. Ask for help from your ST1 on call.

E. Discuss with your consultant the possibility of making a complaint against the medical ST5.

F. Call the ST5 back after 5 minutes and tell her that her patient has neurological signs.

G. Ask a nurse to observe the patient at regular intervals and warn you if the patient deteriorates.

H. Document the conversation you had with the ST5 in the patient's notes.

Scenario 194

Your consultant has asked you to discharge a post-operative patient back to her care home immediately as he urgently requires the bed for another patient who is due to come in for major surgery later that day.

On reviewing the notes of the patient you are due to discharge, you notice that the Occupational Therapist (OT) has stated that she needs to do a "home visit" prior to discharge.

Choose the THREE most appropriate actions to take in this situation.

A. Inform the ward manager of the problem.

B. Tell the consultant that you are unable to discharge the patient and ask him what to do in view of the OT's entry in the notes.

C. Ask the patient to put pressure on the OT to hasten the home visit.

D. Inform the OT that the patient will need to be discharged without a home visit.

E. Call the OT and ask her when is the earliest that she can do the home visit.

F. Tell the OT that she will need to do her home visit today as the patient needs to be discharged.

G. Discharge the patient.

H. Complete a critical incident form.

Scenario 195

During an outpatient clinic, you take a patient's blood pressure and it measures 190/100. She is otherwise well.

The patient tells you that, when her blood pressure is being measured by nurses at her GP practice, it is always normal. She is scared of seeing the doctor about it.

Choose the THREE most appropriate answers to this scenario

A. Tell the patient that, when she has her blood pressure measured at her GP practice, she should ensure it is always done by a nurse.

B. Review the notes and her medication.

C. Advise her she needs to be admitted to the hospital.

D. Ask her to use a blood pressure monitor at home and record the results ensuring she sees her own GP with the results.

E. Ask the patient to sit in the waiting room for a while and get a nurse to take her blood pressure in 30 minutes' time.

F. Advise her she needs more medication to control her hypertension.

G. Start her on bendroflumethiazide.

H. Ask your consultant to review the patient.

Scenario 196

In an outpatient clinic, your patient has not attended his appointment for which he was referred by his GP. When you look in his notes, you notice that this is the fifth consecutive appointment that he has not attended. He has never tried to cancel an appointment before.

Choose the THREE most appropriate actions to take in this situation.

A. Document the non-attendance in the notes.

B. Inform the clinic manager of the non-attendance, asking her to write to the patient to explain the clinic's policy on missed appointments.

C. Call the patient, asking his whereabouts and checking if he is okay.

D. Call the patient and ask why he has not attended this and the last five appointments.

E. Call the patient and inform him that, since he has taken up a large number of slots already, he can no longer attend the clinic. Advise the patient to go back to his GP for a referral elsewhere.

F. Write to the patient and inform him that, since he has taken up a large number of slots already, he can no longer attend the clinic. Advise the patient to go back to his GP for a referral elsewhere.

G. Call the patient's GP to enquire about possible reasons for non-attendance.

H. Call the patient's home and ask his wife whether the patient is okay as you are concerned about his non-attendance.

Scenario 197

You are working in Obstetrics and Gynaecology, doing a pre-admission clinic.

You see a 20-year-old woman who is attending the day unit for her fourth termination of pregnancy (TOP).

Choose the THREE most appropriate actions to take in this situation.

A. Refer the patient to Psychiatry.

B. Advise her that the consultant can insert a coil at the time of TOP if she consents to it.

C. Offer her a supply of the combined oral contraceptive pill.

D. Offer her a supply of condoms.

E. Advise her that surgical TOP is potentially dangerous and is not a form of contraception.

F. Offer her counselling.

G. Tell her she needs to be sterilised.

H. Give her information on adoption.

Scenario 198

You are working on a Paediatric assessment unit, reviewing an 8-year-old child who has a mild chest infection. While his mum leaves the bedside to go to the toilet, the child discloses that his father keeps hitting him.

Choose the THREE most appropriate actions to take in this situation.

A. Admit the child before the mother gets back and inform the registrar on call for child protection.

B. Remind the child gently that he must not lie about such things and then ask him to tell you the truth about what happened.

C. Listen to him and document everything he says.

D. Listen to him. Document the abuse only if the child repeats the same allegation.

E. Wait until his mother returns to talk to the child.

F. Call the nurse on the admission unit to sit in with you while you listen to the child.

G. Ask the child if this has ever happened before.

H. Ask the mother whether she is aware of the fact that the father is hitting the child.

Scenario 199

Your ST5 has asked you to go through his blood results.

On reviewing his results, you uncover a problem. A blood test that your ST5 has documented as "normal, no action" is in fact grossly abnormal. The CRP (C-reactive protein) and ESR (Erythrocyte sedimentation rate) are both elevated and there is a positive rheumatoid factor.

On review of the notes, you discover that the patient is a 36-year-old man with newly experienced joint pain. You are concerned that this is a missed diagnosis of early onset rheumatoid arthritis.

Choose the THREE most appropriate answers to this scenario

A. Do not tell the ST5.

B. Share with the ST5 your concerns about the results and ask him to teach you on the topic.

C. Tell the ST5 that a critical incident form will need to be completed.

D. Inform your consultant of the ST5's mistake.

E. Inform your ST3 of the ST5's mistake.

F. Report the ST5 to the GMC.

G. Arrange for the patient to be referred immediately to a rheumatologist.

H. Contact the patient and apologise for the mistake.

Scenario 200

You are working in General Surgery. Part of your role is to assist the running of the pre-assessment clinic for patients who are to be admitted for major surgery.

One of the patients you saw in clinic last week has just arrived on the ward, ready for surgery today. On review of the notes you realise that you forgot to listen to her heart in the clinic. You do this immediately and hear a murmur.

Choose the THREE most appropriate answers to this scenario

A. Ignore the murmur.

B. Tell the anaesthetist that he may want to listen to the patient's heart before proceeding.

C. Document the murmur.

D. Inform the patient of your findings and possible delay.

E. Inform your consultant that the patient will need further investigations that are likely to delay the surgery.

F. Contact the echocardiography department requesting an echocardiogram to be performed within the next 15 minutes.

G. Complete a critical incident form.

H. Tell the consultant that the patient is ready for surgery.

Scenario 201

A 92-year-old patient tells you that he no longer wants to take his medication for hyperlipidaemia (high cholesterol) as he is ready to die.

Choose the THREE most appropriate actions to take in this situation.

A. Assess the patient for capacity.

B. Ask him to explain why he feels he wants to die, offer support but explain that stopping his medication for high cholesterol is unlikely to hasten his death.

C. Offer to help him die.

D. If he has capacity, explain that he is entitled to make his own decision.

E. Give the patient details of a Swiss clinic that could help him die.

F. Write a Do Not Resuscitate (DNR) order for the patient.

G. Inform his relatives.

H. Tell the patient that his decision is not rational and that he is therefore not competent. Explain that, in such circumstances, doctors must act in the patient's best interests and can therefore impose that he should continue the treatment.

Scenario 202

Your consultant asks you to make a backdated alteration to the notes in order to cover up for a past mistake made by the team.

Choose the THREE most appropriate actions to take in this situation.

A. Make the change requested by the consultant as you are worried that she may give you a bad reference.

B. Refuse to make the entry.

C. Make a note of the conversation that you have had with the consultant and contact your defence union.

D. Report the matter to the Clinical Director at the earliest opportunity.

E. Inform the patient of the consultant's request and of the mistake made.

F. Inform the GMC.

G. Inform the police as there are potentially legal implications.

H. Complete a critical incident form.

Scenario 203

You have written a case report for publication and your consultant has recently reviewed your final draft. When he returns the manuscript, you notice that he has added two names to the list of authors.

When you enquire, he tells you that they are his wife and his ex-ST4 who both need publications on their CV to enhance their chances of employment. Neither were involved with the case discussed in your paper and, to the best of your knowledge, neither have provided any input.

Choose the THREE most appropriate actions to take in this situation.

A. Tell the consultant that you cannot publish the case reports with their names on and that you will submit the case report with your name and the consultant's only.

B. Discuss the situation in confidence with the Clinical Director and envisage contacting the GMC about the two other doctors.

C. Agree to add the two names to the publication as it is only a case report and not a research paper.

D. Check with other colleagues whether something similar has happened to them and contact the GMC about your consultant if it has.

E. Discuss the matter with the consultant in a private meeting.

F. Report your consultant to the GMC.

G. Contact the editor of the paper in which the case report is due to be published to inform him of the situation.

H. Inform your registrar.

Scenario 204

During a busy clinic you overhear a ward clerk talking to one of the regular patients in front of other patients. She is making fun of an ugly patient who came in earlier.

Choose the THREE most appropriate actions to take in this situation.

A. Firmly tell the ward clerk to stop the discussion there and then.

B. Tell the ward clerk you will raise the issue with the clinic manager if it happens again.

C. Raise the matter with the clinic manager.

D. Apologise to the other patients present and reassure them that it will not happen again.

E. Draw the ward clerk away from the discussion by telling her that you need her help with another patient. Have a private word with her.

F. Discuss the matter with your consultant.

G. Document the issue in both patients' notes.

H. Complete a critical incident form.

Scenario 205

One of the nurses on your ward is complaining about the bad body odour of one of your FY1 colleagues and asks you if you could have a word with him.

You were aware of the problem and have in fact already raised it with the colleague in the past.

Choose the THREE most appropriate actions to take in this situation.

A. Tell the nurse that this is really an issue for the consultant to deal with and that she should go and talk to him.

B. Talk to the consultant about the issue.

C. Ask a few other colleagues whether they agree with the nurse's point of view.

D. Raise the issue at a team meeting when the colleague in question is present.

E. Raise the issue at a team meeting in the absence of the colleague in question.

F. Raise the issue directly with the colleague in question again.

G. Send the colleague an anonymous note asking him to sort the issue out.

H. Inform the Human Resources department.

Scenario 206

You work with an ST3 who is often unobtainable. For the fifth time in a week, you have bleeped him to review a very sick patient urgently and he has failed to turn up.

Whenever you ask him where he has been, his only excuse is that his bleep functions erratically and that he wasn't aware that you had bleeped him.

Choose the THREE most appropriate actions to take in this situation.

A. Contact your consultant to inform him about the problem.

B. Ignore the problem but make sure that whenever you require help on a patient-related matter you seek advice from an ST3 on another team.

C. Ignore the problem but make sure that whenever you require help on a patient-related matter you seek advice from another junior doctor at your level.

D. Initiate a meeting with the ST3 to get to the bottom of the problem.

E. Ask some of the nurses whether they have heard the ST3's bleep go off so as to check whether he is telling the truth.

F. Complete a critical incident form.

G. Complain to a senior nurse about the problem.

H. Report the ST3 to the GMC.

Scenario 207

One of your patients has suspected bowel cancer for which a biopsy was organised. The patient's sister has been moaning constantly that the test results are taking their time to come back and that this is making the patient and the whole family anxious.

Your consultant asked you to chase this earlier in the day as a matter of urgency. The results have now come back and confirm invasive bowel cancer.

Choose the THREE most appropriate actions to take in this situation.

A. Inform the patient of the diagnosis.

B. Call the oncologist and ask him for a consultation regarding radiotherapy and/or chemotherapy.

C. Call your consultant and inform him of the result.

D. Ask the Clinical Nurse Specialist for bowel cancer to come and see the patient to explain what will happen next.

E. Write the result in the patient's notes

F. Inform the ward nurses as the patient will need support when she is being informed of the diagnosis.

G. Inform the patient's sister of the diagnosis and ask her to be present when the news is being broken to the patient.

H. Ask the patient's sister to put her complaint in writing.

Scenario 208

A patient whom you have been looking after on the Elderly Care ward has died in hospital. It was an expected death and you have been asked by the nursing team to certify the death.

Choose the THREE most appropriate actions to take in this situation.

A. Tell the patients sharing the bay with the deceased that he has died.

B. Write the death certificate as soon as possible.

C. Check the deceased patient for signs of life.

D. Check the deceased patient for evidence of a pacemaker.

E. Write the cause of death in the patient notes.

F. Review the case with the coroner.

G. Follow the ALS algorithm for checking signs of life.

H. Tell the nurse you don't need to see the patient.

Scenario 209

You have finished your work early and have no additional tasks to complete. All the notes are up to date and your patients all appear stable.

Your shift normally finishes at 6pm. It is 3.30pm and you would love to go home. You are tired after working three long shifts in a row. At the back of your mind is an audit that you are currently working on, and which you have been asked to present in 6 weeks' time. Your bleep is long range and works at home.

Choose the THREE most appropriate actions to take in this situation.

A. Stay on the ward.

B. Go home.

C. Go to the doctors' mess.

D. Keep your bleep.

E. Hand over your bleep to the ST1.

F. Relax.

G. Work on your audit.

H. Offer help to your colleagues.

Scenario 210

You are an FY1 on the Acute Medical Unit (AMU).

Just as you are about to discharge a 16-year-old patient with community-acquired pneumonia, she asks whether you could prescribe the oral contraceptive pill as she regularly has unprotected sex with her boyfriend who is also 16 years old and is due to come back from holiday with his parents in 2 weeks' time.

She asks that you do not tell her mother.

Choose the THREE most appropriate actions to take in this situation.

A. Prescribe the contraceptive pill.

B. Ask the patient to see her local GP or the local sexual health/family planning clinic.

C. Advise the patient that you can only prescribe or refer her to other services that can prescribe if she attends a local "safer sex" learning course.

D. Inform her mother.

E. Report the matter to social services.

F. Do not prescribe the contraceptive pill.

G. Tell the patient that you cannot prescribe the contraceptive pill in AMU.

H. Offer the patient some leaflets on "safer sex".

Scenario 211

You are the Vascular FY1 for a small DGH. You notice that your fellow FY1 work colleague has just come into work unshaven, and that his breath smells of alcohol. He seems to be slurring his speech a little.

To your knowledge, this is the first time this has ever happened.

Choose the THREE most appropriate actions to take in this situation.

A. Give your colleague some chewing gum to hide the smell of alcohol.

B. Assess your colleague with the CAGE questionnaire to ascertain whether he is an alcoholic.

C. Report the incident to your consultant immediately.

D. Ask your colleague to go home.

E. Complete a critical incident form.

F. Make a note to raise the issue with a consultant next time this happens again.

G. Approach your colleague with your concerns and tell him you are available to discuss anything if he needs help.

H. Tell your colleague that he should only be seeing patients with a chaperone.

Scenario 212

You are currently doing a taster week at a GP practice. You have been given your own clinics to run. You see a patient who says he has a problem with his weight and takes oral ephedrine, which he orders online via the internet.

He has come to you because he has been getting some palpitations when he uses it. Having gathered information from several websites, he asks that you monitor his blood pressure and heart rate regularly.

His BMI is within the healthy range. You have read previously that ephedrine is a drug that is banned due to its cardiotoxic effects.

Choose the THREE most appropriate actions to take in this situation.

A. Prescribe Orlistat on the NHS to stop the patient from taking the potentially harmful ephedrine.

B. Advise the patient to stop taking the ephedrine. Measure his blood pressure and heart rate whilst he is on ephedrine even if he declines your advice.

C. Prescribe Orlistat as a private prescription to stop the patient from taking the potentially harmful ephedrine.

D. Talk to the patient about why he wishes to lose the weight.

E. Refuse to see the patient further if he continues to take the ephedrine.

F. Write a formal letter to the patient regarding his behaviour, warning him that he may be taken off the practice's list if he continues to use ephedrine.

G. Refer to a psychiatrist regarding possible eating disorder behaviour.

H. Advise the patient to keep taking ephedrine with regular GP monitoring.

Scenario 213

You are the FY1 on call for Paediatrics. You have just clerked in a 7-year-old boy who has presented in the past to the Paediatrics A&E unit with several episodes that did not seem related.

Today, the child is being brought in with a suspicious burn and bruise mark on his arm. You ask the father whether anyone has struck his child. The father responds angrily and threatens to sue you.

Choose the THREE most appropriate actions to take in this situation.

A. Inform the consultant of the incident and ask for advice.

B. Give reassurance to the father and treat the patient's injury appropriately.

C. Let the father discharge the child from the hospital.

D. Call the police and report the incident.

E. Ask the mother in private whether there has been any abuse.

F. Speak to the hospital legal team asking for advice regarding the possibility of a lawsuit.

G. Admit the child to the ward for further assessment.

H. Report the family to social services.

Scenario 214

You are the FY1 on call on AMU (Acute Medical Unit) on a Sunday. On Friday, you printed and signed a discharge summary with drug list for an elderly patient who was due to be discharged that day. Unfortunately this patient suffered an episode of acute cardiac failure prior to discharge. She made a good recovery and is now stable due to changes to her cardiac medications. The consultant advised that she is ready for discharge today.

You are preparing a new discharge summary with drug list using the signed version from Friday as a guide. Whilst in the middle of doing so, you are called into an emergency. When you return, you realise that the first discharge summary and drug list have been sent off, and that the patient has already gone home without the new drug combination.

Choose the THREE most appropriate actions to take in this situation.

A. Inform the consultant of the incident and ask for advice.

B. Do nothing more.

C. Call the patient, apologise for the mistake and ask her to come back to collect the new medications immediately.

D. Call the patient, apologise for the mistake and tell her to take double the dose of her previous heart failure medications from now on.

E. Fax a letter to the GP with the new medication list and ask him to review the patient in a week's time.

F. Complete a critical incident form.

G. Document the mistake in the patient's discharge summary and send an updated copy to the GP.

H. Call the patient, apologise for the mistake and get her to see her GP on Monday. In the meantime fax over an updated medications list for the GP.

Scenario 215

You are an FY1 in Endocrinology & Diabetes. You notice that one of your patients has low serum magnesium levels on routine blood tests. You decide to top it up with an IV infusion of 8mmol of magnesium sulphate in 50ml of normal saline over 30 minutes (the speed and dose of magnesium sulphate is reasonable in this situation).

The nurse giving out the medications refuses to administer the IV magnesium sulphate to the patient as she feels that the infusion is going in too fast.

Choose the THREE most appropriate actions to take in this situation.

A. Administer the IV magnesium sulphate yourself.

B. Complete a critical incident form.

C. Speak to the nurse and find out why she feels the infusion is going in too fast.

D. Double the length of time for the magnesium sulphate to be infused over (which you know will not harm the patient or change the drug's efficacy) and ask the nurse to administer the medication again.

E. Cross the magnesium sulphate prescription off.

F. Speak to your Endocrinology & Diabetes registrar for advice.

G. Document in the notes that the nurse has refused to administer the magnesium infusion.

H. Order the nurse to give the infusion, making it clear that you will take full responsibility as you prescribed the medication.

Scenario 216

You are an FY1 on call for AMU (Acute Medical Unit).

A patient is about to be discharged and just needs a final infusion of Venefer (IV iron) before discharge. The nurse gives you a tray containing a syringe with the fluid already drawn up, which you administer to the patient. The patient is then discharged without incident.

Later on you notice that the IV iron was not actually infused (the ampoule of active powder is still intact in the tray). Only the saline solution was given.

Choose the THREE most appropriate actions to take in this situation.

A. Inform the consultant of the incident and ask for advice.

B. Take no further action.

C. Phone the patient's GP for him to organise another IV iron infusion in the community next week.

D. Fill in a critical incident form and write a reflective e-portfolio essay.

E. Inform the ward sister of the nurse's mistake.

F. Document in the notes that this has occurred and name the nurse involved.

G. Contact the patient and explain what has happened immediately.

H. Drive to the patient's home with an IV set and infuse the IV iron at their home after your shift has finished.

Scenario 217

A patient with slightly unusual facial features and a port wine stain is being treated on your ward.

One afternoon, you overhear two junior nurses and one of the medical students openly mock the patient's appearance in the corridors.

At the same time, a relative of the patient who is in the bed next to his grabs your attention at the end of his visit and tells you that he overheard the medical student ask the patient if he "got the port wine stain by drinking too much".

Choose the THREE most appropriate actions to take in this situation.

A. Talk to the patient who has been mocked and to the other patient's relative about the incident, emphasise that such behaviour is unacceptable and reassure them.

B. Contact the Human Resources department.

C. Complete a critical incident form.

D. Take the junior nurses and medical student aside and make it clear that their behaviour is unacceptable.

E. Tell both the patient and the other patient's relative that they are entitled to make a complaint. Offer to provide the information required.

F. Report the issue to the consultant and the ward sister.

G. Tell the patient who has been mocked and the other patient's relative that you are aware of the problem from previous occurrences you have personally witnessed and reassure them you will deal with it.

H. Send the nurses and the medical student home.

Scenario 218

You are on the ward, being shadowed by a medical student. As you approach a male patient to catheterise him, the medical student asks you if he could do the catheterisation.

You ask him to explain to you how he would perform it and are satisfied with his explanation. He says to you that he has done it three times before with other doctors.

The patient was already consented for the procedure on the basis that you were going to perform it yourself.

Choose the THREE most appropriate actions to take in this situation.

A. Allow the student to catheterise the patient unsupervised.

B. Document the procedure in the patient's notes.

C. Ask the patient to provide consent again, but this time for the procedure to be done by a medical student.

D. Do the catheterisation yourself.

E. Ask the medical student to seek approval from the registrar or the consultant.

F. Ask a nurse to supervise the medical student.

G. Tell the patient that the procedure will be done by a medical student.

H. Supervise the medical student whilst he performs the procedure.

Scenario 219

You commence antibiotic therapy for a patient who has cellulitis with skin ulceration. You misread the antimicrobial sensitivities; the isolates were in fact of intermediate sensitivity to the antibiotics that you have started.

You only notice this mistake when reviewing the patient after the second day of treatment. Despite this, the patient has made an improvement.

Choose the THREE most appropriate actions to take in this situation.

A. Apologise to the patient about the mistake and inform the registrar.

B. Record it as a clinical event in your reflective NHS e-portfolio.

C. Cancel the antibiotic prescription on the drug chart.

D. Do not inform the patient.

E. Tell your clinical supervisor about the mistake, reassure him that it won't happen again and that, since the patient was not harmed, there is no need to write a critical incident form.

F. Stop the old antibiotics and prescribe new ones that the bacterial isolates are sensitive to.

G. Continue the old antibiotics until the course is finished then start a new regimen.

H. Continue the old antibiotics and commence the new antibiotics in parallel.

Scenario 220

The nurses on one of the wards that you cover are constantly bleeping you for non-urgent tasks. It is making your working day difficult and you are beginning to resent attending that particular ward.

Choose the THREE most appropriate actions to take in this situation.

A. Continue to answer the bleeps from that ward. Whenever the matter is non-urgent, send an email to the ward sister to inform her.

B. Ignore the bleeps from that ward but ensure you call them every hour to ask if there is anything urgent.

C. Ask the FY1s to meet to discuss the general bleep policy of the hospital, asking specifically about the ward in question at your meeting.

D. Ask the ward sister if she could have a meeting with you to discuss the bleep policy of the ward.

E. Inform your registrar of the situation.

F. Ask a consultant to arrange a ward meeting.

G. Ask one of the nurses you get on with the most to place a note at the nurses' station to remind them that the bleep is for urgent matters only.

H. Discuss the situation with one of the nurses you get on with the most on that ward and seek her perspective on the matter.

Scenario 221

Your consultant is doing a ward round and you are the only other doctor present. The ward nurse is also in attendance. Your ST5 is away on a course and is due back tomorrow.

A 63-year-old woman has confirmed lung cancer and the consultant breaks the news at the bedside. You are shocked at the manner in which he broke the bad news. The patient was on her own, with no privacy (the curtains were drawn back), and he was very blunt: "I'm afraid that it is lung cancer, Mrs X."

Choose the THREE most appropriate actions to take in this situation.

A. Excuse yourself from the ward round temporarily, bleep the specialist lung cancer nurse and ask her to attend.

B. Ask the ward nurse to leave the ward round.

C. Ask the consultant to stop the ward round.

D. Find a suitable time to discuss with the consultant your discomfort about his communication skills.

E. Inform the ST5 of the incident when he gets back the next day.

F. Return to talk to the patient in question at the end of the ward round.

G. Complete a critical incident form.

H. Excuse yourself from the ward round and stay with the patient straight after the consultant has finished talking to her about the diagnosis.

Scenario 222

Your mobile phone was stolen from the doctor's office yesterday.

You have now managed to review the CCTV images at the hospital and can clearly see that the culprit is a relative of Mr Jones, one of the patients on your ward who is due to be discharged from your ward later on today.

The images clearly show the relative going into your office and taking the phone. They also show him looking briefly at some patient notes that had been left in the office.

Choose the THREE most appropriate actions to take in this situation.

A. Call the patient after he has been discharged and ask him to ask his relative to send your phone back.

B. Write to the patient after he has been discharged, asking him to ask his relative to send your phone back.

C. Contact the police immediately and ask them to speak to the patient away from the ward before he is discharged.

D. Contact the police and give them Mr Jones's contact details so that they can deal with it once he has been discharged.

E. Ask your consultant and service manager to ban Mr Jones from the hospital.

F. Document the theft in the patient's notes.

G. Talk to the patients whose notes were seen by the relative.

H. Raise the matter at the next team meeting and complete a critical incident form.

Scenario 223

You are working on a busy ward and are doing as much as you can to do everything asked of you. However, you have found that, on occasions, some of the nurses made your life harder by not communicating effectively.

Despite this, the ward sister pulls you to one side and tells you that several nurses feel that you are inefficient and don't work fast enough.

Choose the THREE most appropriate actions to take in this situation.

A. Reassure her that you feel that you are working as much and as fast you can.

B. Ask the sister to provide examples of situations where you have underperformed.

C. Ask the sister which of the other nurses have been saying that you were underperforming.

D. Explain to the ward sister that, though you are sure that there are situations where things could have been done better, it is also true that this has not been made easier by some of the nurses' behaviour.

E. Ask the sister to address the issue with your consultant directly.

F. Talk to your consultant about the confrontation.

G. Discuss the sister's comments with some of the nurses whom you feel are causing problems to understand their point of view on the situation.

H. Ask the sister to organise a meeting with you, the consultant and the nurses concerned.

Scenario 224

You are called by the ward pharmacist.

You have prescribed penicillin as a take home medication for a patient and the pharmacist is telling you that the patient is allergic to it.

Choose the THREE most appropriate actions to take in this situation.

A. Ask the pharmacist to change the script to erythromycin.

B. Explain the mistake to the patient and apologise.

C. Write the incident up in your reflective journal as a learning point.

D. Immediately attend the ward, double check for allergies and rewrite the take home prescription with an alternative antibiotic.

E. Inform the consultant of your mistake.

F. Inform your registrar of the mistake.

G. Complete a critical incident form.

H. Document your mistake in the patient's notes.

Scenario 225

Following a team evening out, you are now dating a fellow FY1 in the same service. He/she occasionally shows you affection at work and often comes to help you out if you're busy and he/she has completed his/her work.

Choose the THREE most appropriate actions to take in this situation.

A. Tell him/her that he/she must keep his/her distance at work as it is unprofessional.

B. Accept his/her help graciously.

C. End the relationship.

D. Sit and have a talk with him/her to come to a mutual decision on how much time you will spend together at work.

E. Try to find time to help him/her out too to ensure you are working as a team.

F. Sit and have a talk with him/her and tell him/her to keep his/her distance at work.

G. Ask to be transferred to a different team.

H. Tell the consultant about the relationship.

Scenario 226

You feel that you are being pressured by your ST6 to perform tasks beyond your expertise.

On one occasion, you raised your concern to the ST6 in question. He told you that, in medicine, it is "see one, do one, teach one" and that you should "pull yourself together and stop complaining".

Choose the THREE most appropriate actions to take in this situation.

A. Comply with his requests until you can find a solution to the problem.

B. Find a quiet time to raise the issue with the ST6 again and explain in clear terms that you need more supervision.

C. Escalate the matter to the consultant.

D. Share your concerns with the ST3 and ask for his guidance

E. Take the matter to medical personnel and discuss with them the possibility of starting the bullying procedure.

F. Complete a critical incident form.

G. Warn the ST6 that his approach is compromising patient care and that you will have to address the matter with your consultant if that carries on.

H. Discuss the matter with your medical defence organisation.

Scenario 227

You suffer from migraines from time to time.

You are just starting to get a headache. You know that if you do not take some analgesia within the next 15 minutes your headache will get out of control, forcing you to take the rest of the day off work to recover.

You have no analgesia of your own and your repeat prescription for sumatriptan ran out last week.

Choose the THREE most appropriate actions to take in this situation.

A. Take some analgesia from the drug trolley.

B. Ask someone to hold your bleep and go to the local pharmacy to buy some simple fast-acting analgesia.

C. Ask one of the other doctors to go to the pharmacy to buy some simple fast-acting analgesia.

D. Fax your GP to arrange a repeat prescription of sumatriptan.

E. Ask someone to hold your bleep so that you can take a break whilst your migraine settles.

F. Go to A&E and book in as a patient.

G. Tell one of your seniors that you need to take the rest of the day off sick and go home.

H. Write a private prescription of sumatriptan for yourself.

Scenario 228

You are looking after a patient who has a fractured femur. She tells you she is being physically abused by her partner and that it was he who broke her leg.

She tells you in confidence and insists that you must tell no one else.

Choose the THREE most appropriate actions to take in this situation.

A. Agree to keep her secret and tell no one.

B. Call the police and report the assault.

C. Inform your consultant immediately.

D. Reassure the patient that neither the police nor her partner will be able to access her notes unless she agrees to it. Insist that you have no option but to document the fact that she said that her partner was responsible for the abuse.

E. Talk to the patient. Explain that she is at risk, that you have a duty to look after her welfare and that you must divulge this matter to a more senior member of the team.

F. Document the conversation that you had with the patient but leave out of your notes the fact that she said that her partner was responsible for the abuse.

G. Do not document the conversation.

H. Tell the patient that you will need to discuss the issue with her GP.

Scenario 229

One of your patients has taken a romantic interest in you. The patient constantly asks you about what you do when you are off duty and has offered you their telephone number so that you can become friends with them. You actually happen to like the patient too.

Choose the THREE most appropriate actions to take in this situation.

A. Refuse the patient's number.

B. Take the patient's number.

C. Report the patient's behaviour to your consultant.

D. Tell the patient that you would be interested in meeting up but only when they have been discharged.

E. Tell the patient that their behaviour is unethical.

F. Tell the patient that it is nice of them to think of you as a friend, but that, although you do find them very friendly and would consider being their friend in a different context, as a doctor it would be inappropriate.

G. Tell the patient firmly but in a friendly manner that befriending them is against your code of practice.

H. Document in the patient's notes that they may have mental health issues.

Scenario 230

You are off duty and see a man collapse in a supermarket.

You went shopping for last minute food shopping. You have guests coming for lunch in 30 minutes' time and nothing is ready yet.

Choose the THREE most appropriate actions to take in this situation.

A. Call 999 from your mobile phone.

B. Carry on shopping. You are off duty.

C. Assess the situation checking for danger and then approach with care.

D. Ask one of the members of staff to go and get the store manager so that he can call 999.

E. Assess the man for a response and then proceed to check his airway if there is none.

F. Take the man to A&E.

G. Ask the staff to clear all other customers from the area where the man collapsed.

H. Leave the supermarket without declaring that you are a doctor so as not to be obliged to intervene.

Scenario 231

You have just started as an FY1 on a Renal ward. During a weekend shift, your registrar asks you to consent a patient for a catheter insertion. The patient is hyperkalemic and requires emergency dialysis.

As the registrar starts talking to the patient, you see very quickly that the patient can't understand a single word of English and you ask a nurse who speaks his language to translate. However, the nurse seems sloppy, does not seem to care much about what the patient says, tells you that she doesn't know how to translate all the terms and ends up saying them in English.

The registrar, however, seems eager to go ahead and says as the patient nods "That'll do for consent".

Choose the THREE most appropriate actions to take in this situation.

A. Tell the registrar that you are not happy to assist until all options to obtain proper consent have been tried.

B. Call the consultant on call immediately.

C. Assist the registrar with the catheterisation on the basis that it is an emergency.

D. Call the Trust's official translators and consent the patient yourself.

E. Tell the registrar that the patient has not been consented properly.

F. Advise the registrar to contact the Trust's official translators.

G. Complete a critical incident form.

H. Ask the nurse to go and find someone else who speaks the same language but with a better grasp of technical terms.

Scenario 232

You are bleeped to attend a crash call for Mr Smith who has arrested. On reading the notes, you do not find any Do Not Resuscitate (DNR) order and proceed with the resuscitation attempt. Unfortunately this attempt is unsuccessful and Mr Smith is pronounced dead.

A little while later, while reading another patient's notes, you notice a DNR order for Mr Smith, which had evidently been misfiled. The relatives have witnessed the arrest. They are upset and are still with the patient.

Choose the THREE most appropriate actions to take in this situation.

A. Contact your consultant and complete a critical incident form.

B. Contact your consultant. Complete a critical incident form only when/if such misfiling happens again.

C. Let the resuscitation team know about the recently discovered DNR form.

D. Do nothing, since the patient has died.

E. Talk to the relatives in a separate room.

F. Wait until your consultant comes back to talk to the relatives.

G. Inform senior managers at Trust level.

H. Throw the newly discovered DNR order in the bin.

Scenario 233

During a bedside teaching session, your consultant asks you a range of questions, some of which you struggle to answer.

Towards the end of the session, you are left with the feeling that the consultant has been rude and has embarrassed you in front of the patient.

Choose the THREE most appropriate actions to take in this situation.

A. Contact the Human Resources department to complain about the incident.

B. Complain about the incident to a senior nurse.

C. Take some time out to think about the incident and how you might want to react to it.

D. Next time, tell the consultant at the bedside that he is being harsh on you.

E. Once the session is over, apologise to the patient about the consultant's behaviour.

F. Arrange a meeting with the consultant to discuss the incident.

G. Complete a critical incident form.

H. Discuss the incident with your educational supervisor.

Scenario 234

A patient has been found to have a potentially malignant tumour, for which surgical removal has been agreed by the multidisciplinary team to be the best option.

Your registrar has asked you to check on the patient before he seeks the patient's consent for this procedure. The patient tells you she knows that the registrar is coming soon and that she would rather not know anything about the procedure. She tells you that you can just go ahead with the procedure – there is no need to explain.

Assume the patient is competent.

Choose the THREE most appropriate actions to take in this situation.

A. Explain to the patient that, since the surgeon thinks the operation is in her best interest, the consent is only a formality and the current verbal consent she has given you will be sufficient.

B. Ask the patient why she does not wish to hear the details and whether it would be okay to involve some of her relatives in the discussion.

C. Document your conversation with the patient.

D. Explain that consent is only valid if the patient has been given the information and therefore the procedure can't take place unless the registrar or someone else who knows about the procedure explains it.

E. Explain to the patient that since she is consenting to the procedure, it will go ahead.

F. Document that the patient has given verbal consent to the procedure.

G. Give some details of the procedure to the patient to show her that there is nothing to be worried about.

H. Tell the patient that, if she could pretend not to have mental capacity, the surgeon could operate without requiring her consent.

Scenario 235

You are on the ward and it is the start of visiting hours. Mrs Peacock, one of the inpatients, has been taken to the radiology department for a scan. Her husband has arrived to visit her but is surprised that she is not in her bed.

He catches up with you in the corridor. He grabs your arm firmly, takes you aside and tells you that the receptionist is a total waste of time who can't be bothered to answer questions directly and that people like her should really be taught a lesson. He seems very angry. It is not the first time that patients or relatives have expressed their frustration about this particular secretary.

Your department has a zero tolerance policy.

Choose the THREE most appropriate actions to take in this situation.

A. Tell him that you have a zero tolerance policy and escort him out.

B. Tell the husband that you will have no choice but to call security if he doesn't calm down.

C. Tell him that you are aware that other patients and relatives have complained about this particular secretary and assure him that the issues will be dealt with.

D. Explain to him that his wife is currently in the radiology department for a scan and that she will be back soon.

E. Explain to him that his wife won't be long and ask him politely to leave the ward and wait near the coffee machine until she returns.

F. Tell him that you have registered his comments about the secretary but that it doesn't justify this type of abuse.

G. Ask another secretary to give him a cup of tea.

H. Tell the secretary that there have been quite a few complaints against her and that she should consider doing something about it.

Scenario 236

You work with only one other junior colleague on the ward. It is 3pm and all ward jobs have been completed.

The shift normally ends at 5pm but your colleague says that he is going out for a birthday meal and would like to leave straight away so that he has time to go home, get ready and drive to the restaurant.

Choose the THREE most appropriate actions to take in this situation.

A. Make sure that he has agreed it with the ST3 before he leaves.

B. Let him slip away without a word so that no fuss is made.

C. Take his bleep from him.

D. Insist that he stays.

E. Tell him to clear it with Medical Staffing.

F. Make him double-check that there is nothing left to be done before he leaves.

G. Ask him to redirect his bleep to the doctor on call for the evening.

H. Explain to your colleague that, in the event of an emergency, the lower level of cover is likely to affect patient care.

Scenario 237

You walk into the doctors' mess and see one of your ST3s is watching standard adult pornography on a hospital computer.

Choose the THREE most appropriate actions to take in this situation.

A. Notify medical personnel, as this is clearly an abuse of NHS property.

B. Tell your colleague that it is not really appropriate to watch these kinds of images on hospital property and that he should be careful as some people may find it offensive.

C. Discuss the situation with other junior colleagues and confront him as a group so as to have maximum impact and make him stop.

D. Have a word with your consultant if this occurs too often.

E. Have a word with your consultant if the ST3's performance is affected by his activities.

F. Contact the IT department so that they can monitor the computer's activities.

G. Notify the police.

H. Try to keep your colleague away from the mess, for example by bleeping him for advice whenever he's going for a break.

Scenario 238

Your FY2 colleague looks permanently tired. You know that he has been working very hard over the past few months.

He seems to be burning himself out and makes simple mistakes every day, though none has actually had any adverse effect on patients so far.

Choose the THREE most appropriate actions to take in this situation.

A. Approach the FY2 and express your concerns about his health and the simple mistakes that he has been making.

B. Inform the FY2 that all mistakes, even small, are a danger to patients and that you will have no choice but to talk to the consultant if the situation does not improve.

C. Discuss with him the possibility of your taking on some of his work.

D. Encourage him to raise the issue with his consultant to find a workable solution to the situation.

E. Contact Medical Staffing to see if they can get a locum to relieve the pressure on the FY2.

F. Inform Occupational Health and encourage them to contact the FY2 before it is too late.

G. Complete a critical incident form the next time a mistake occurs.

H. Complete a critical incident form the next time he makes a mistake that causes patient harm.

Scenario 239

In the past few minutes, you have flushed an intravenous cannula with lidocaine instead of saline. There appears to be some problem with the labelling of the drug.

The patient does not seem to be experiencing any adverse reaction.

Choose the THREE most appropriate actions to take in this situation.

A. Tell the patient that you have made a mistake, apologise and offer him the means to make a complaint if he so wishes.

B. Bleep your registrar for information and further advice.

C. Wait 5 more minutes and if the patient appears to be fine then do not take any further action.

D. Write down the mistake in the notes but do not notify the patient, as there was no adverse reaction.

E. Tell the patient that you have injected a bit of local anaesthetic (which is a procedure that is sometimes carried out) so as to be open but not to worry him.

F. Explain to the patient that you have made a mistake caused by wrong labelling, which is the nurse's responsibility. Give the patient the means to make a complaint against the nurse if he so wishes.

G. Complete a critical incident form.

H. Tell the patient what happened but only if he asks.

Scenario 240

You have noticed that one of the consultants on your team is often making remarks of a sexual nature to one of the secretaries. On the surface she does not seem to be affected by this.

Choose the THREE most appropriate actions to take in this situation.

A. Encourage the secretary to check the staff manual to determine what action she should take.

B. Let the secretary know that you have observed the consultant harass her and that she should raise the issue with her seniors.

C. Arrange a discussion with the consultant in question to let him know that such behaviour must stop.

D. Approach a senior colleague whom you can trust to discuss the matter.

E. Contact the GMC, who will handle the situation from then on.

F. Inform the Human Resources or Medical Staffing department.

G. Wait until the next incident to mention something to the consultant in the presence of the secretary about how inappropriate his remark was.

H. Talk to another secretary about the problem, asking her to provide support to her colleague.

Scenario 241

Another FY1 on your team confides that he has contracted Hepatitis C and needs your advice. He would appreciate that you keep the matter confidential.

Choose the THREE most appropriate actions to take in this situation.

A. Inform the Medical Staffing department.

B. Refer your colleague to Occupational Health to be vaccinated.

C. Discuss the matter with a senior colleague.

D. Discuss the matter with a senior colleague if you see that your colleague performs risky procedures.

E. Ask a senior sister to alert you if he is doing any exposure-prone procedure.

F. Recommend to your colleague that he should get advice from his defence union.

G. Recommend to your colleague that he should discuss the matter with his seniors.

H. Inform Occupational Health.

Scenario 242

You are a new FY1 doctor in a busy service. You are having a 5-minute break to escape the hectic pace of the ward. One of the nurses who has been working on your ward for over 10 years is not well liked by doctors and other nurses because she is difficult to work with. She is otherwise good at her job; there are no concerns about her clinical abilities.

She comes to you for a chat, and complains that most doctors in the department tend to ignore her. The other day, one doctor was busy talking to another nurse, and he made her wait at least 3 minutes before he acknowledged her. Some doctors can make her wait up to 20 minutes to sign a prescription when "it only takes 5 seconds to just sign a piece of paper".

Choose the THREE most appropriate actions to take in this situation.

A. Tell the nurse that she should really approach the ward sister as this is something that she needs to discuss with her rather than with you.

B. Wait for an appropriate time when you can grab your consultant and the head nurse at the same time and mention the conversation you had with the nurse.

C. Later on, email all doctors in your team, asking them to be more attentive.

D. Listen to the nurse for 5 minutes, apologise for the brief nature of the chat and ask if you could meet with her after work to discuss her issues.

E. Ask one of your colleagues to cover for you for a small amount of time so that you can talk to the nurse straight away.

F. Tell the nurse in the most empathetic manner that this is really not something that you can do much about.

G. Ask the nurse to complete incident forms if patient care is delayed because doctors are not responsive.

H. Tell the nurse that she can't criticise others without also looking at her own behaviour.

Scenario 243

You are an FY1 doing a taster week in a GP practice. You have your own patient list. A 15-year-old boy comes in with his mother.

The mother tells you that she would like the boy to have an HIV test because she thinks he is gay. The boy denies it and there is nothing in the son's notes which suggests he is sexually active.

Choose the THREE most appropriate actions to take in this situation.

A. Take a sexual history from the boy.

B. Give the mother some leaflets about HIV transmission and tell her she can contact you further if she needs any more information.

C. Tell the mother that her son is unlikely to have HIV at such a young age.

D. Obtain the boy's consent to perform an HIV test.

E. Tell the mother that she is probably over-reacting.

F. Ask the mother to leave the room so that you can talk to the son alone.

G. Explain to the mother that nothing in the notes suggests he is sexually active; reassure her that therefore he is unlikely to be HIV positive but that if he consented you could go ahead with the test.

H. Tell the mother that "there is nothing wrong with being gay" and that her son will need her approval if he is to lead a happy life.

Scenario 244

You are an FY1 in Endocrinology & Diabetes in a small District General Hospital (DGH). There are normally two consultants, one registrar and a nurse practitioner (who has not yet achieved her prescription status) running clinic lists.

The registrar is on holiday; he has pre-signed a full prescription pad for the nurse practitioner to use. Both consultants have gone to a meeting and will be back in 30 minutes' time. There is no prescription script left on the pad and the nurse has just asked you nicely if you wouldn't mind signing another pad for her.

Choose the THREE most appropriate actions to take in this situation.

A. Pre-sign a whole prescription pad for her.

B. Pre-sign enough prescription scripts to last her 30 minutes and ask her to get one of the consultants to sign the rest.

C. Refuse to sign the prescription pad.

D. Report the matter to one of the two consultants.

E. Address the matter with the registrar when he comes back.

F. Ask the nurse to provide you with a list of patients to whom she gave pre-scriptions.

G. Ask a secretary to recall each patient for follow-up.

H. Praise the nurse for coping so well in the absence of the registrar and re-assure her she can count on you for support if she needs it.

Scenario 245

A nurse gives a patient an intravenous drug as a bolus injection. Looking at the discarded drug vial, you realise that the medicine has expired. Despite that, the patient has come to no harm.

Choose the THREE most appropriate actions to take in this situation.

A. Explain to the patient that a mistake has been made and apologise to him.

B. Report the mistake to the ward sister without naming the nurse involved.

C. Explain to the nurse that her mistake could have caused serious harm. Ask her to complete a critical incident form.

D. Report the incident to the ward sister and name the nurse involved.

E. Go through the drugs cupboard with the nurse and ensure that no other expired drugs are present on the ward.

F. Complete a critical incident form yourself.

G. Send an email to the other doctors in the team to explain what happened.

H. Tell the nurse that there is no need for a critical incident form as no harm was caused, but that she will need to be more careful in future.

Scenario 246

A patient has revealed to you that she has a history of taking illegal substances.

She begs you to delete any mention of drug-taking from the notes as it could compromise her medical insurance if the information ever came to light.

Choose the THREE most appropriate actions to take in this situation.

A. Reassure the patient that you are bound by a duty of confidentiality and you simply cannot divulge any information about them to a third party without her consent, except in very specific circumstances.

B. Tell the patient that you cannot guarantee her confidentiality but that you will inform her first if you need to breach it.

C. Tell the patient that you simply cannot delete any information from the notes.

D. Delete the information from the notes.

E. Delete the information from the notes if it has no relevance to the patient's current health problems.

F. Tell the patient that you will have to reveal the information if asked by the insurance company.

G. Contact the insurance company, name the patient, inform them of the issue and ask them if drug-taking information is important for the patient's policy.

H. Tell the patient that you would only consider removing the information if she could prove she is no longer taking drugs.

Scenario 247

During a discussion with a fellow FY1 in the mess, you notice that a bag of marijuana has fallen out of his bag.

Choose the THREE most appropriate actions to take in this situation:

A. Inform the GMC as it is not appropriate for any doctor to take drugs since it can endanger patients.

B. Call the police as marijuana is an illegal substance.

C. Recommend that your colleague considers professional help.

D. Have a discussion with your colleague about the incident to understand what the situation is.

E. Seek his reassurance that he is not using the drug, and tell him that you will keep quiet about the incident if he flushes the drug down the toilet.

F. Discuss the incident with your consultant.

G. Complete a critical incident form.

H. Report the incident to the Clinical Director.

Scenario 248

This morning, one of your consultants arrives at work obviously drunk.

You have advised him to go home but he has dismissed you and is about to start his regular clinic.

Choose the THREE most appropriate actions to take in this situation.

A. Call the GMC.

B. Discuss cancelling the clinic session with the outpatients' administrator or clinic manager.

C. See another consultant to discuss the situation.

D. Let the consultant run the clinic and ask him to contact another consultant if at any point he feels unable to continue running the clinic so that some-one else can take over.

E. Report the matter to your registrar (ST3).

F. Sit in the clinic with the consultant to ensure that patients are safe.

G. Tell the consultant that he needs to go home and offer to pay for a taxi.

H. Warn the patients that they should not agree to be seen by the consultant as he is unwell.

Scenario 249

You are working on a busy ward, having to deal with many admissions every morning.

You share the workload with another FY1 who has been consistently late by 20 minutes every day for the past week.

Choose the THREE most appropriate actions to take in this situation.

A. Call your colleague's husband to see whether your colleague has personal problems that may explain her delay.

B. Arrange a discussion with your colleague, express your discontent and tell her to make sure that she comes in on time as her delay is slowing you down.

C. Arrange a discussion with your colleague to enquire about the reasons behind the delay.

D. Work harder to compensate for her absence, in the knowledge that her delay is likely to be short term.

E. Discuss your concerns with a group of nurses from your ward to gain insight into your colleague's behaviour at work.

F. Mention the delays to your ST3 and ask him whether he can deal with it.

G. In order to avoid confrontation with the colleague, do nothing for the time being, knowing senior colleagues will soon notice her behaviour.

H. Complete a critical incident form.

Scenario 250

During a very busy shift, a nurse informs you that the relatives of a recently deceased patient want to see you to discuss "things".

Choose the THREE most appropriate actions to take in this situation.

A. Ask the nurse to talk to the relatives to get an understanding of the type of "things" that they want to discuss so that you can be fully prepared when you see them.

B. Tell the nurse to let the relatives know that you are aware they are waiting, and that you are detained right now; but that if they go home you will call them as soon as you are free.

C. Ask one of your colleagues to let the relatives know that you cannot see them because you are busy; ask him to deal with any queries.

D. Tell the nurse that you can only grant the relatives a maximum of 5 minutes as you are busy.

E. Inform your registrar (ST3) of the relatives' request and ask her whether she can cover for you whilst you go and talk to the relatives.

F. Tell the nurse to send the relatives to PALS, as your involvement with the patient is over.

G. Tell the nurse to find an excuse to send the relatives home; as the patient is dead, the matter is less important than those patients with whom you are currently dealing.

H. Tell the nurse to inform the relatives that they should contact the consultant as he would be a more appropriate person for them to talk to.

6 Answers

Scenario 1 ANSWER: CEDBA

1. In this scenario, there are several strands to consider:

   - It is inappropriate to make comments in front of patients (this applies to both the nurse and you). Something needs to be done about it but it needs to be handled sensitively.

   - The conversation has now moved on; so what was said is now in the past, meaning there is no longer a need for an immediate intervention. However, this may not be an isolated incident and a solution that helps resolve the problem systemically is preferable to one that just addresses the incident itself.

2. Option A (interrupting the nurse and telling her that she is being inappropriate) and Option B (telling the patient that the nurse is lying) are both inappropriate options. The conversation has already moved on, so intervening straight away will have little value. Both options should therefore rank last. Telling the nurse off in front of the patient is the worst option because it will embarrass the nurse and will lead to a confrontation which will seriously undermine the patient's trust in the team. So Option A is less appropriate than Option B and therefore ranks last.

3. Out of the remaining options, Option E (contacting the ward sister) would ensure that something is done about the situation at a systemic level. However, you should first give the nurse a chance to explain her comments (Option C). You could use the opportunity to remind her of the inappropriateness of her comments. Talking to your consultant (Option D) would only help you get some advice on how to address the matter but would not actually resolve much.

Scenario 2 — ANSWER: CDBAE

1. The key issues to consider are as follows:

   - The blood needs to be retaken before the next morning's surgery but, although it is important, it is not an emergency.

   - You must ensure it happens on time. As such, any options which consist solely of passing on a message without a clear idea of the deadline, or which run the risk of the deadline being missed, should be ranked down.

2. Documenting (Option E) is important, as it will ensure that there is a clear trail. However, the option does not involve retaking the sample, and as such it does not actually resolve the problem. Since all the other options ensure that the blood is taken again, Option E will rank last. Option A (getting the phlebotomist to retake the blood the next morning) will come too late. It therefore ranks fourth.

3. Option B (handing the form to the ward sister) is not ideal because you have not given her a deadline. However, there is a better chance that it will get done on time than if you simply get the phlebotomist to do the test the following morning (Option A). Therefore Option B ranks over Option A.

4. Option D (taking the blood yourself immediately) and Option C (ensuring it gets done at some time today) both ensure that the blood is taken again on time. Both options will ensure that the mistake is corrected; however, since the situation is not an emergency (the sample needs to be taken before surgery, i.e. before the next day, but that doesn't mean that you have to drop everything else for it), there is scope to conclude that Option C is more realistic and therefore more appropriate than Option D.

Scenario 3 — ANSWER: ACDBE

This scenario tests your honesty, your reliability, your impact on others and your ability to communicate. As a doctor, you have a responsibility to get to work (it is in your patients' interests to ensure that there is appropriate cover). If you can't get to work, then you need to ensure that patient care is not compromised. Overriding all that is your own safety.

1. Calling in sick (Option E) is dishonest. It is the least appropriate option.

2. Driving to work if you are not confident in snowy conditions (Option B) could put your life and others at risk. This should be avoided as much as possible. That option ranks fourth on the basis that it is potentially unsafe, though if you decide to drive you will probably be more inclined to be extra careful in view of the poor road conditions. Driving slowly will also limit the risk. Option B is better than Option E because the risk is limited by the slow speed and it is more honest.

3. The remaining three options all involve communicating with the registrar honestly on different grounds:
    *   Option A = Try public transport
    *   Option C = Wait and see
    *   Option D = Not coming in.

    Option D essentially means you have given up and therefore you are not demonstrating that you are trying your best to fulfil your responsibilities. Option C at least shows that you are willing to give it a go; and, in Option A, you are actually trying to find an alternative to your troubles. The ranking of those three options should therefore be ACD.

Scenario 4   ANSWER: ADBEC

1. Looking at the list of options, two of them (A and D) involve you covering the shift. This is what will be expected of you: firstly because your contract mentions you are expected to provide emergency cover and secondly because you are expected to work with the team to ensure that patient care is provided adequately. Therefore those two options will rank at the top.

    Option A (offering to cover "on this occasion") is a fair approach since the situation has arisen as a result of a failure by the department to organise cover and you want to make sure it doesn't become a habit. It also goes one step further by ensuring that you deal with the problem in the long term. Therefore Option A ranks higher than Option D.

2. Options B and C both involve you not running the shift. Option B (asking a colleague to cover) is the more helpful option because you are trying to find a solution to the problem. Option C (say no and leave at 5pm) is the least helpful as you are just essentially walking out. Refusing to help with

no reason given is not good teamwork. It is not your fault that the locum was not booked, but it is everyone's responsibility to provide cover to ensure that patients are safe and well looked after. So Options B and C will come next in that order.

Important note
The exam requires you to rank according to what you SHOULD do and not what you WOULD do. In this case, in practice, some candidates may well first ask another colleague to cover the on call, especially if they have already made plans for the evening, but the "theoretical" answer sought by the examiners will most likely involve you getting out of your way to cover the on call before you start dumping the problem onto someone else.

3. So far we have established the order ADBC. We simply need to determine where option E fits amongst those four options. Option E simply mentions that you will complain to medical personnel about their lack of planning. That would be a legitimate complaint to make but it is not very constructive. It is, however, slightly better than just walking out as it keeps the dialogue open and may help sort some issues out. As such it will rank higher than Option C (walking out), but lower than Option B (asking a colleague to cover).

Scenario 5   ANSWER: CBEAD

1. Patients fall under the responsibility of the consultant; therefore, if there is a risk to patient safety (which would be the case if there is no senior cover), the on-call consultant should be called (Option C). Once you have informed him of the situation, he can make a decision on how the situation should be handled and may come into hospital to cover the take team (at least until the workload is more manageable for everyone concerned).

2. Staying behind to continue to clerk in patients (Option B) is a noble sacrifice, but you need to be aware that you are tired as well after having done a whole day's clerking. However, given the potential patient harm that could occur if you do go home with such a depleted night team, this will be an appropriate thing to do.

3. Out of the remaining options:

    *   Completing a critical incident form (Option E) won't do much for the current situation as it unfolds but will at least ensure that the problem is recorded and investigated.

    *   Asking the NNPs to clerk in medical patients (Option A) would not be appropriate as they will not have received suitable training; as such Option A is equivalent to leaving the depleted team on its own, i.e. do nothing.

    *   Asking a potentially infectious doctor to come in to work (Option D) is completely inappropriate as he may do more harm to patients than good.

Scenario 6   ANSWER: ABECD

1. The nurse said that she is concerned about the patient deteriorating. Therefore you will need to give preference to the options that indicate immediate action. That means that Option C and Option D will be ranking lower than the other options.

    *   Option D (moving on to the next patient) leaves the situation in a state of limbo. You are leaving the situation with no real closure.

    *   Though equally unhelpful, Option C at least has the benefit of offering some kind of solution by inviting the nurse to seek help elsewhere. So Option C will rank higher than option D.

2. Option A contains all the right elements, i.e. you are dealing with the matter straight away, you are demonstrating an awareness of your limitations by stating that you will contact the registrar if you encounter any problems and you are communicating with the nurse in an appropriate manner. Option A will therefore rank towards the top.

3. Option B is playing the "I'm a doctor" card and sounds quite brutal. However it does place an emphasis on dealing with the situation straight away and on safety. The main issue here is poor communication. Option B will therefore rank lower than Option A.

4. Option E essentially entails taking the nurse's comments to the registrar. There are several issues with this option:

    - You are leaving the patient unattended and so patient care will be delayed for a short while (this is still better than Options C and D where we are not sure what the plan is).

    - The registrar is busy dealing with a sick patient. He may well be able to assist you by providing advice, but he will most likely only be able to do so if he has a better appreciation of the clinical situation. In fact, he will expect you to come for advice only once you have gathered all the information he needs to make decisions. For example, he will need to know why the nurse is so concerned, why she felt you couldn't deal with it, what the basic observations are, what prompted the call for review, etc. So, before you talk to him, you would at least need to review the patient quickly or get some information from the nurse. Failing that, he will only be able to advise you on how to handle the relationship with the nurse. As such, Option E is likely to result in your being sent back to the ward for more information.

    - The option does not mention any communication with the nurse; therefore Option E ranks below Option B on grounds of both safety and poor communication with both the nurse and the registrar.

Scenario 7   ANSWER: BCEDA

1. This scenario is testing your professionalism, patient focus and ability to work as a team. The patient has made a rather bold statement and you need to make sure that you handle the situation effectively but sensitively. Even though the patient is not your patient, you are covering the ward and you therefore have a duty of care. Looking at the options on offer, there are a number of decisions we can make straight away:

    - Options B and C are of a similar nature, with one trying to ascertain signs of depression and the other one her capacity. It is essential to assess her capacity (if you feel able to) but if there is an element of depression (which is very common in the elderly) then she will need to be treated for it before you can be sure she has full capacity. Therefore Option B will rank above Option C.

- Option A does not actually involve doing much, other than letting the patient sort out the problem herself. She may have approached you because she felt she could confide in you or because she finds some of your colleagues intimidating. Although she is not your patient, you have a duty of care and you must honour that trust by ensuring that her remarks are acted upon. All options involve doing something about it, except Option A. Therefore Option A will rank last.

2. Option E: leaving the patient after you have finished the cannulation is not ideal (it would be better to engage with her), but by going straight to the nurse looking after her, you are at least ensuring that someone is aware of the problem and can deal with it effectively. Before you alert other colleagues, it would be better to have a discussion with the patient. As such Option E will rank lower than both Options B and C.

3. Option D: by asking if she wants to say goodbye to anyone, you are assuming she is dying or is about to die; this is not what the question says. In cases like these, it is advisable to contact family members, particularly if there is an element of loneliness (making sure, of course, that you maintain confidentiality and do not divulge the diagnosis). With this option, you are engaging with the patient and getting the family involved, but you are not really addressing the core of the matter. As such, Option D ranks lower than Options B, C and E but higher than Option A.

Scenario 8   ANSWER: CDEBA

1. You should not breach a patient's confidentiality except in certain exceptional circumstances. Therefore both Options A and B would be the least suitable. Out of those two options, Option B is the nicer one because you are at least making sure that the discussion is taking place in a suitable setting (as opposed to simply explaining the diagnosis).

2. The other three options all entail respecting the patient's confidentiality in different ways:

- Option C explains to the son what the position is in respect of confidentiality.

- Option D achieves the same thing but in a less helpful way as it does not actually explain to the son why you do not wish to reveal the diagnosis to him. He may perceive this as being obstructive or even rude. In addition, by revealing that the patient is aware of the diagnosis, you are potentially placing her in a difficult position as she may have opted not to share the diagnosis with this particular family member.

- Option E is a lie. As such, it is worse than Option D which is truthful, though slightly dismissive. The lie is better than a breach of confidentiality because it has no significant consequences on the relative or the patient. The lie is also directed towards the relative rather than the patient.

Scenario 9   ANSWER: CBAED

1. Option A (forgetting about the application form) seems a sensible approach but then you will lose out (admittedly by your own fault). There are better options that you can try first.

2. Option B (calling your ST3 in the morning to see if you can take time off) seems sensible too, as you are involving your senior and are asking for a favour from your team whilst playing by the rules. You are taking a gamble because he might refuse, but, if he does, then you are no worse off than under Option A. Besides, you will at least have tried to find a solution by using the appropriate channels. This shows good insight and also a good approach to teamwork. Therefore Option B ranks over Option A.

3. You have nothing to lose by asking for an extension to the deadline (Option C). This should therefore be the most effective option as it would save you having to disrupt the team. Thus Option C ranks first.

4. Both Option D and Option E are dishonest. Plagiarism is an offence taken seriously by the GMC, and if you were found out you would be reported. It is therefore more serious than lying by saying that you are sick (which may lead to being reprimanded by your seniors but nothing more in the short term). Therefore Option E ranks above Option D.

Scenario 10 ANSWER: CEDAB

In some cases you will find it easier to determine the level of appropriateness in reverse order (i.e. least appropriate first):

1. Option B (calling the police) has to be the least appropriate. We are only talking about a small amount of cash here. The culprit could be anyone ranging from a patient or a visitor, to a nurse, a doctor, a porter, etc. The police will not be able to do anything about it and you will have achieved nothing by calling them. If the thefts were of controlled drugs, or if the thefts were a regular occurrence, then there would be a stronger case for doing so. However, there would need to be a discussion with the Clinical Director and head nurse first (i.e. someone in charge would call the police, not you. Otherwise you will alienate the whole team).

2. Option A (asking the culprit in your team to replace the money) looks good at first glance but it makes the assumption that the culprit is a member of the team. This will create conflict. Do you sincerely think that the culprit will replace the money? Therefore Option A can be placed as the fourth least effective option on the basis that it risks alienating the team without achieving much.

3. Options C, D and E all talk about reassuring patients or warning them to be more careful. Those options are therefore stronger candidates for appropriateness as they are more in line with common sense. Two of the options involve reassuring the victim himself (Options C and E). Option D only talks about sending an email to your colleagues to warn patients. This may well be appropriate but your first concern should be with the victim and not the potential future theft of the other patients (this comes later). Therefore, out of the three options, Option D is the least appropriate.

4. Out of Options C and E, Option C is a softer and more caring approach. Option E is slightly patronising to the patient (he probably already knows he should have been more careful) but still within acceptable limits. In this context, a softer, reassuring approach is required; Option C is therefore better than Option E.

Scenario 11 ANSWER: DCBAE

1. Option E makes no practical sense. If the colleague is sick (and we must take his word for it at this stage), then it would make no sense to expect him to come in an hour later. It is also unsafe because, once the hour is over, it leaves a sick colleague in charge of patient care. This is the least appropriate option.

2. Option A is unsafe. You simply cannot expect to do a double shift and remain safe, at least not in comparison to the other options on offer. It is, however, less unsafe than Option E discussed above because, if you do the double shift and start feeling tired, you always have the option to ask for support from other colleagues later; whereas leaving your sick colleague in charge would be unsafe from the start. This is therefore the second least appropriate option. In addition, anyone absent through sickness is, by definition, officially on sick leave, and cannot be expected to make up for such absence later.

3. Options B, C and D all involve contacting the ST3 on call but at different times:

   - Option B: you stay 2 hours and then involve him
   - Option C: you involve him and leave
   - Option D: you involve him, offer to stay for a while and then leave.

   If an FY1 is ill, the ST3 will need to know at the first opportunity so that he can manage the situation appropriately. In addition, you should not take additional responsibilities without informing a senior colleague. Therefore, involving him early is best. This places Option B in third position.

   Between Options C and D, Option D is best because you show solidarity and willingness to help. The ST3 might accept or refuse your offer to stay but that is down to him. In any case, he is also on call and therefore it will be down to him to cover for the FY1. By involving the ST3 as early as possible you will ensure that the right decision is made for patient care, demonstrating both professionalism and team playing.

Scenario 12 ANSWER: EABCD

1. At first glance, the following observations come to mind:

    - Quoting the EWTD as an excuse to leave (Option B) seems a bit over the top, especially to a consultant. It creates a big drama when there is no need to do so. Why not simply argue patient safety, since the question clearly states that you are sleepy?

    - Patiently waiting and covering (Option C) when you are exhausted could be unsafe. The wait could be long!

    - Handing over to a nurse could be disastrous. This may lead to miscommunication and errors. You are also assuming that she will know what to do with the information.

    - Your colleague may have been delayed for a good reason and there may not be long for you to wait. The sensible thing to do is to find out more about the situation before you can take any action. Option E therefore seems the obvious starting point. Even if you are tired, it won't take long.

2. Both C and D are unsafe: C is unsafe because you are tired and D is unsafe because the information may never get to the doctor or may be miscommunicated. Also, it is unfair on the nurse (and it is against team spirit) to place the responsibility onto her. It is also bad practice simply to disappear without notifying your colleagues (in particular your ST); therefore, Option D is worse than Option C.

3. We have now established that Option E should come first and that Options C and D should come last. This leaves us with A and B to place in second and third positions. It makes no sense to hand over to your consultant if the ST3 is available (nothing in the question states that he is not available and the other options suggest that he is). This places Option A ahead of Option B. The fact that you used the EWTD as an excuse for handing over to your consultant also confirms that Option A ranks above Option B. Quoting regulations may be the right thing to do, but it does not give the impression that you are helping the team to deal with a difficult problem. Regardless of the excuse given, it is the grade that will dictate the answer here: i.e. ST3 first, then consultant.

Scenario 13   ANSWER: EBADC

You are expected to rank the options according to what you SHOULD do and not what you WOULD do. As such, you will be expected to attend the teaching session unless you really have a very strong reason not to do so.

1. There are two options which involve attending the session:
   - Option B: enquiring about whether the session is strictly necessary
   - Option E: cancelling your plans.

   As a doctor you are required to keep up to date and your seniors would expect you to attend the teaching; in this case even more so because your reason for not attending would be purely social and the text states that the teaching is mandatory. So, although enquiring about the relevance/ importance of the session (i.e. Option B) may be the preferred option in practice, Option E is what would be expected of you and therefore ranks above Option B. If you have an issue with the fact that it is all rather last minute then you should take this up with the relevant person afterwards.

2. All other options involve not attending the teaching session. The issue now is to determine in what circumstances you will be leaving your workplace. This is testing your teamwork ability:

   - Option D (the nurse). Why involve her since she is probably not even going to the meeting? This is a teaching session for FY1s and your approach would place the responsibility on her to pass on a message that she could not care less about, on a topic that she knows nothing about.

   - Option A (the fellow FY1). This is better; you are involving a relevant member of the team as well as offering your apologies. Therefore Option A will rank third and Option D will rank fourth.

   - Option C (slipping away). Although you might find that it saves you having to justify there and then why you have to leave, people will be wondering what has happened to you. The uncertainty surrounding your departure, particularly if one team member remembers telling you about the meeting, could develop into resentment towards you and this is bad news. Such behaviour is unprofessional and therefore ranks last.

Scenario 14 ANSWER: DAEBC

1. The best option would be to send him to his GP as this should be the natural course of action. It is not an emergency and therefore it would be better than to send him to A&E. Therefore Option D comes first, and Option A comes second.

2. Options B and C both involve stealing, which is a disciplinary matter. So those two options will rank at the bottom. If you had to choose between stealing from A&E and stealing from the ward, stealing from the ward would be the most inconvenient as you would effectively be taking an inhaler that was reserved for one of your patients. Therefore Option B ranks higher than Option C.

3. Option E (asking one of your more senior colleagues to write a prescription) is a possibility though in practice you are likely to face rejection. Your colleague would only really be able to prescribe once he has met your friend and asked a few pertinent questions. By asking him, you will also place him in an awkward situation where he might feel pressured. Therefore this option ranks after the more mainstream Options D and A, but higher than the two options involving theft.

Scenario 15 ANSWER: DABCE

The key to this question is to identify how effective each option will be in resolving the matter and how sensitive your approach is. We will look at each option in reverse order of appropriateness.

1. Option E (keeping records) might sound good if you ever have to make a case to a senior colleague later on, but it really feels like you are spying on your colleague and not addressing anything. Watching and waiting (for what?!) is also counterproductive as it implies that you hope someone else will do your dirty work for you. It is the worst option.

2. Option C (approaching your colleague and not going straight away to a senior) might have a surface appeal, but your actions would be highly patronising. Your colleague might have personal problems which are causing the delay; Option C gives no indication that you have an understanding, or are trying to gain an understanding, of what these might be. Telling your

colleague off will only cause conflict. If someone needs to reprimand him, it will need to be someone more senior than him.

3. Option B (discussing with other juniors) is better. Your other colleagues will have no doubt been affected by his late arrivals and therefore it makes sense to discuss the matter with them. Note that this option is only ranking highly because it mentions "junior doctors". If it had mentioned "nurses" instead, then your actions could simply be considered as gossip. It would therefore rank much lower.

4. Option A (telling his senior) is preferable to Options B and C because you are involving someone who can make a difference and who will try to get to the bottom of the problem with your colleague. This will include investigating any particular problem that may be causing the delay. You might not find out what is causing the delay but at least you are ensuring that the problem gets resolved. However, there are other things that you can do before you get to this stage.

5. Option D (asking your colleague for reasons and offering your help) is the most helpful and therefore the highest ranked option. It is seeking to resolve the matter in a helpful and supportive manner.

Scenario 16 ANSWER: CDAEB

This question is about professionalism and teamwork. You are expected to show a helpful attitude while ensuring that the system works the way that it should, and that patient safety is ensured.

1. Don't confuse being a good team player with being taken for a mug by your colleagues and giving up your own life for their own comfort. Here are a few things to think about:

   • You might have been asked to review a patient but, since you are leaving your shift, the FY1 on call is the one who should be handling this (the question doesn't state that the case is urgent).

   • As a junior doctor, you need to take your own responsibilities; so asking a consultant to take over would not rank highly as a response to a routine case.

- Patient safety should also be a major consideration (this is why trying to see the patient quickly is not a good idea; it may end up taking much longer than you initially thought).

2. Your first approach should be to encourage the team to function the way it should function normally. This means getting your colleague to track the on-call FY1 (Option C). If she is too busy for that, you should consider doing it yourself (Option D), the reason being that it is really the on-call FY1's job to deal with the patient and not yours. The primary responsibility to delegate to whoever is on call is your colleague's, not yours.

3. If the on-call FY1 is not available then you are now faced with three remaining options:

   - Giving the patient to the consultant (E)
   - Seeing him yourself (A)
   - Seeing him quickly (B)

   Giving the patient to the consultant will place you in a bad light. Option E says "Tell your consultant". This makes it a direct command rather than a request for assistance. If the option was worded as "Ask the consultant if he would not mind seeing the patient" then it would rank higher. In any case, it should be down to your colleague to tell the consultant. You will therefore have to see the patient yourself.

   Seeing the patient quickly is simply unsafe, which makes it the worst option. Once you have seen him, he may need further care which will take you longer to organise. What would you do if, once you have seen the patient, you need to stay behind? We are back to square one.

   In addition, Option B says that your family will be waiting for you in the hospital restaurant during that time. This is bad news as they will be a constant reminder for you that you are late and this will bring extra pressure onto you. The order for the remaining options is therefore A, E B.

Scenario 17 ANSWER: CEDAB

In this question, you need to ensure the safety of the patient, whilst minimising the impact on your colleagues.

1. Option C (asking a colleague to attend) is both safe for the patient and convenient for the team. It will only inconvenience one single colleague.

2. Option E (asking a colleague to fill in whilst you get information) sounds like a good idea though it could be embarrassing for your colleague if he is not well prepared. Still, it is a safe option; it ensures that the team gets its session and only inconveniences one colleague.

3. Option D is very safe but will inconvenience everyone in the team. It is slightly over the top; you cannot cancel educational meetings every time there is an emergency otherwise no one would ever get trained. Still, it is better than just slipping away (at least people know what is going on and know where things stand) and therefore will rank higher than Option A.

4. Option A is very safe for the patient but awful for your colleagues, who will be sitting around wondering what is going on. It shows poor communication abilities and poor team playing skills. There are better options.

5. Option B is the most unsafe of all. The scenario says that it is an emergency call.

Scenario 18 ANSWER: BACED

1. Option D comes last because it poses a danger to patient safety. You simply cannot ignore such an important issue. Patients may be placed in danger because of his addiction.

2. All the other options involve reporting the matter in various circumstances. When faced with such a choice, it sometimes helps to rewrite the options in a clearer, more concise manner:

   • A: report after telling your colleague
   • B: report after giving the colleague a chance to address the matter
   • C: report without telling the colleague
   • E: report only if you have concerns about his performance.

   E is potentially unsafe as you should not just be concerned about his current performance but also his future performance. Your colleague might be fine for now but his addiction might escalate and spiral out of control. Will you wait until he kills a patient to act?

Out of the other three, the order is fairly obvious: B, A, C, the order being determined by a decreasing level of friendliness and sensitivity.

Scenario 19   ANSWER: DACBE

1. You must look at the nature of the gift, the circumstances surrounding the gift and the impact that a refusal would have on the doctor-patient relationship. Your main concern is to ensure that the situation cannot be construed as bribery; but on the other hand, you do not want the refusal of a gift to affect the doctor-patient relationship negatively, so the matter needs to be handled sensitively.

2. In the scenario, the gift is of high value, particularly in view of the short-term relationship that you have had with the patient. The wording of the question goes out of its way to emphasise a detachment (short admission, only contact was during ward rounds, patient not expected to come back). Therefore it would make sense to refuse the gift. There are two options to do this: Option D (politely refusing the gift) which is polite and also shows a degree of care and empathy, and Option A (telling them it would be unethical to accept) which is a bit more bureaucratic but still acceptable. Therefore Option D and Option A should rank at the top, in that order.

3. We are now left with three options to accept the gift:

   - Option E (keeping quiet) has to be the least appropriate. In fact it is verging on unethical and dishonest (and might actually expose you to blackmail from the patient in the worst possible scenario).

   - Giving the gift to your loved one (Option B) might sound like a good idea but it is still for personal gain. It is not as good as using the money for the good of everyone on the ward (Option C). After all, the gift was for care given to the patient and therefore rendered by the whole ward. Also, giving the gift to the team will make it less likely to be construed as bribery. It is also an excellent demonstration of selflessness and teamwork. Therefore Option C is more appropriate than Option B.

Scenario 20   ANSWER: DBEAC

1. The situation is tricky. On one hand you must respect the confidentiality of the patient but on the other hand maintaining such confidentiality is hard to achieve if the person he wants to keep in the dark is actually working on the ward where he is a patient. In particular, you will want to make sure that the care of the other patients is not compromised (bearing in mind that the safety of the other patients will always be more important than the confidentiality of one patient). You also have to make sure that you do not give in to patients too easily, particularly if their requests appear unreasonable.

2. Based on the above, it seems sensible to try to reach a compromise with the patient in order to avoid any disruption. Option D explores the reasons behind the patient's request and constitutes the most appropriate action. You might find that his fears are unfounded or that, simply by reassuring him about the team's professionalism, he will accept having the nurse around.

3. Option B is the second most suitable option because it looks after the patient's confidentiality without disturbing any team member (or not much anyway). However, it is less appropriate than Option D (reaching a compromise with the patient), which at least attempts to eliminate the constraint of confidentiality in a diplomatic way.

4. Once you have done your best to sort out the situation without disturbance, either by reasoning with the patient or by issuing directives to the team, then you are left with three options:

   - Option A (telling the patient to accept the situation): it is not the worst idea but it could create problems in terms of your relationship with the patient and his trust in the team, and in terms of the patient's own relationship with his wife and her friend.

   - Option E (transferring the patient to a different part of the ward) is preferable to Option A because at least you are doing something concrete about the problem, with limited disturbance.

   - Option C (telling the nurse to take some time off) is unthinkable; she must have better things to do with her annual leave than to avoid patients. Any such directive would have to come from someone far more senior than you anyway.

Scenario 21 ANSWER: BEACD

1. If the patient is refusing that you examine him then, regardless of his reasons, you should not examine him yourself, with or without a chaperone. Therefore Option D should rank last.

2. Asking a nurse to conduct a clinical examination and describing the details to you is inadequate as vital clinical details can be missed out and the examination will have to be redone. It is, however, better than to ignore the patient's wishes (which would constitute an assault). Hence Option C ranks fourth.

3. The remaining three options all involve getting a male doctor to examine the patient and should be ranked in the order of timescale, i.e. the sooner the patient can be seen, the better. Ideally you should ask the male SHO to see the patient when he is free (Option B), failing which you could hand over to the on-call team (Option E) or refer to urology for next day appointment (Option A).

Scenario 22 ANSWER: BEACD

Ensuring patient safety is essential; all tests that have been ordered should be followed up in a timely fashion. All the options allow the possibility of effective follow-up of blood results; however, they differ in the urgency and the effectiveness of the communication of the need to check the results and act upon them.

1. Option B is the most appropriate and timely option. If you know another FY1 who is working on another ward, then it would be most appropriate to relay the relevant clinical information directly to him rather than via a third party. In that way, he will not only be able to check the blood results; he will also be able to act upon them.

2. Asking the ward sister to contact the on-call FY1 (Option E) is also appropriate, though less so than Option B because you should avoid involving

third parties if you can. The on-call FY1 is currently not responding and could be in the middle of an arrest call, or in the middle of a procedure. The message would then be relayed by the sister, allowing the on-call FY1 to deal with your request when his more immediate concern has been addressed.

3. Calling the on-call medical registrar (Option A) will ensure that the results are checked; however, he may be busy with more serious patient reviews. As such you should try Options B and E first. The registrar may not appreciate your asking him directly to check blood results and would most likely simply relay the information to the on-call FY1 so that he can check the results and act upon them. You would be adding an extra layer of complexity and hierarchy to the problem in return for no real further benefit; so Option A ranks lower than Options B and E.

4. Option C (going back to the hospital) is a harder option to rank. On one hand, one may think that the responsibility lies with you to do a proper handover when your shift ends, and there is no doubt that going back to the hospital would be a good thing to do. However, it will take you a while to get back to the hospital and if the blood results require a medical intervention, you would still have to hand the job over to the on-call team. In such a situation, your responsibility is therefore to make sure that the current team is aware of the situation and acts upon it. As such Option C ranks lower than Options B, E and A.

5. Option D (leaving a note for the FY1 on call) is the least effective option because your FY1 colleague will not necessarily know that a message has been left for him. If he does not get notified by the ward, by you or other colleagues, the results may never get checked. This option is potentially unsafe and therefore ranks last.

Scenario 23 | ANSWER: ECABD

1. Option A is a very sensible thing to do because you are being honest with the patient, you apologise and you seek their consent for the new sample. If you handle the situation sensitively, in most cases the patient will not mind. And if the patient complains, then at least you can show that you acted vey professionally. However:

- It would be sensible to first check with the lab that the sample has indeed been lost. Hence, Option E ranks higher than Option A.

- Before you tell the patient that their blood sample has been lost, you may wish to approach a consultant (Option C) as he may be able to provide some advice on how to handle the matter. He may also be able to put some pressure on the lab, suggest other non-invasive ways of investigation and advise you on the relevance of doing another tap. He may also decide that he would be the most appropriate person to break the news to the patient. You would be expected to have done some ground work yourself first (e.g. checking with the lab yourself) before you approach the consultant. Hence Option C ranks between Option E and Option A.

2. This now leaves Options B and D, both of which involve probity issues that reflect a lack of professionalism.

- Option B: It is not entirely true that the results haven't come back but on the other hand, it is a small lie with no real consequences other than delaying the moment when something will have to be told to the patient.

- Option D: Obtaining a further blood sample from the patient by telling them that more tests need to be done is a total lie. You would essentially be obtaining the other sample under false pretences and, aside from the lack of probity this demonstrates, it could also worry the patient about the nature of those other tests. Telling the patient that another sample is needed from an invasive procedure with potential complications without any discussion with senior colleagues is completely inappropriate (and may in fact constitute assault).

So, though both Option B and Option D are inappropriate, Option B has the least consequences and would therefore rank higher than Option D.

Scenario 24 ANSWER: CADBE

1. Mrs Smith is inherently unstable and will therefore require a medical escort. This makes Option E (leaving the porters with Mrs Smith) the worst option because it is the only one which leaves the acute patient in the hands of non-medical staff; as such it is therefore unsafe.

2. Option B (ask the nurse to stay with Mrs Smith whilst you review the other patient) is equally unsafe because an unstable patient is made to wait whilst you are reviewing the patient who has fallen; but at least during that time Mrs Smith is in the care of a nurse. Having a nurse on standby next to the patient is safer than having non-medically trained staff escorting a potentially highly unstable patient, as she will be able to monitor the patient's vital signs and recognise if the patient is in distress. Therefore Option B ranks higher than Option E.

3. The other three options (A, C and D) all involve taking Mrs Smith to ICU straight away, which is the safest approach, but with varying consequences for the patient who has fallen:

   - Option A: The patient will be assessed by you whilst another doctor will accompany Mrs Smith to ICU.

   - Option C: The patient will be assessed by a registrar who has been informed by the nurse, whilst you take Mrs Smith to ICU.

   - Option D: The patient will be assessed by you on your return from ICU.

   Option D means that the patient who has fallen will have to wait to be seen. Since both Option A and Option C would ensure that both patients are dealt with effectively and much more quickly, Option D will rank third.

   This leaves Option A and Option C as the top two options. Because you have developed a good rapport with Mrs Smith, it would be best that you escort her whilst someone else assesses the other patient. Doing it the other way round would require a handover between doctors as you assess a fallen patient and another doctor has to escort Mrs Smith to ICU without knowing the background. Therefore Option C ranks higher than Option A.

Scenario 25 ANSWER: EDABC

1. Atorvastatin is contraindicated in pregnancy and therefore you need to take action before the patient has a chance to take it, otherwise the foetus may be harmed. Options A, D and E will ensure it and therefore should rank as the top three options.

- Option E (cancelling the prescription and contacting the registrar) is the best option. By cancelling the atorvastatin you guarantee that it cannot be given. It also gives you the opportunity to establish the facts with a senior colleague.

- Option D (taking the drug chart to the pharmacist and changing the prescription) is good too, and shows that you are proactive. However, before you change the prescription, it would be best to ask for advice from a senior colleague whether directly or via the ward pharmacists. For that reason, Option D ranks second.

- Option A would also ensure that safety is preserved, but again it makes no mention of involving a senior or anyone else. Such unilateral action would be fine in this context, but you really ought to run it past a senior colleague first, something that Option E does, and that Option D gives you an opportunity to do (checking with the pharmacist is better than checking with no one).

2. Option C (communicating via patient's notes and not notifying anyone directly) is totally ineffective as it relies on (i) someone checking the notes and (ii) that person acting on the information. Discussing the matter at the next ward round introduces a delay that could prove problematic if the patient takes the medication in the meantime. Option C is the worst and therefore ranks last.

3. This leaves option B, which ranks fourth on the basis that, although a discussion with the FY2 may clear the problem, we are told that he is out of reach. As such, the wait may be detrimental to the patient and the foetus if the patient ends up taking the medication before you can reach the FY2.

Scenario 26 ANSWER: BACED

In this scenario, there is an immediate emphasis on patient safety (i.e. the FY1 must tuck his tie in as soon as possible to minimise risk to patients), followed by a longer-term concern of non-compliance.

1. Options A and B are the only options that will result in immediate remedial action and therefore rank first. Reporting the issue to the infection control nurse sounds a little over the top given that it is only the second occurrence but it will ensure that the situation is being addressed in the longer

term too. If there is a recurrent risk of infection (and in this case you have already told the FY1 to sort things out once before) then she should be informed. Therefore Option B ranks over Option A.

2. Option C will also ensure that the situation is addressed in the short term but there will be a delay in communication which will result in a greater risk of infection. As such, it is not as good as Options A and B. In addition, it is the coward's way out, involving a nurse to do your dirty work. Still, it will be more effective in the short term than informing your education supervisor or emailing his consultant. As such Option C should rank third.

3. Option E (emailing his consultant) may help resolve the situation but you are relying on the fact that he actually reads his emails and acts on them. Nevertheless, this is more direct and therefore more effective than informing your own educational supervisor (Option D), who will have to contact your colleague's educational supervisor so that he can have a word with him.

Scenario 27 ANSWER: DACEB

1. Of all the options, Options A, C, D and E are proactive actions, which may lead to the scan being granted. Option B will result in neither the scan being done nor other people being informed that there is an issue until they actually read your notes. Option B is therefore the least effective option as it will cause the greatest delay to patient care and is unsafe.

2. The fact that the consultant radiologist nearly always queries the paperwork may prompt some candidates to involve their own consultant straight away. In reality, it would not be appropriate to involve your consultant unless you have first attempted to resolve the problem yourself. The best thing to do is to contact the radiology department to sort out the paperwork and get the scan done as soon as you can. Indeed, the additional information that you will provide may prompt the radiologist to advise that there are tests which are more suitable than CT CAP. Therefore Option D ranks first.

3. Options A and C will come next in terms of suitability because they both get the two consultants talking to each other and therefore ensure that the scan is being discussed. It is your team's responsibility to make sure that the appropriate information is provided to the radiologist and therefore it

should be your consultant who contacts the radiologist rather than the other way round. As such, Option A ranks above Option C.

4. Option E provides no further clinical information to the radiologist and merely emphasises that you are a junior passing on a message. Mentioning that the radiologist is potentially compromising patient safety is very inflammatory and directly questions the radiologist's integrity. Not only is this option unlikely to get the CT CAP granted, you might also find yourself with an official complaint against you for inappropriate behaviour, with the radiologist insisting that you are in fact the one compromising your own patient's safety by never giving the information required to make suitable decisions with regard to scans. Option E will therefore rank low, though higher than Option B, where nothing at all is being done or discussed.

If there are issues to discuss with regard to paperwork for scan requests, they should be handled at senior level between the two departments. It is not your job to deal with it and you should not let your frustrations get in the way of patient care.

Scenario 28   ANSWER: ADECB

1. Any option that involves ignoring the advice given by the microbiologist would rank low. Indeed, there is a strong possibility that the antibiotic you are giving to the patient is ineffective and by ignoring the guidelines you are exposing your patient to harm. Therefore Options B and C would rank last. Option C is slightly better than Option B because you are documenting the advice given by the microbiologist, which increases the chance that someone else might see it and act upon it.

2. Your consultant is in charge of the patient, therefore it would be most appropriate to discuss the advice given by the microbiologist with him before any change is made. It may be that the consultant is well aware of the Trust guidelines but felt that his choice of antibiotic was justified. Following your approach, he may then instruct you to switch to the recommended antibiotic or to discuss the matter further with the microbiologist. Option A will therefore rank top as it is the only option that gives full consideration to all aspects of the situation so that a considered decision can be made.

3. This leaves Option D (you change the prescription in accordance with Trust guidelines) and Option E (you give the new antibiotic on top of the

old one). In both cases, you are switching the patient to the new antibiotic and will therefore likely enhance his chances of recovery; however, in Option E, you are going against Trust policy because the advice was to replace one antibiotic by another, and not give it on top of the other. You are also potentially harming the patient because you are increasing the risk of resistance to the antibiotic which is not needed or not effective. Therefore Option D ranks second and Option E ranks third.

Important Note
In practice, most doctors would simply follow the advice given by the microbiologists without necessarily discussing the matter with the consultant. They would simply inform him retrospectively. But remember that you are asked to rank options in accordance to what you SHOULD do and not what you WOULD do. Those who answered in accordance with what they would do may have ranked D before A. This would be acceptable (and therefore would probably score high too in the exam) but it is not best practice.

Scenario 29   ANSWER: CDEBA

Patient confidentiality is extremely important, and is a cornerstone of medical professionalism. According to the GMC, patient information can be provided to the police in the case of 'serious crimes' only (meaning mostly crimes against the person, e.g. murder or rape). Benefit fraud does not fall into that category.

1. Issues of confidentiality are often difficult to deal with outside of the normal clinical context. As a junior doctor faced by a police request, and without full knowledge of the legislation, you would need to ensure that the request is addressed by a senior member of the team. It would be inappropriate for you to handle the matter personally without ensuring that proper consideration is given by the team to the request. Referring the matter to a senior consultant will ensure that the right thing is being done, whilst maintaining a good relationship with the police though proper communication. As such Option C will rank first.

2. Following on from that, the next two options will be Option D (ask for a court order) and Option E (refuse the request bluntly) as these still maintain the confidentiality of the patient. Out of those two, Option D is the most constructive, Option E being slightly rude.

3. We are then left with the two options that involve breaching the patient's confidentiality: Option A and Option B. Option B is the option which is the least damaging to confidentiality and therefore ranks above Option A.

Scenario 30 ANSWER: BADEC

1. Your colleague is placing a burden on the team because of his own behaviour and risks compromising his own professional image and that of the medical profession. It is clearly not acceptable, but on the other hand the stupidity of his behaviour calls for personal support more than an administrative punishment, at least in the short term. The situation may be different if the problem is recurrent. Option B would achieve both a withdrawal of the pictures and would ensure the situation does not recur, and should therefore rank first.

2. Option C (ignoring the matter) and Option E (keeping copies of the pages) achieve nothing at all. They both leave the colleague and the team exposed to accusations of lack of professionalism and demonstrate little support towards your colleague, who could get into trouble if someone were to find out about the existence of the pictures. Therefore both options should rank bottom, with Option E ranking higher than Option C as you are at least gathering information and showing an intention to do something about it at some stage.

3. This leaves Option A (asking your colleague to take the pictures down and informing the consultant) and Option D (informing the consultant) in second and third position respectively on the basis that informing the consultant may be a little too harsh for a one-off event which did not cause any patient safety issues. However, should you feel the need to do it, it would be best to do it once you have asked your colleague to take the pictures down. This will minimise the danger of someone else seeing them, and will also ensure that you communicate directly with the colleague, as opposed to simply going to the consultant behind their back. Therefore Option A ranks above Option D.

Scenario 31 ANSWER: CBDAE

It is not the patient's fault if the registrar is late. The patient has specific needs relating to his work and you should ensure that these are taken into account by seeking to reach an appropriate consensus; communication will be key to reaching that consensus. Therefore, provided it is safe to discharge the patient, there is no reason why he couldn't be discharged.

1. Calling the registrar to enquire about his reasons for holding the patient back (Option C) is the most sensible thing to do as it will help you ascertain whether it is essential to delay the discharge or not. If the discussion with the patient can wait, the registrar may ask you to discharge the patient and recall him at a later date. If the discussion can't wait, the registrar may decide that another senior colleague should get involved in talking to the patient (or maybe even you).

2. All the other options make the assumption that you don't know whether the information that the registrar wants to convey is important or not. As such you will need to rank them in an order which ensures that you can optimise your chances of conveying that information to the patient without inconveniencing him too much:

   • Option E essentially entails holding the patient against his will, otherwise known as false imprisonment or kidnapping! Except in very specific circumstances (e.g. if a patient has been sectioned), if the patient wants to leave, he is entitled to do so by self-discharging. Option E will therefore rank last.

   • This leaves us with Options A, B and D to rank. Option B is the most flexible of all as it informs the patient of the situation and encourages him to stay without being too coercive. This gives the patient a clear choice. As such it will rank top of those three options.

   • Option D comes next because it sets out an action plan; however, it does not explain to the patient that the registrar needs to talk to him. It also does not offer the patient the full choice between all available options. It is a good option but not as comprehensive as Option B.

   • Option A does not inform the patient of the need to talk to the registrar at all and does not provide any proactive solution to the problem; though on the plus side, you are informing the registrar.

Scenario 32 — ANSWER: ADBCE

1. Post-thyroidectomy patients may suffer from laryngeal oedema; this requires emergency intervention. The question is telling you that the patient is struggling to breathe; because you are by yourself, your immediate priority will be to get help and commence resuscitation to maintain the patient's airways. Two of the options (A and D) will result in immediate help, whereas the other three (B, C and E) will result in delayed help. Therefore Options A and D will rank at the top.

2. Out of A and D, Option A ranks highest because the CCOT comprises a number of specially trained nurses in critical care medicine whose role is to stabilise critically-ill patients. The patient they are currently reviewing has been stepped down from ITU and is therefore stable; that means it would be safe for them to come to your help and commence resuscitation whilst freeing you perhaps to contact your consultant. Alternatively, other members of the CCOT could break off and contact an anaesthetist to secure definite airway. Option D ranks lower because, although the surgical registrar would be able to provide immediate assistance to you, the CCOT would have more personnel to help out, and are trained and equipped to deal with critically-ill patients. Their intervention would therefore be safer.

3. Option B (calling the resuscitation team) would allow you to raise the alarm and recruit a number of doctors very quickly. This option ranks higher than options C and E, which both result in potentially much delayed care.

4. Options C and E would rank bottom because they are leaving the patient with no care. Out of those two, Option E is the worst as you are essentially doing nothing about the problem. With Option C, you will at least get some input from the consultant.

Scenario 33 — ANSWER: CADEB

1. Options A and C both give you the best chance of prescribing the correct antibiotic. Out of the two, Option C is the definitive choice since, by asking microbiology for advice, you will get the latest microbiology Trust protocol for HAP treatment. Asking the registrar for advice (Option A) is also a good bet, though there is still a risk that he may not fully or correctly re-

member the protocol. So Option C ranks above Option A, and both rank at the top.

2. The other three options (B, D and E) all involve guessing to an extent. The less you have to guess, the safer your actions will be and therefore the higher the option will rank:

- Option D (asking the other FY1 doctors) is the best choice because you are seeking advice from local colleagues, who have a small chance of remembering the local Trust guidelines.

- Option E (looking up another hospital's protocol on the internet) is less appropriate than Option D because there is no guarantee that the information is accurate and that the external protocol is similar in any way to that in your hospital.

- Option B (prescribing your best guess) is the least safe option as you are simply hoping that the antibiotics mixture is right without asking for any kind of help. This is the most unsafe of all options and there-fore should rank last.

Scenario 34 ANSWER: CABDE

1. Your priority in this situation is to ensure that the patient gets his usual dose of his medications. The optimal and safest approach would be to contact the GP to obtain a collateral drug history, i.e. Option C.

2. Options A (contacting the next of kin) and B (looking at the previous dis-charge summary) would also help you with this task, but the next of kin may miss out medications if he/she is not familiar with them; also the last discharge summary is 2 years old and may not be up to date. On the basis that dealing with the next of kin may lead to greater accuracy, Option A will rank higher than Option B, though both options will rank lower than Option C.

3. There is no real clinical need to prescribe a stat dose of medications (Op-tion D) to slow the heart down as the heart rate is only slightly elevated for the moment. However, by doing so, you will buy time to find out the real dose of medication that the patient normally takes.

4. Option E will rank lower than option D because there is no guarantee that the on-call team will see your note or titrate the medications up, and so the dosages may be inadequate. This approach would rank higher if there was a proper handover rather than a written instruction in the patient's clinical notes.

Scenario 35 ANSWER: CEBDA

1. The best approach to start with would be to ask the patient to remain quiet and wait for their turn. By adopting a soft approach you may win the patient's goodwill and you would then have a better chance to gain their trust. So Option C would be the top ranking option.

2. Option E (advising them of the zero tolerance policy) is also an appropriate response but it is asking the patient to comply with rules which they may not be able to fully comprehend in their current state of mind. By taking the conversation to a "legal" level, you are possibly exacerbating the situation too. So this would be a less preferred option than Option C.

3. In dealing with unruly patients, one has to take into account their health status. This patient's intoxication may be masking a more dangerous pathology. Thus refusing to see the patient and asking him to leave immediately (Option A) would stop you from being able to determine that. In addition, there is a risk that, having been told to leave, the patient may in fact become violent. Option A would therefore be one of the least favoured options. It would in fact be preferable to call security first (who may be able to calm him down or at least keep him in check) or see the patient straight away.

5. Between Option B (calling security) and Option D (seeing the patient straight away), calling security is preferable because the patient should not be allowed to jump the queue simply because of his threats. The priority should be to see him whenever he is due to be seen, but to make sure that his behaviour is being controlled.

Scenario 36 ANSWER: ADBEC

1. The person breaking the bad news should be responsible for the patient's care, and be able to fully inform the patient of the possible management and prognosis. Bearing that in mind, the consultant in charge of the patient's care would be the best suited to break the news (Option A), as he will be able to answer both the possible management and prognosis.

2. The doctor who performed the colonoscopy (Option B) is not in charge of the patient's care, and he will only have met the patient a few minutes before the operation. In fact, you, the FY1 in the team looking after the patient's care, would be better suited to breaking the bad news (Option D) than the doctor conducting the colonoscopies.

3. Option E: Writing to the GP and getting him to notify the patient of the results after discharge could delay the management process. Besides, the GP may not be in the best position to answer questions regarding management and prognosis.

4. Notifying the next of kin and asking him to relay the news to the patient (Option C) is breaching patient confidentiality. In addition there is a risk that the information may not be adequately or fully relayed to the patient. This would be the worst option from the whole list.

Scenario 37 ANSWER: CADEB

1. The situation is cause for concern as falsifying the observations may result in wrong decisions being made by the team in relation to patient care. Ignoring the issue would be very unsafe and so Option B ranks last.

2. Because patient safety is compromised, your first approach should be to make sure that someone in charge is made aware of the issue. Since this is a nursing issue, it would be appropriate to inform the ward sister so that she can investigate (Option C). Your consultant would need to be informed too (Option A); however, this is secondary to Option C because he doesn't have any direct influence on the nurse.

3. Whereas in normal circumstances, talking to the individual concerned would be the most appropriate option, in this scenario you have already

approached the nurse and she denied it. You would therefore only seek to approach her yourself again if senior colleagues were not around. Hence it ranks third.

4. Option E (making sure that your own patients are safe) is a good idea but other patients, who are not under your care, are still exposed to danger. The remaining safety issue means that the option should rank fourth.

Scenario 38 ANSWER: CEBDA

1. Your own assessment of brain-stem death would not be sufficient to request that the ventilator be switched off. It would be more appropriate to inform the relatives first so that they can take in the news, organ donation can be discussed and the switching-off can be discussed with them. As such Option A will rank last.

2. The options that involve confirming the brain-stem death (i.e. Options C and E) would be the most appropriate ones. It is clear that the ICU consultant (i.e. the doctor with overall responsibility for the patient's care) should review the patient first, not only so that he can confirm brain-stem death, but also so that he can notify the next of kin. Conducting further tests on the patient should not be attempted before another senior colleague has reviewed the patient. Thus Option C ranks over Option E.

3. Informing the next of kin about the brain-stem death is not something you would do until death was confirmed and this should preferably be done by the ICU consultant rather than you. As such, Options B and D rank below Option C. It would not really be appropriate for you to discuss organ donation with the next of kin. This role is normally reserved for specific Organ Donation Nurse Specialists or senior doctors who are trained for such scenarios as they can answer the specific questions the relatives may have. So Option D will rank lower than Option B.

Scenario 39   ANSWER: EBCAD

1. This question is evidently about confidentiality. Essentially the less you mention, the more appropriate the option:

- Option A: You are confirming the fact that Mr Jay was admitted.

- Option B: You are just about confirming that Mr Jay is a patient, but not that he was admitted (so that makes it better than Option A)

- Option C: You are updating the head cleaner on status, though this is very vague and could mean anything. This makes it more appropriate than Option A which gives away the fact he was admitted, but less appropriate than Option B, which simply gives away the fact he is a patient.

- Option D: You are telling him he was admitted in the respiratory ward. So that is worse than the three previous options.

- Option E: You are not giving anything away and are simply directing him to HR. That is the best option as it is the option that optimises confidentiality. It is possible that HR may reveal more to him, but that is something for them to consider, your own main consideration being to respect Mr Jay's confidentiality.

Note on Option C: GMC guidance states that "Unless they indicate otherwise, it is reasonable to assume that patients would want those closest to them to be kept informed of their general condition and prognosis." This would normally allow you, as a doctor, to reassure a relative that a patient is "fine", "okay" or "getting better" without feeling that you are breaching confidentiality. However, in this scenario, the head cleaner is not a relative and there is no indication that Mr Jay would want him to know anything. So it would be safer to say as little as you need to, hence why Option C ranks third here whereas if the head cleaner had been a relative instead, that option might have ranked first.

Scenario 40 ANSWER: ADECB

1. This question is testing your ability to use other members of the team appropriately in a context where you have reached your limitations in dealing with a sick patient. Out of the five options, four are about contacting someone more senior. The other one, Option B, simply mentions that you leave a message. Thus option B should be ranked last.

2. The most appropriate option is to contact the surgical registrar (Option A). He is currently on site and can provide immediate review. If, however, you cannot contact the registrar, or the registrar is in the surgery with the SHO and cannot leave the theatre, then the most appropriate option would be to contact the next person up who can stabilise the patient in preparation for a potential emergency operation. This would be the surgical consultant (Option D).

3. The problem is a surgical one, and will require surgical intervention. Therefore getting the anaesthetist to come in to prepare and stabilise the patient (Option E) would be the next best option.

4. Whilst getting a medical opinion (Option C) might be useful, and getting another pair of hands to come and stabilise the patient is important, it is more appropriate to call the anaesthetist before the medical registrar as there is a potential need for surgical intervention. Thus, Option C ranks below Option E.

Scenario 41 ANSWER: ADCEB

1. As you are covering the ward, your duty of care is towards the ward patients, and so your priority should be to assess and manage the patients on the ward. If you have spare time, then it would be feasible (and nice of you) to help out another colleague, but currently, as the pancreatitis patient is in A&E, and you are presented with two unwell patients on the ward, you will have to prioritise them over the A&E patient. In any case, A&E doctors will have already stabilised the patient before referring on for surgical clerking, and thus you would know that they are stable. Therefore leaving sick patients on the ward to review a stable patient in A&E (Option B) would place you in serious breach of duty.

2. In both Option B and Option E, you are dumping your patients onto the night team; instead of spending your time handing over the patients, you should spend it more appropriately by assessing the sick patients on your ward. Therefore Options B and E will rank last, with Option E ranking slightly higher because you are at least reviewing a patient in the process (even if it's not yours).

3. The three remaining options (A, C and D) all involve telling the surgical SHO that you can't clerk the patient and will therefore rank top. In this scenario, it is important to get help from the surgical registrar as a priority (Option A), as he has the ability to lend a hand in assessing and triaging the patients on the ward. So Option A will rank first.

4. The patient with presumed haematemesis is more clinically urgent than the feverish patient. Taking blood cultures would be important for later identification of better antibiotics to use, but if you are not talking to microbiology to ask for advice about what other antibiotic to add for this patient, then taking blood cultures would not be a priority over reviewing the patient that presents with haematemesis. Thus Option D ranks over Option C.

Scenario 42 ANSWER: ECABD

1. The patient has made her intentions clear and you believe she is serious. As such you would have a strong case for breaching her confidentiality but you will need to make sure that you only disclose information that is absolutely necessary and to the minimum number of people necessary. The most appropriate options would involve disclosing the information to the police only (i.e. Options C and E), with E ranking higher because you are asking for her consent first.

2. Options A and B both involve notifying the employer. However, Option B may be counterproductive as it will only serve to warn the employer without anything being done about the threat. Breaching confidentiality will only be effective if the police are informed and therefore Option A ranks over Option B.

3. Option D ranks last because you have already talked things through with the patient and it doesn't address the imminent danger that the employer is in.

Important note: in practice you would most likely report the situation to senior members of your team who can then decide whether to breach confidentiality and how this should be done. So, if they were available, any options which involved senior clinicians or managers within your team would rank towards the top. In some cases you may need to seek advice from lawyers or your defence union. If you were to do that, you would need to do it on an unnamed basis so that the patient cannot be identified as they would not need to know the name of the patient to be in a position to advise you.

Scenario 43 ANSWER: CBDAE

1. Your clinical judgement is being questioned by a nurse. It is of course important that you respect the nurse's opinion and taking his comments into consideration will help you approach the situation from a different perspective. It is perfectly possible that your approach may be over the top or incorrect and that the nurse is correct in his handling of the situation. Conversely the nurse may have misunderstood the situation or might simply be obstructive.

    Ultimately the responsibility for the patient lies with you. Since you have just identified a clinical need for NIV, you should discuss this with suitable medical professionals (in this case the Respiratory registrar – Option C), who will be best able to provide you with advice, or if you feel that another opinion for NIV use is warranted. Since your consultant is in charge of patient care, he should be contacted to help resolve any issues (Option B); however, you will need to discuss the patient with the Respiratory team first, so Option C ranks higher than Option B.

2. We are now left with three options as follows:

    - Option A: Call back 30 minutes later and exaggerate the results;
    - Option D: Call back 30 minutes later after you have reassessed;
    - Option E: Do it yourself.

    It is clear that lying would not be acceptable in any context, but particularly so in a context where it may affect the management of a patient; and so Option A ranks lower than Option D.

The main dilemma now is whether it is more appropriate to set up the equipment yourself (Option E), or to lie to get the NIV set up by the nurse 30 minutes later (Option A).

With Option A, once you have given the CCOT nurse your exaggerated version of events, the nurse will need to come and assess the patient himself before setting up NIV; therefore your lie may result in quicker action and the situation will remain safe (but the nurse will no doubt complain against your behaviour).

On the other hand, if you decide to set it up yourself without having had proper training you may end up with a wrongly fitted NIV and may cause serious harm to the patient. This would be negligent behaviour and Option E is therefore potentially unsafe.

In such a dilemma, patient safety would prevail over your general integrity (i.e. it is better to lie to save a patient than to kill that patient through negligence). Option E therefore ranks last.

Scenario 44 ANSWER: BDECA

1. Your duty is to the patient and not the family, though of course it is important that you deal with the family in a sensitive manner too. Unless there is significant evidence that the patient will suffer psychological or physical harm from being given the clinical information (e.g. a suicidal person, which is not suggested here) then the news will need to be given to the patient directly. Therefore, whilst you have to listen to the family's wishes, these wishes should not make a difference to the way you proceed.

2. You have a duty of confidentiality towards your patient and should not release any information to the family unless the patient consents to it. The only situation in which you could reasonably consider giving a diagnosis to the family without giving it to the patient would be if the patient had told you they didn't want to know and that you should inform their family instead. Such situation would not be ideal because the patient would then not be in a position to make decisions about their own care.

3. On that basis, the options which involve keeping the information from the relatives (i.e. Options B, D and E) will rank at the top. Whether the bad news is being given by you or the SHO does not matter so much; how-

ever, getting the SHO to do it for you whilst telling the relatives that you will follow their wishes (Option D) is slightly sneaky (bordering on dishonest) and may impair the relationship between the family and the medical team. For that reason, Option B ranks first and Option D ranks second.

4. Option E (getting the GP to do it) is not as good an option because he will not have been involved directly in the care of the patient and may not be in the best position to inform the patient about the impact of the diagnosis. On that basis, Option E should rank third.

5. Options A and C remain to be ranked at the bottom of the list. If you are going to comply with the family's wishes, then having some kind of formal request would be best as it would enable clear documentation of what happened. So Option C ranks higher than Option A.

Scenario 45 ANSWER: EDCBA

For this question, you do not need to know much about the ethics of sharing information with the private sector. Suffice to say that patient confidentiality rules will apply as usual and therefore you should not give data to anyone who is not entitled to it. Even if the data is anonymised, there should still be a valid reason for providing it – that would exclude pretty much anything commercial.

This question also tests the manner in which you communicate. Even if you chose to decline the request, you would be expected to do so in a constructive manner.

1. Option A is clearly the least appropriate option as it breaches patient confidentiality. Thus it will rank last.

2. You should not forget that these patients are ultimately your consultant's responsibility. In addition, the release of any data to any external organisation will need to be sanctioned officially by someone in charge within your department – from a professionalism perspective, you can't simply send a spreadsheet out with information taken from patient notes without senior colleagues being made aware of it. Therefore Option B would rank second to last.

3. Out of the three remaining options (C, D and E), Option C (telling the rep it is unethical) is the least constructive. Options D (asking the rep to put his

request in writing) and E (asking the rep to email the consultant) would at least give your consultant or someone in charge a chance to consider the request and, as senior author, to formally deal with it. Out of those two options, the least formal option would be preferable – there is no point getting the rep to write a formal letter if the answer is nearly certain to be no. Therefore Option C ranks third, Option D second and Option E first.

Scenario 46   ANSWER: EADBC

1. In this scenario you should consider the following:

- The patient is reporting a form of abuse and you should obviously consider her words seriously, particularly as she is confiding in you.

- The abuse does not seem to be frequent and, though she has lost some weight and has several bruises, she does not appear to be in danger of serious harm or death.

- The patient is competent and tells you explicitly not to breach confidentiality.

The most important thing to do here will be to preserve the relationship with the patient and retain her trust. Any hasty moves may make the situation worse for the patient, particularly if she lives with her son-in-law.

2. In view of the above, involving other agencies would be premature. Aside from the issue of breaching confidentiality, the patient seems worried about the consequences of discussing the issue with any other party, and so she may not engage fully with the process. In the end you may actually make life worse for her. Therefore, in this particular case, Options B (making a safeguarding referral) and C (reporting to the police) will rank bottom, with Option C being the most extreme option and therefore ranking last.

3. The abuse seems to be linked to the son-in-law's drinking and addressing that issue may be an idea. Option A (discussing the drinking with her daughter) involves doing precisely that (with the patient's consent) but this carries risks too and, before you consider doing so, it would be wise to put the patient in contact with support groups who may be better experienced in handling such matters (Option E). Therefore Options E and A will rank top in that order.

4. Option D (advising the patient that she should be admitted in a nursing home) ranks after Options E and A simply because, though it may address the issue of abuse in the long term, it is not aligned with the patient's wishes, which are that she wants to carry on living with her daughter and son-in-law. Advising her to move to a nursing home may make her feel that you have not been listening to her. Moving her to a care home could also prove detrimental as she would lose her immediate support network.

Scenario 47   ANSWER: EADCB

1. Giving the patient anaesthetic cream and leaving it for 30 minutes (Option E) should be your first choice because it would reduce the pain of the blood taking and would ensure that you get what you need. It would be more suitable than explaining the importance of the test and attempting to take the blood straight away (Option A) because it provides a solution to the dislike of the "prickly feeling" that causes an issue to the patient. Option A does not help that much in reassuring the patient. She is probably well aware of the need to do the blood test; what bothers her is the pain associated with it. Forcing the issue too soon may actually be counterproductive and give the patient a mental block. There is no major urgency here. Therefore Option E ranks above Option A.

2. Admitting the patient for observation (Option D) is also suitable, but it will delay care substantially. Ideally you should get a sample of baseline blood sooner rather than later; younger people have larger physiological reserve and can appear well, but can also deteriorate rapidly. Thus Option D ranks below Option A.

3. Option C is essentially giving up on the patient, hoping that she may come back if the situation deteriorates. This does not really address the issue of the needle phobia; nor does it help in managing the patient. Admitting her overnight (Option D) is a safer and more productive option.

4. Getting a nurse to hold the patient down would be considered battery as you would be performing a procedure on a patient without her consent. Therefore Option B ranks last.

Scenario 48 ANSWER: CBADE

1. The perception that doctors can be influenced by the pharmaceutical industry has resulted in the implementation of tight regulations. The GMC follows guidelines set by the Association of British Pharmaceutical Industry's Code of Practice for the Pharmaceutical Industry, which states that during scientific conferences and meetings it is fine for delegates to accept a "modest meal", and entirely fine to accept educational activities (i.e. the lecture). However, no money should be paid to doctors either directly or indirectly. Thus Option C is the best choice (lunches do also provide a good opportunity for networking amongst peers), followed by B and A.

2. Options D and E accept the book voucher and should therefore rank last as this is akin to receiving money. Option E is the worst option ethically, since you take the hospitality items (book voucher and dinner) without actually going to the educational activity.

Note that, even without awareness of the regulations, you should be able to get to the ranking using common sense.

Scenario 49 ANSWER: DBCAE

Small gifts, such as food, flowers, etc. are perfectly acceptable and help enhance the patient-doctor relationship without unduly influencing the standard of care that patients may expect from you. In other words, you are unlikely to change your management of the patient for the sake of a marble cake, but there is a risk that gifts of an expensive nature (e.g. a watch, large sums of money, etc.) may influence your behaviour. Refusing small gifts may in fact harm the doctor-patient relationship as the patient may not understand your refusal (particularly elderly people) or may feel that your refusal goes against their principles or culture.

1. In this scenario, the gifts are common items and are harmless; as such it would be appropriate to accept them, making Options B, C and D the top ranking options. Out of those three options, Option D shares the gifts with the team whereas, in Option B, you simply keep them for yourself. Therefore Option D will rank above Option B. Option C only partially accepts the gifts when there is no need for such refusal; it will therefore rank last out of the three.

2. Option A and Option E will rank last. Out of the two, Option E is the worst because it links the gifts to a specific activity. Gifts cannot be tied to a specific expectation of care such as a particular prescription, or completion of paperwork. Thus Option E ranks below Option A.

Scenario 50   ANSWER: ACDEB

1. Though there is a possibility that refusing the gift may upset the patient, given its size, you cannot risk to be seen to be influenced by the gift. As such, refusing the gift (Option A) is the safest thing to do. You will need to be sensitive in your refusal.

2. Simply accepting the gift for yourself would be the least appropriate thing to do, so Options E and B will rank last, in that order.

3. The remaining options entail accepting the gift and sharing it with others, which is more appropriate than keeping it for yourself. Donating it to charity (Option C) would be more appropriate than flooding the ward with chocolate (Option D) as it still represents a lot of money overall and the department should not be seen to be "bribed" in such manner. A nice thing to do may be to involve the rest of the staff to decide which charity it should go to. So Option C ranks above Option D.

Scenario 51   ANSWER: ADECB

1. A child over the age of 16 who has capacity can consent for treatment. In this scenario the child seems competent and has given her consent, therefore you should be allowed to proceed with the transfusion. So any option which involves transfusing the girl straight away (i.e. Option A and Option D) would come at the top. Option A contains an element of communication and apology that Option D does not contain. Advising the parents that they can seek a High Court injunction is pretty pointless anyway if you are going to transfuse within minutes. Such point is therefore likely to aggravate the anger the relatives are feeling.

2. The other three options would cause a potentially fatal delay. If you are going to delay a decision, your priority will be to ensure that you get the best advice for yourself and so contacting the hospital lawyers will be

more beneficial to the situation than getting the family to contact the Jehovah's Witness society, who will be advising the patient rather than you. Therefore Option E will rank above Option C.

3. Option B ranks last because there is no attempt to do anything constructive.

Scenario 52 ANSWER: DABCE

1. Reporting child abuse is mandatory, even if you only have a suspicion. The doctor does not have authority to remove the child from the parents; only social services or the courts can do that (Option D).

2. Failing that, admitting the child to the ward will remove him from harmful environments and the staff can observe the child so that there can be no further abuse whilst the child is an inpatient (Option A).

3. The police should be called if the assault is happening at the exact moment, but the police are not appropriate to investigate child abuse (Option B).

4. When you have a suspicion of child abuse, <u>it doesn't matter what the parents have to say</u>. Talking directly to the mother or father is inappropriate, and could in fact result in retribution to the child on discharge (Option C).

5. Discharging the child (Option E) without follow-up or investigations is completely inappropriate.

Scenario 53 ANSWER: EABDC

1. The girl is 16 and competent (nothing suggests otherwise so assume she is) and therefore she is able to make her own decisions. As such there is no reason why you should not provide prenatal care. Therefore Option C will rank last.

2. We are now left with options which involve providing prenatal care and we now need to look at the confidentiality aspect. The girl is entitled to full confidentiality and you should do your utmost to respect it. Therefore Op-

tion A (saying nothing) is more appropriate than Option B (saying something only when asked), which in turn is more appropriate than Option D (Informing the mother).

3. Option E (encouraging the girl to talk to her mother) is a better option than A, B or D because it is a matter of time before the parents find out that she is pregnant. It will be important for the girl to receive support from her family both before and after the birth. Therefore Option E ranks first.

Scenario 54 — ANSWER: ACEDB

1. Both the husband and the wife are your patients; however, though you have a duty of care towards both, it doesn't mean that you can breach the confidentiality of either of them. You could only do that if the behaviour of one of them placed the other one in serious danger of harm or death; that isn't the case here. Therefore, the less you say to the husband, the better. As such Option A (saying nothing due to duty of confidentiality) will rank first, with the added bonus of the apology.

2. Option C (saying that his wife is better placed to answer the question) will rank close second on the basis that, although you are saying nothing, there is no apology and you are hinting that his wife knows the answer (which is inadvertently saying something, even if it is minimal).

3. Options B, D and E all involve communicating something to the husband. Option B is breaching patient's confidentiality, whereas Options D and E involve deflecting from the truth; so option B will rank last.

4. Option D is actually a lie whereas Option E is something which is possible, though not true in this case. In both cases, the patient may be angry that you are not specific but with Option E you are not actually lying as such; you are just being evasive. Option D is basically rubbish and could undermine your credibility and therefore the patient's trust in you (with the internet, it won't be long before he works out that you lied to him). Therefore Option D ranks above Option B.

Scenario 55 ANSWER: BACED

1. If an individual is deemed to be competent, they can refuse treatment for a <u>physical</u> illness if they understand the consequences of refusing it; they cannot be compulsorily detained for this reason. It is possible, however, to detain under the Mental Health Act an individual who is mentally ill, in order to treat the mental disorder only. This is because the mental disorder could affect the capacity of the patient to make decisions about the treatment of the mental disorder itself, which clearly has happened in this case. Options A and B allow the patient to be treated for her mental disorder, with Option B ranking ahead of Option A since only her schizophrenia needs to be treated under the Mental Health Act.

2. Of the remaining options, detaining the patient for treatment of her abscess (Option C) is wrong, but will allow the patient to be safe in a hospital monitored environment, as opposed to letting her go without adequate treatment (Option D). Following the patient up with a home visit (Option E) is preferable to just discharging the patient (Option D).

Scenario 56 ANSWER: DBACE

1. Anorexia nervosa can lead to a loss of functional ability to make competent decisions. For example, the physical illness of starvation may impair cognitive function (through hypoglycaemia) making it hard for patients to weigh the risks and benefits of their decisions.

2. This does not mean doctors are always ethically right to force treatment onto the patient. If she is competent, respect for autonomy is a major consideration. It requires a full psychiatric review in order to assess what treatments are available rather than commence her on treatment straight away. Thus Option D is vital in getting a psychiatric opinion and should be ranked highest, before considering admitting her under the Mental Health Act (Option B) for treatment via the psychiatric team (Option A).

3. Forcing a nasogastric tube down her and force feeding her (Option C) should be ranked fourth since it should not be attempted in the A&E setting, and it would also disrupt the patient-doctor relationship. Option E (discharging her) is completely wrong, since we have established she has hypoglycaemia and deranged electrolytes. This should be corrected.

Scenario 57 ANSWER: CBDAE

1. Referring the man to a specialist needle exchange centre (Option C) will result in managing the patient in a safe clean environment under an established programme. Giving the man needles and syringes from the hospital (Option B) will only encourage him to do whatever he does in a less suitable environment. However Option B is better than not giving the man needles at all (since it will incentivise him not to reuse or share needles with others).

2. If you are to refuse to give him needles and syringes, referring him to a drug cessation programme (Option D) would be better than simply turning him away (Option A).

3. Calling the police in (Option E) to search the man is the worst possible option as it may put the man off from seeking medical care in future.

Scenario 58 ANSWER: BCEDA

1. The GMC advises that you, wherever possible, avoid providing medical care to anyone with whom you have a close personal relationship. Examining and assessing the child outside a clinical practice setting may mean that she does not receive the same standard of care as other patients, and puts you in a position where your clinical judgement may be clouded by your relationship with the child and her parents. Therefore Options A, D and E would rank lower than the other two options.

2. For a suspected throat infection, the best option would be to ask the father to take the child to the local out-of-hours service for assessment (Option B), rather than the local A&E (Option C). The child could then be properly assessed and managed.

3. Assessing and examining the child and giving a suspected diagnosis to the father would be the next appropriate option (option E). Your diagnosis may not be correct and may lead the father to take decisions which are inappropriate, but at least you are not prescribing anything.

4. Option D (telling him that it is probably nothing) would be gambling that it is indeed nothing. If the father is worried then he should seek medical at-

tention for his daughter and he would also expect something more proactive from your part. If you are going to risk giving a diagnosis, you should at least examine the daughter. Options B, C and E are all more appropriate.

5. Option A is inappropriate since you cannot write private prescriptions as an FY1.

Scenario 59   ANSWER: DEBCA

1. In a question like this, it is easy to jump to conclusions. Some may think that the consultant is behaving inappropriately with the patient; others may think that there must be a good reason for his behaviour. After all, he may have been reassuring a patient who was distraught. Never ignore the issue; but, equally, don't take drastic action until you have got your facts right.

2. Option A (doing nothing and making assumptions) is the worst option. If there is a potential problem, you cannot ignore it.

3. Option C (reporting to the Clinical Director) is a possibility but it is quite strong. You would have to have reasonable concerns about the situation before you can go to the Clinical Director and therefore there are steps that you should take before pursuing this option. The fact that it ranks fourth does not mean that it is a wrong thing to do. It is just not as appropriate as some of the other options given the scenario and its ambiguities.

4. The three remaining options (B, D and E) are all about finding out more about the situation and seeking advice. They are therefore to be preferred over the other two.

   • Option D (enquiring with the consultant once the patient has left) is the preferred option because it enables you to discuss the situation with the consultant in a non-confrontational manner. Based on the outcome of that discussion and whether you believe the consultant, you can then act appropriately.

   • Option E (seeking advice from the ST5 next door) comes next because you can get a different perspective from an appropriate trusted colleague. He may know the consultant's manner with patients better than you do and might think that it is more likely to be appropriate for that consultant than not. On the other hand, he might have come across complaints from other people before and can make a more informed decision than you can. The fact that he is running the clinic next door also means that the advice will be immediate, which is an advantage.

- Option B comes third because sending the patient out would be quite a brave thing to do, especially if nothing untoward was happening. If the consultant was simply reassuring the patient, the consultant and the patient might find your actions a little bit offensive. You would need to think twice before doing this because you could irritate your consultant and the patient (hence why it comes third) but it might still be an appropriate action to take if you feel strongly that there is cause for concern.

Do not jump to conclusions
Generally speaking, most doctors conduct themselves ethically. If you notice something strange, there is usually a good explanation for it and you should avoid jumping to conclusions. It does not mean that you have to ignore warning signs, but simply that you should approach the situation tactfully to make sure that you do not create more problems than there were in the first place. Explore the facts as appropriately as you can before escalating the matter.

Gauge the level of appropriateness of the physical contact
The question talks about a consultant with his arms around the shoulder of a patient. Although you should avoid physical contact with patients if possible, there may be situations where such behaviour could be accepted. If you are given a question with a more suggestive wording (such as seeing a consultant in an embrace with a patient or kissing a patient), your approach should be a bit less subtle because the breach of duty will be more obvious.

Scenario 60   ANSWER: CDBEA

1. As the patient has offered you a small gift with no obvious bad intentions (i.e. there is nothing that the patient wants in return), there is arguably no reason to refuse the gift. In fact, refusing the gift may upset the patient and may negatively affect the doctor-patient relationship. The best option is Option C (informing your seniors). This would ensure that the patient is

happy about it and will also ensure that you are not seen to be behaving inappropriately.

2. Option D: accepting the gift (as it is small and therefore within guidelines) and then making sure you tell the patient it is not necessary is the second best option. This means that the patient is fully aware that your ongoing care is in no way related to their gift. It is not as transparent as Option C though.

3. Option B: accepting the gift and thanking her is third best. Again the acceptance is within guidelines but there is no declaration of the gift here (as there is in Option C) or anything to ensure the patient knows this is not a "bribe" or will in any way change the care they receive.

4. Option E: stating that you would check the guidelines AFTER accepting the gift implies that you do not know what the rules are. If that were the case, you ought to decline the gift until you have checked the guidelines.

5. Option A: refusing the gift as it is against guidelines is incorrect. Most Trusts will allow small personal gifts as stated above which is why this is the worst option.

Scenario 61 ANSWER: ADCBE

1. It is best not to jump to conclusions, and to get your facts right first. Hence, Option A (asking the patient and your colleague for more details) is the most appropriate. After all, your colleague might have had a perfectly good reason for performing the examination but simply failed to record it.

2. Option D (seeking advice from trusted senior colleagues) is also a good idea as it ensures that the issue is investigated without being too formal for the time being. It will help establish the facts before you decide whether to take the matter further. However, it would be inappropriate to go to a senior colleague without first identifying whether there is a real cause for concern. Therefore it comes second in order of appropriateness.

3. The three remaining options are harsher in their approach and are each, in some way, flawed:

- Option C sees you failing to elicit information from the patient as you report to the Clinical Director straight away. This is not necessarily a bad move, but you would consider it once you have raised the issue more informally with other senior colleagues first (Option D).

- Option B informs the patient that your colleague is in some way guilty; it is therefore inappropriate. If the patient has been the victim of an unscrupulous doctor, then you will need to have a discussion with your seniors about the matter before approaching the patient. You cannot tell the patient that the examination might have constituted an assault without having first gathered all the facts. The best that you can do in the first instance is to tell the patient that you will look into it and get back to her.

- Option E (contacting the GMC) is worse than Option B because it ignores the hierarchy within your team and launches the full systemic procedure against your colleague when there may not be a cause for concern. You would only consider going to the GMC if your seniors failed to act appropriately. Hence Option E must follow Option B in the order of appropriateness.

Scenario 62   ANSWER: CABED

1. Though strictly speaking, DNR orders are the doctor's decision, the decision to issue an order should be taken within the context of the patient's thoughts on the matter (it is after all their life that we are talking about here). It would also be important to involve the relatives in the discussion– the dream outcome being that everyone agrees with the decision made. As such, though there is an element of truth in Option E, it is not quite correct that the patient's and relatives' stance does not matter. Such response could be seen as insensitive.

2. Having said that, Option E is not as bad as Option D (documenting that the patient should be resuscitated), which (i) contradicts your own stance on the matter, and (ii) only takes into consideration what the relatives have said (you don't know if the patient agrees with this since you haven't talked to him). In addition, documenting that the patient should be resuscitated may give the impression that this was discussed with the patient and may therefore mislead colleagues who read your notes. Therefore Option E and Option D rank bottom, in that order.

3. Options A, B and C are more appropriate as they take the time to establish the best way forward. Involving the patient in the discussion directly and documenting his thoughts (Option C) would be important. It would be important to make note of the fact that the patient gave his opinion in front of his relatives (they may give a different opinion when the relatives have gone) so that the notes reflect the context in which the discussion took place. Asking for help would also be appropriate if you felt you may not be able to handle the discussion. Calling the on-site on-call registrar (Option A) would be your preferred option as (i) the hierarchy is there for a reason and (ii) he is on site and will therefore be of more use than a consultant at the end of the phone (Option B). So Options C, A and B rank top in that order.

Scenario 63   ANSWER: CBDEA

1. In this situation, it is important not to jump to conclusions. We are told that the patient is physically impressive and has been in prison in the past for violence, but that doesn't mean that he will be violent in the hospital environment today. So far there is no indication that he is threatening at all. Having said that, it would be wise to be cautious. Therefore, asking for a chaperone (i.e. Option C) would be a good idea. It will make you safe and will also be the least inconvenient option for the patient. Therefore this option ranks top.

2. Failing this, the other option which enables you to remain relatively safe is to ask to see the patient in a room where you are close to others whom you can rely upon if the situation turns sour. Option B will therefore be the next appropriate option.

3. Both Options D and E involve someone seeing the patient on their own. Sending a nurse on their own to see the patient is the coward's way out. You should take responsibility for your own actions and not expose others to harm simply because it suits you. So Options D and E will rank next in that order. Note that both of these options rank below Option B (bringing the patient to a closer room) because your safety is more important than a mere inconvenience to the patient.

4. Option A comes last because you can't refuse to see a patient unless you really feel so threatened that it will result in your being harmed or it will impair your judgement. Because there is no threat so far, it would be prefer-

able to go and see the patient, even if it means popping your head round the door to ask a few questions than to simply refuse to see the patient. You would only refuse to see a patient if you felt that you were at risk of being assaulted, for example if you were told here that the patient was to see you in an isolated room, was drunk and agitated and had threatened staff and patients. In practice, you would most likely involve a security guard, but unfortunately the option is not part of the list here.

Scenario 64 ANSWER: CDBEA

1. There is a definite problem here, and you cannot "do nothing"; therefore Option A comes last.

2. Option E (confronting the colleague at the team meeting) is the least effective of the remaining options. It will probably ensure that she never does it again, but it will humiliate her and will cause a problem within the team.

3. Option C (talking to the colleague and warning her) is the best option. You should try to discuss the situation with the colleague first and make her realise that she has done wrong. She must understand how her behaviour affects the team and that it is not acceptable. Because there is no discernible effect on patient safety, there may not be a need to report the matter straight away; hence why warning her is a better option.

4. Option B (informing your consultant) is harsh because it does not give your colleague the opportunity to redeem herself. Because it is an issue that has affected the junior doctors directly (they have had to cover for her), it makes sense to address the situation as a team first (Option D). The team can then decide how best to address the matter, either by having a strong word with the colleague, or by reporting the matter to one of your seniors (particularly if it happens often). Hence Option D will come before Option B.

5. Some candidates may find it hard to decide whether the first option should be Option D (discussing the matter with fellow junior colleagues) or Option C (discussing with the colleague directly and warning her). The reason Option C ranks before Option D is that it does not spread the word too much and gives your colleague a chance to put things right without feeling that she is being picked on by all her fellow junior colleagues. Although Option C seems a little harsher, it is commensurate to the nature of the

problem and allows the situation to be sorted out, whilst enabling her to save face.

Scenario 65 ANSWER: DEBCA

1. The fact that he is watching the images on his own computer makes no difference: it is the very act of looking at the child pornography that matters. Therefore Option A should rank last.

2. Options B (police), D (senior colleague) and E (medical personnel department) are fairly easy to rank. An "inside to outside" policy here, as elsewhere, is best so, in order of appropriateness, you should first consider talking to:

    *   A senior colleague; then
    *   Medical personnel; and then
    *   The police.

    You do not want to undermine the people you work with, so you should always go to a senior before going any higher. If one is not available or if, collectively, they are not doing anything about the problem (highly unlikely in this case) then you may consider escalating the matter by taking it to a different level (first to Trust level, then outside). Ranking the police as the least appropriate of these three options does *not* mean that it is inappropriate to call them. We are simply saying that it is not necessarily your role to call them and that, before the police are called, a range of internal people (senior, HR) should be involved.

3. The main problem is with Option C (sending an anonymous note) because, although it looks like you are doing something, it is rather counterproductive. It might stop him watching it at work but it won't stop him watching it anywhere else. You are also instilling fear in your colleague (which may have an impact on his performance), while not actually trying to resolve the fundamental problem. The real issue here is child protection. No need to be too subtle about it. This would rank just before "doing nothing".

Scenario 66 ANSWER: ABCDE

1. This question is a trick question where doing nothing is actually the right thing to do! The scenario deals with gossip about someone you don't know getting drunk at a Christmas party at which you were not present. Why bother? Option A is therefore the most appropriate.

2. The rest follow in the order of escalation, i.e. the higher up you go and the more people you involve, the less suitable the option.

Scenario 67 ANSWER: BACDE

Most people would tell you that they would just ignore it. However, since we are in a medical selection context, you could at least make an effort to see if he is okay! It does not cost much and no one could fault you for doing this. Hence B has to be the most appropriate option.

1. The truth is that you would not want to launch a full medical team after every drunken person in the street if there is no real emergency. Therefore C, D and E, which are quite involved when there is nothing to suggest an emergency, would be over the top (he is only vomiting; there is no mention of haematemesis). Option A is therefore second best.

2. If you did decide to do something then E would be pointless since you are near A&E and the tramp hardly justifies monopolising an ambulance in such circumstances. Therefore E comes last.

3. After that, it is a case of choosing between taking him to A&E yourself or fetching someone from A&E to take him in. If you want to be a Good Samaritan, do it in a way that is least disturbing for your colleagues. There is no need to take an A&E member out of A&E for this. You should do it yourself.

Scenario 68 ANSWER: DAEBC

1. Option D (reassuring the consultant and taking over) is the most sensible and safest approach since you are well trained. Whether you can get away

with it will very much depend on the consultant's ego. But in this case his ego will come second to patient safety.

2. Option A (basic life support whilst waiting for the arrest team) is also safe. In fact this is what would happen if no one in the team had ALS training. However, it comes second to Option D because you are only providing basic care to the patient (albeit safe care) and not the maximum care that is provided for under Option D.

3. Option E (letting the consultant lead the arrest whilst another consultant arrives) is unsafe because you have to wait for help and you are doing nothing in the meantime to stop an unsafe situation; but at least expert help should be quick arriving.

4. Option B (allowing the consultant to continue and discussing with him later) is unsafe and you are not acting in the patient's best interest.

5. Option C (not following his orders but doing your own thing) is chaotic. Team members will get confused between mixed messages. The consultant will be undermined and all this will build resentment. In fact, the patient is likely to be worse off than if the consultant handled the whole event by himself (Option B).

Scenario 69 ANSWER: DAECB

1. This is a situation where we don't know if the colleague has had one gulp or more, why he is drinking and whether he has a chronic drink problem or is succumbing to a temporary weakness. Therefore it is important to act with a degree of diplomacy.

2. On the other hand, there is an issue of fitness to practise. In the worst-case scenario, the colleague may be unsafe. In the best-case scenario, he may not be unsafe but he will smell of alcohol, which is unprofessional.

3. Options B and C both encourage you to drop the matter and are therefore the least appropriate options. In cases of alcohol intake while at work, you cannot ignore the patient safety aspect. Out of the two options, C is marginally preferable because at least you are warning your colleague of potential future action on your part; in Option B you are simply giving up.

4. Options A and D are both appropriate options because you demonstrate that you understand the gravity of the situation and that you are (i) talking to your colleague about it and (ii) involving senior colleagues. Option D involves a greater degree of tact than Option A and is probably more appropriate in the circumstances. If the question had actually said that the colleague was visibly drunk then you may have preferred the stronger approach dictated by Option A.

5. We know that Option D should be the first option and that Options C and B should be the bottom options. The main problem is whether Option A (informing his educational supervisor) is better than Option E (discussing the issue with the other juniors) or vice versa. Whereas Option E allows you more flexibility and is less draconian than Option A, by seeking advice from other colleagues you are spreading rumours/gossip which could undermine the drinker's standing in the team. The key to the dilemma is in the level of efficiency achieved by each option in helping the matter to a resolution. In Option A you are being upfront with the colleague and, with your colleague's knowledge, you are going to a relevant person who will be in a good position to discuss and resolve the matter. With Option E, you are going to the rest of the team behind your colleague's back. Furthermore, those colleagues will only be able to advise you and, having received any advice, you will still be on your own in making your decision. Option E therefore looks attractive but will yield little, while Option A, although more unforgiving, will ensure that something gets done. It is also the more open approach of the two. Therefore Option A ranks over Option E.

Scenario 70 ANSWER: CBDAE

1. The question says that the patient is 17 years old. She is therefore still a minor (being under the age of 18) and you have a child protection responsibility. This scenario deals with a disturbing situation but there is no hint in the question that you must deal with it at this very minute; indeed, whilst she is in MAU she is safe. Therefore, if in doubt, and given that you have time in front of you, you should seek advice from other members of your team before doing anything. If you are about to breach a patient's confidentiality, it is always best to make sure that you have got it absolutely right. Therefore Option C ranks top.

2. Your duty is to protect the patient. Had the patient been over 18 and with old small bruises then you could argue that the onus would be on her to

make a decision for herself and that all you could do would be to provide advice. However, the scenario is quite clear that she is only 17 and that the bruises are very severe. Therefore there is some justification for breaching confidentiality to ensure that she is not placed in danger physically, socially or mentally. Option B (contacting social services with or without consent) and Option D (asking permission to contact social services, and doing it without telling her if she refuses) are both possible candidates. Option B is the most drastic but you are breaching confidentiality with the patient's full knowledge. Option D takes a more cautious approach but leads you astray by stating that you will notify social services without her consent. If you are to breach her confidentiality then you should at least tell her otherwise it could impair the relationship and trust that she has in you. Therefore Option B, although seemingly harsher, is more suitable, closely followed by Option D.

3. It remains to allocate Option A (doing nothing) and Option E (contacting her partner) to the last two places, which means having to decide whether it would be best to have a discussion with the patient's partner or to do nothing. Going to the patient's partner could have disastrous consequences; he may feel threatened and, given that we are told that he is a violent criminal who takes drugs, one could ask what would be achieved by such a discussion other than more trouble for the patient. We can therefore conclude that, on balance, it would be safer for the patient if you did nothing than if you had a discussion with her partner. By giving her time to reflect, she may well come to a safer decision by herself later on. This places Options A and E in fourth and fifth position respectively. This is a rare example when doing nothing may actually be better than taking an action which, on balance of probabilities, could prove very detrimental to the patient.

Scenario 71   ANSWER: EACDB

1. This is an urgent job; this person may need a blood transfusion. Calling the FY1 on call (Option E) and asking him to chase the result urgently is the best option as he has access to the patient files and can document the findings clearly in the notes. This is essential because, if something happens later on during the night, the team will have all the information at its fingertips.

2. Calling the nurses on the ward (Option A) to hand over the responsibility of contacting the FY1 urgently is your second best option because it allows access to the notes and there is a ward team member who will chase it up. It is obviously not as good as contacting the FY1 directly.

3. Chasing the result over the phone from home (Option C) is an option, particularly if you ensure that any abnormal result is then handed over. There is no comment in the stem as to what you would do if the result was normal. Even if a result is normal, it needs documenting in the patient notes, which makes it more difficult if you are not on site. Now that you have gone home, it would be more appropriate for the matter to be handled directly by people who are on site as (i) it is their shift and therefore their direct responsibility and (ii) they have everything they require at their fingertips. Handling the matter from home might lead to some confusion and so your role should be ideally confined to assisting them rather than doing it yourself. This option therefore ranks third.

4. Asking the registrar to review (Option D) is not ideal. You, as the FY1, were tasked with chasing the blood result. The registrar may need to review them later but to make best use of a senior doctor's time, it is essential that the blood result is there first.

5. Adding it to the nurse's list of "ward jobs" (Option B) does not address the urgent nature of this result and is therefore not appropriate. It may be several hours before the FY1 on call gets to the ward to complete the non-urgent list of jobs. By that time, it may be too late.

Scenario 72 ANSWER: DABEC

1. The simplest thing to do would be to extend the deadline (Option D). You made a mistake in leaving it to the last minute and therefore any solution that doesn't make other people pay for it is preferred. Under Option D, you will have to own up to your mistake, and you will take full responsibility for getting the audit done. A delay in the audit will have no real consequences.

2. Options A and B involve making someone else suffer an inconvenience because of your mistake. In Option A, the department will be inconvenienced by having to pay a locum (unless the consultant decides that another colleague should cover for you, in which case that other colleague

would be inconvenienced). In Option B, you are asking a colleague directly to cover for you. There are two reasons why Option A is more appropriate than Option B: (i) it would be inappropriate to get a colleague to cover for you without the consultant being informed, so Option A is best; and (ii) you can't just impose your will onto the other FY1. The consultant may be able to come up with an alternative idea. So Options A and B rank next in that order.

3. Option E: by staying overnight and working through the night you will get tired and may be potentially putting your patients at risk the next day. The question makes it safer by telling you that you have the option not to go to work the next day, but that would still put pressure on your other colleagues. Option E ranks fourth because it is potentially unsafe or may cause substantial disruption to the team.

4. Option C (using a reduced set of data and multiplying the results) is unethical. You would get into serious trouble for doing that. It is dishonest and would call into question your integrity as a doctor

Scenario 73   ANSWER: BADCE

1. Option B: by approaching your consultant, and informing him of the prescribing policy, you are raising this issue without confrontation. The consultant will then be able to justify his actions or choose an alternative.

2. Option A: by saying nothing you are not addressing the problem directly, but by contacting the microbiologist you are checking whether the Augmentin is approved in this case. If it is, you can then prescribe; if it isn't, you can then ask the microbiologist for advice. This option is less effective than Option A because, although you maintain the patient safety, you are not making the consultant aware of the problem. You are therefore helping perpetuate the issue.

3. Option D: by saying nothing you are not addressing the problem directly. The ST3 will be able to give you advice, but cannot tell you if the drug has been approved by the microbiologist and is unlikely to override your consultant's decision. At the end of the day, someone will still need to contact the microbiology department; you might as well do it yourself. That makes Option D less appropriate than Option A.

4. Option C: by refusing to prescribe the drug, whilst you are adhering to the prescribing policy, you are not communicating the problem to your consultant, or doing anything to look for an alternative.

5. Option E: this goes against hospital prescribing policy and, even if you prescribe it, the nurses will not be able to give it. Protocols are written for a reason and we should always adhere to them. Documenting will not achieve much here. It shows your honesty, but it does not do much for patient safety. If you disagree with an order given to you or you feel it is not appropriate then you should not go ahead.

Scenario 74 ANSWER: CDABE

This scenario is about balancing important personal issues with work related issues, in a context where patient safety is not affected (the ST2 is currently assisting and, at worse, he may have to delay going to his course). The criteria for ranking will therefore mostly be linked to the impact your actions have on other colleagues and your ability to communicate with others.

The phone call to the bank is important and urgent. Having your bank account frozen could seriously impact on your finances, your stress level and your life, which in turn may impact on your performance. One important criterion which features in the list of attributes tested by the SJTs is your ability to take responsibility for your own health and well-being. As such, and considering that there is no impact on patient safety, it will be important that you make that quick call if possible.

1. Option C: with this option you are clearly communicating the truth. The ST2 will be slightly inconvenienced but you are being honest and realistic and the others will know where they stand.

2. Option D: this will equally signal to the team that you are coming, although it will cause a delay without any explanations. In practice you will be in theatre within 10 minutes, ready to fulfil your responsibilities, but it would be nice to let the team know how long they are likely to wait for you. Hence Option D ranks lower than Option C.

3. Option A is not ideal because it involves another FY1 who has nothing to do with the problem. It will ensure that the theatre is covered and that the ST2 can go to his course. But with this option you are pleasing one col-

league (the ST2) at the expense of another (the FY1). Under the previous options, the ST2 would only have been inconvenienced for 10 minutes. Under this option, the other FY1 could be inconvenienced for a long time. Hence this option ranks below Options C and D.

4. Option E is the worst option because (i) it is dishonest – you are not too busy, you just need 10 minutes to sort something out; (ii) it places the burden on the theatre team to find someone else when they are busy and (iii) it is not very proactive. It is also fairly rude. On the basis that sorting out your personal problem comes at a disproportionate cost to the team, this option ranks last. It would be more appropriate to simply turn up and leave the call until later (Option B).

Scenario 75 ANSWER: DACEB

1. Option D: nurse practitioners are very experienced and valuable members of the team. If she is working alongside you in the clinic, she should be the first person you go to for advice.

2. Option A: calling your ST3 is a good idea as he will have more experience than you and will be able to advise you, or come to review the patient. You should respect the other members of your team and not bypass them by going to your consultant (as in Option E).

3. Option C: the anaesthetic team is always involved in the pre-operative work-up of complicated patients and they should definitely be informed of this complicated case.

4. Option E: your own consultant should be involved in the case, but from a pre-operative assessment point of view the junior members of your team (STs) and the anaesthetic team will be the best guides for you; hence this is ranked fourth.

5. Option B: if you are unsure, you must always ask for help. Knowing your own limitations is one of the key aspects of being a good doctor. By only doing the routine investigations in a patient who is potentially very complicated, you may cause more problems down the line, particularly if their operation has to be cancelled due to lack of pre-operative work-up. For this reason, Option B comes last.

Scenario 76 ANSWER: DCABE

1. Option D: by talking to senior members of the team, you are asking for help and advice. If you are fatigued and are potentially putting patients at risk, you should stop working. However, you cannot just "abandon ship" and need to make sure that the team knows what is happening.

2. Option C: once you have spoken to the medical team involved, the next port of call is management. In the daytime, this would be medical personnel. At night, there is always a bleep holder for emergencies, often a senior member of the nursing team.

3. Option A: by Leaving at 10pm, you are addressing your fatigue problem and you are still showing signs of good teamwork by helping out the late FY1 and the rest of the team on call. It would be much better, however, to be honest as in options D and C above.

4. Option B: by simply leaving because your "shift is over", you are paying no attention to the team, who will be one person down whilst waiting for the other FY1 to turn up.

5. Option E: the question clearly states that you are exhausted. By staying indefinitely, you are not looking after yourself or your patients. If you stay, your colleagues will assume that you are fit, whereas if you leave they will be able to take steps to ensure that patient care is properly covered. Therefore Option E ranks last.

Scenario 77 ANSWER: CBADE

1. The question states clearly that one mistake has endangered a patient's life and therefore there is no time to waste. The ST5 could harm patients in the very near future and immediate action should be taken to stop him. Option C (going with the other FY1 to see the on-call consultant) would ensure this happens, whilst also providing support to your colleague.

2. Option B (advising the other FY1 to go straight to the consultant with his concerns) would also be appropriate. The option does not contain the element of support that Option C offers and so ranks second.

3. Options A, D and E do not have an immediate impact on the situation and therefore rank afterwards:

    - Option A will not stop the ST5 there and then but has the major benefit of ensuring that at least the mistakes come to light and are dealt with at some stage by senior colleagues.

    - Option D does not achieve much in terms of sorting out the ST5, but at least it will protect you from being exposed to difficult situations.

    - Option E will achieve nothing other than placing your fellow FY1 in a difficult position.

    Therefore options A, D and E will be ranked in that order.

Scenario 78 ANSWER: ADBCE

1. Option A: if a problem is brought to your attention then it needs dealing with. By spending a few minutes working out what the relative's concerns are, you can point her in the right direction to resolve her worries. For example, if the concerns are clinical then you should direct her to your consultant; if there are nursing concerns then you should direct her to the ward sister. By dealing with concerns promptly, we can often avoid formal complaints; therefore anything that you can do immediately to ensure that the relatives feel they are listened to and that the problem is dealt with will avoid an escalation of the complaint.

2. Option D: the PALS service is the patient's advocate. They should be involved if patients and relatives have concerns about standards of care, not just for formal complaints. By explaining PALS' role and directing the relatives to the service, you will ensure that the complaint is addressed properly.

3. Option B: by advising the relative to talk to the nurses, you are avoiding dealing with the concerns yourself and are simply transferring the problem to someone else. If the nurses can't deal with the complaint and consequently end up referring the relative to someone else, she will feel that she is being messed about. If you are going to send the relative to the nurses, you should at least make sure it is a senior nurse. For that reason, Option B is not as appropriate as Option D.

4. Option C: you can discuss general matter with relatives provided the discussion mentions nothing about confidential patient matters. The concern from this relative may be a general comment relating to all patients, e.g. the ward is dirty, the food is cold, etc. and not necessarily about the patient in question. Even if it relates to the patient in question, the complaint may be of a general order, e.g. the test results that are awaited are not yet available and the patient is becoming anxious about it. Until you find out what the concern is, quoting patient confidentiality as a reason not to talk to the relative is inappropriate and could decrease the patient's and the relative's trust in your team.

5. Option E: by confronting the patient about his relative's comments, you are placing both the patient and the relative in a difficult position. You are effectively intimidating the patient by putting him on the spot; this cannot be good for his morale and your relationship with him.

Scenario 79 ANSWER: CEABD

1. The patient has informed you he wants you to stop and get someone else. Therefore by continuing to attempt the cannulation (Options B and D) you are going against his wishes. Option D (getting a nurse to hold the patient down) is the extreme version of it (i.e. physical assault). It should therefore rank last. Option B represents a more gentle approach; you are apologising and explaining that you are junior, which is good, but, at the same time, the explanation comes rather late and you are essentially telling the patient that they have no option but to stick with you. By proceeding against the patient's wishes, you are also committing an assault but in a more gentle way than under Option D.

2. Option C is the most appropriate option because you are retaining control of the procedure and therefore can learn from it, the patient's request will be granted because a senior colleague will be present, and you have taken the trouble to talk to the patient about the problem that he is experiencing. By offering this compromise, you are also asking for his consent, which he still has the option to refuse to give.

3. Option A and E are virtually identical except that Option A does not offer an apology and therefore ranks below Option E.

Scenario 80 ANSWER: BDCEA

1. The whole point of protected teaching is that it is protected. As such, unless there is an emergency which can't be dealt with by anyone else then you shouldn't have to be disturbed. Therefore Option B (telling the nurses that you are unavailable and that they should contact someone else) will rank highest.

2. Option A (ignoring the bleep), however, will rank last. You should never ignore a bleep; there has to be some response to it. You should at least get further information or offer alternative personnel to ensure patient safety.

3. The other three options all involve you leaving the teaching session:

   • Option D (calling the ward to ask them to call someone else) will enable you to answer the bleep and will give an opportunity to the nurses to mention the nature of the problem and therefore mention any emergency if required.

   • Option C is about the same as Option D except that you are actually going to the ward. It will make you absent from teaching for a longer period of time. Once you are there, it may be hard to leave again. Calling is a preferable option.

   • Option E: going to review the patient may not be necessary if someone else can do it, and you will miss out on the protected teaching. You should not do this routinely.

Scenario 81 ANSWER: EBADC

1. Option E would be the most productive approach. By asking for a list of patients, you are not wasting valuable time trying to find suitable cases (it should be quick for the consultant to give you that list since he was just about to run the session himself) and you are helping out. Doing something is better than doing nothing.

2. In Option B you are essentially complaining about your inexperience. It is not a very proactive move, but it leaves the door open for the consultant to

give you some quick advice and reassurance. So whatever the outcome, you will have raised your concerns and he may have listened to them. It is better than just cancelling the session.

3. Options A and D are both cancelling the session. If you were to do that, it would be better coming from you (Option A) since the consultant has a genuine emergency and should not be delayed.

4. Option C is very aggressive and unfair if the emergency is genuine. You would only consider complaining to the postgraduate tutor if the consultant made a habit of cancelling the teaching, which is not the case here.

Scenario 82 ANSWER: EDCAB

1. This is a potential complaint and, if the patient has concerns, her health, well-being and recovery may suffer. If there are genuine concerns regarding her care, they need addressing. The main issue here is that you can't actually get any useful information from the patient. Without knowing more about the problem, it is hard to deal with it. So, although informing the consultant (Option C) seems like a good idea, it won't actually help much in the first instance. A better option would be to discuss the issue with the son, so that you can understand exactly what the nature of the problem is in his own words. This would be best done face to face with the patient being present, but an alternative would be to discuss it over the phone with the son, with the patient's consent. Therefore Option E will rank first, and Option D will rank second.

2. Before thinking of sending the patient to PALS, it would be more appropriate to involve the consultant. If you do that, it would be preferable if the move came from you (Option C) instead of leaving it to the patient to raise the matter when she next sees him (Option A).

3. PALS is there as the patient advocate and not just for complaints. Whilst it is desirable to give PALS information to any patient who wishes to discuss issues (whether good or bad), this option states that the reason is to "formalise" their complaint. At the current time, there is no complaint; the patient is simply worried. The priority should be to have a good dialogue with the patient and her son, rather than go down a formal route which will delay the handling of the matter. Hence Option B ranks fifth.

Scenario 83 — ANSWER: CADEB

1. If you feel a colleague may be getting overworked, the most appropriate approach would be to ask whether they need help, without forcing yourself onto them. This is what Option C achieves safely since you are waiting for the end of the day to use your spare capacity to help them out. As such you are not neglecting your own patients.

2. Option A (just keeping an eye on the colleague) ranks second because it is less proactive but it still ensures that you look after him whilst not interfering too much. If he is happy, why not leave him to it? It is less appropriate than offering your help, but nevertheless a workable solution.

3. Alternatively you may wish to raise your concerns with the FY2 (Option D). Note that at this stage you are not concerned by your colleague's performance; you only have a feeling that he may be working too hard. Hence, sharing your concerns with someone more senior would rank lower than trying to help your colleague or looking after him. In any case, in most circumstances, it is best to address any issue directly with the individual concerned rather than involve a senior too early.

    The ranking would be different if the question had mentioned that the colleague had already made several mistakes. If that were the case, you would need to rank Option D (informing the FY2) before Option A (doing nothing but keeping an eye on him).

4. You should never "insist" that another team member does something (unless of course a patient is at risk, which is not the case here). You can offer to help, or ask others to offer to help but, at the end of the day, it is the doctor who has to take responsibility for his/her own work pattern and workload. So Option E ranks fourth.

5. Option B ranks last because you are placing a heavier burden on yourself early on in the day before you have even started dealing with your own patients. You have a patient list to look after and you should always ensure that your patients are safe and that all tasks are completed before taking on other doctors' responsibilities. If you don't do that:

    *   You run the risk of burning out.
    *   You may end up neglecting your own patients.

- Some of his patients may take longer to deal with because you are busy with your own patients.
- It blurs the boundaries of responsibility and increases the risk of error.

This option is therefore not entirely safe. If you want to help with his patients, the safest way to do it would be to wait until you have completed all your jobs (Option C) so that you know how much spare capacity you have.

Scenario 84 ANSWER: EBCAD

1. This question is about blood taking and in many circumstances the patient will give you implied consent, e.g. by extending their arm to give you access. In this scenario, you should do your best to get the patient to consent but if she can't speak English, the fact that she is cooperating will be sufficient. However, in the exam you will need to rank the options in accordance to what you should do and not what you would do; therefore any options which consist of actively seeking consent will prevail. The best and safest approach should therefore be to call a family member so they can translate, i.e. Option E.

2. Approaching the patient with simple English (Option C) will not be much use since she can't speak a word of English, but showing the procedure using the equipment (Option B) will be more useful. Therefore Option B will rank next, followed by Option C.

3. Option A (taking the blood) is not that different to Options B (showing the equipment and mimicking the procedure) and C (attempting to explain in simple English), since you will be showing the equipment to the patient as and when you are about to take the blood and the patient can't speak English anyway. However, there is no hint that you are attempting to communicate with the patient, and therefore Option A will rank fourth.

4. Option D comes last because the question states clearly that the blood is needed today. And in any case, this will leave the phlebotomist with the same problem of not being able to explain the procedure to the patient.

Scenario 85 ANSWER: BAEDC

1. Option A (discussing handover expectations with all FY1s) and Option E (asking the colleague why there are so many jobs on the list) are two options which will tackle the problem head on, with Option A being the least threatening. However, it would more appropriate in the first instance to raise the issue with the colleague directly in a sensitive way (Option B)

2. Option D (avoiding the colleague) simply pushes the problem onto someone else and so does not constitute good team playing. Still, it is better than Option C (i.e. teaching the FY1 a lesson by giving him more work). That approach is vindictive and will simply put more pressure on him. It will also mean that he will hand over even more jobs at the end of his shift.

Scenario 86 ANSWER: BCEAD

1. You are missing part of the ward round and therefore not attending to your patients. It would be tempting to rush to the ward without taking any coffee; however, you also need to eat and drink in order to make sure you provide your patients with the care they deserve.

2. We are all occasionally late. As long as there is a genuine reason for being late and it is not a recurring event, you will be forgiven for this short absence. It is imperative, however, that you look after yourself and ensure that you eat and drink regularly to prevent yourself becoming ill whilst on long days. Paging your registrar and informing him of the delay (Option B) would be the best approach. It will only delay you for a short while but you will soon be there and, when you get there, you will be fully performing.

3. Option D is potentially unsafe. You don't know how long the ward round will be or if you will have time afterwards to fetch your coffee. If there is an urgent matter to deal with, you may not be fully functional. As such, Option D should rank last on grounds of personal and patient safety.

4. Option A is not professional at all. Others (including patients) won't necessarily understand why you are jumping the queue. It will give a bad image of doctors and should therefore be avoided. It is, however, a better option than Option D because it is safer.

5. Option C (waiting for your turn) is more appropriate than Option A (jumping the queue). There is no emergency and the ward round is in hand. Waiting 10 minutes won't make much difference to the situation. In this context, waiting your turn is more appropriate than playing the "I'm a doctor" card (Option A).

6. We have now ranked options BCAD in that order. Option E (asking the secretary to queue for you) remains to be ranked amongst those. Consider the following:

    • Joining the ward round without food or drink may make it difficult for you to focus.

    • The ward round can run without you (indeed, they did not wait for you to start it).

    • Your secretary is not your slave and she also has her own work to do in relation to patient care so that would cause her some inconvenience.

    • You would get food and drink quicker if you waited yourself.

    On the premise that there is no major urgency in joining the ward round, that it would be quicker to wait yourself and that it would inconvenience someone else, Option E ranks third.

Scenario 87   ANSWER: CBDEA

1. If the GP has prescribed the medication then he should be the one correcting the mistake (Option C). The patient won't be admitted for another 2 weeks so the GP has time to sort things out. You could do it yourself on advice from the ward pharmacist and then inform the GP of the change in a letter; however, the contradictory advice may confuse the patient. Therefore though both Options B and C would be appropriate, Option C is better.

2. Leaving a message with the GP's receptionist is not ideal. The message may not get to the GP intact and a mistake could be made. But at least you have raised the matter with someone who is likely to help out with the problem. This would therefore rank third.

3. Placing the onus on the patient to discuss the matter with the community pharmacist (Option E) causes several problems:

- That will only happen in 3 days' time.

- The patient may not fully understand the problem.

- The community pharmacist does not have the power to change the prescription and so will either do nothing, or will contact the GP (which he should already have done before anyway if he had spotted the error when the patient first went to pick up his medication).

- It alerts the patient to the error behind the GP's back without proper communication. There are more effective ways of raising awareness.

This is therefore not an effective way of dealing with the problem, though it does at least make someone aware of it.

4. Option A (writing a critical incident form) would be pointless since the mistake was not made by you or any of your hospital colleagues. This is a matter for the GP. So Option A would rank last.

Scenario 88	ANSWER: BCEAD

1. If you are having a meeting, whether impromptu or not, you should make sure that there is proper cover on the ward. The text does not specify whether the patient needs antibiotics because she has an infection (in which case you would need to resite the venflon soon) or as a preventive measure for surgery (in which case, you still wouldn't want to leave it too long so as not to inconvenience the rest of the team). Either way the care of the patient will be more important than your impromptu meeting, which can be rescheduled.

At the same time, you are having a break after a very long ward round and you are also discussing important matters. One of the criteria tested in the exam is your ability to take responsibility for your well-being and your own health, so if you can find a solution that enables you to get the work done by appropriate people whilst enabling you to have your break then that's even better. As such Option B is the best approach.

2. Option C (going to the ward straight away) is a suitable alternative, as you will put patient care first, but not as ideal as Option B, which enables you to get everything done (break and patient care). This is followed by Option E (recommend that the nurse finds someone else), which will get the job done, though not with the same team spirit as you are putting the onus on the nurse to sort the matter out.

3. Option A (making the nurse wait) is inappropriate without knowing the degree of urgency; it does not give the impression that your patients take any kind of priority. Option D (telling the nurse that you are on a break) is rude and does not remotely give the impression that you will get round to doing the job anytime soon. Those two options rank last in that order.

Scenario 89 ANSWER: EBCDA

1. From the clinical presentation, it is unclear whether the patient has high risk factors for HIV. Rather than agonising over whether and how you should get blood from the patient and whether you may be at risk of having HIV, the best approach would be to contact someone in the HIV team or in Occupational Health so that they can advise you on what you should do, the need to test yourself, the possibility of being medicated and the risks that you are exposed to. You can then make a decision about what should be done. So Option E would come first.

2. If you were to do a blood test on the patient then you would need their consent (unless there are exceptional circumstances, e.g. the patient is unconscious – and even then the matter is contentious because the test is not in the patient's best interest, but in your best interest). So Option A (using the pre-operative blood samples) will rank last. If the patient has not been consented for HIV testing then you can't just use an existing blood sample taken for something else in order to test for HIV.

3. All three remaining options involve consenting the patient for HIV and then testing if consent is given. Those options are all valid but at various levels:

   • Ideally you should not get involved in the process because the matter concerns your own health. It would be more appropriate to get the ward sister to do it. So Option B ranks above Options C and D.

- Using a disposable number is not advisable since the patient would need to be treated if they were found to be HIV positive. The more you document, the better. So Option D ranks lower than Option C.

Scenario 90 | ANSWER: ECDBA

1. Out of all options available, Option E (deleting the prescription from the drug chart until the allergy is confirmed and prescribing an appropriate antibiotic) is the safest option as it allows you to actually stop the penicillin from being given and causing a possible anaphylactic reaction. This should rank first. The other options do not confirm possible reaction to penicillin before the new medication is given.

2. Options B, C and D allow you to confirm whether the patient is actually penicillin allergic, though there is a possibility that all those sources could actually be mistaken. The best source of information would be the patient himself (he might even be able to tell you the severity of the reaction). Asking the patient would also allow you to complete the drug chart allergy section (the patient may have more than one drug allergy), so that in the future you can refer to it. So Option C ranks above Option B (asking the nurse) and Option D (asking the registrar).

3. Asking the registrar (Option D) is the next best option, as the antibiotic of choice might have been discussed at the ward round, and the team would normally have taken care to check any drug allergies there and then before prescribing. However, you cannot rely on the registrar's memory specifically; you should check it directly with the patient himself, especially if the drug allergy section was not completed.

4. Nurses also have a duty of care to ensure that the patient is not penicillin allergic before giving the penicillin, by checking for any penicillin allergic red wristbands. However, asking the nurse (Option B) would be less preferable than asking the registrar as the decision to prescribe penicillin would have been made during the ward round with the FY2 and the registrar present; thus it should be discussed with them first.

5. Apologising to the patient (Option A) when the situation is unclear, the penicillin allergy is not confirmed, and the drug has not been stopped is the least appropriate option of them all and should rank last.

Scenario 91   ANSWER: CBDEA

1. The boy is 18 and competent. Therefore his decision to refuse transfusion will have to be accepted. Hence Option B (respecting the boy's wishes and refusing to transfuse) will rank high.

2. However, it would be more appropriate to contact the Jehovah's Witnesses society (Option C) as they may be able to provide advice to the patient and to you on a suitable compromise and/or replacement products. Since you were simply going to stand back and refuse the transfusion (as you should do), Option C is more appropriate because it opens other possible avenues to enhance the patient's chances of survival. Basically you have nothing to lose and everything to gain by involving the Jehovah's Witnesses society.

3. Option D (contacting the lawyers to seek a court order to enforce the transfusion) will be pointless since the patient is competent and therefore no court order will overrule his wishes. That would therefore not be an appropriate response to the situation (basically you are wasting your time) but since it will still result in the patient not being transfused then it ranks third.

4. The other two options may or will result in the boy being transfused and therefore are the least appropriate:

   - Option A is the more inappropriate since it totally defies the boy's wishes.

   - Option E is inappropriate too because the decision does not belong to the parents but since there is a possibility that they will refuse the transfusion and that you will comply with their wishes, that makes it less inappropriate than Option A.

Scenario 92   ANSWER: EDABC

It is the patient's prerogative to refuse an HIV test, even if this potentially goes against her own interest and the interest of the foetus. In addition, the patient here is the woman, and not the foetus, which has no legal rights until it is born. As a doctor though, you have a duty of care towards the woman and in this case it means that you will have to explore every possible avenue before you can admit defeat. Therefore:

1. Option E (leaving it to the next appointment) is the most appropriate option because you are respecting the patient's wishes for not being tested, but you are leaving the door open to ask her again next time you see her, without being coercive. By that time she might have changed her mind, talked to other people, looked at internet resources, etc.

2. Option D (offering a referral to an O&G consultant) is the next most appropriate option because you are also respecting her wishes but you are allowing someone else with a different degree of expertise to review the situation and provide advice to the patient. The O&G consultant will have more experience than you in dealing with such matters and may have a better understanding of the issues that are causing her refusal. The patient will also have the option not to attend the appointment if she doesn't want to.

3. Option A is essentially giving up on the patient and will rank third.

4. The two remaining options (B and C) rank last in that order, on the basis that you are going against the patient's wishes. If you are going to do so then you might as well be honest with the patient about what you are doing. Hence, Option B ranks above Option C because you are informing the patient.

Scenario 93   ANSWER: EADBC

1. Patients who are 16 years old or above have the same legal capacity to consent for medical procedures as anyone above 18, without requiring consent from the parent/guardian.

2. When it comes to refusing treatment, the situation differs in England & Wales and in Scotland:

   - In Scotland, a competent minor can refuse treatment.
   - In England, Wales & NI, a competent minor cannot refuse treatment. If they refuse then the parents' opinion will be taken into account. If the parents also refuse, then you cannot go ahead. If the parents consent, then you have a problem because it is hard to do an intervention or

give treatment to someone who doesn't want it. In a situation where the parents agree and the child disagrees, it is always best to make sure that the child is on board; you really want to avoid having to re-strain the child to force a procedure onto them.

Therefore, whether you are in Scotland, England, Northern Ireland or Wales, your purpose will be to convince the child that the procedure is in their best interest without coercing them. The SJT questions are tested and used throughout the UK, and are specifically written in a way that lo-cality does not matter. So although the law may differ between countries, this question will have a universal answer.

3. By discussing with the patient her thoughts and fears of going for surgery, you will be able to identify what is driving their refusal. Perhaps they have a phobia of needles, or one of their friends had a bad experience. Thus Option E should be ranked first.

4. Giving the patient a stat dose of sedatives and sending them for surgery (Option C) is the least appropriate of all the options. In all countries within the UK, this would lead to loss of the child's trust; in Scotland, it would ac-tually be illegal. It should be ranked last.

5. Option A (admitting the patient for observation) is more appropriate than Option B (discharging her and telling her to come back to A&E if needed) or Option D (asking the mother to talk the child into having the procedure):

   • By admitting the child for observation (Option A) you can clinically monitor their pain levels and deterioration. You can also send the pa-tient for surgery if it becomes more urgent; you won't be able to do that if you discharge the patient (Option B).

   • Her mother can try to discuss, with the child, her decision again (Op-tion D). This may bring into light any fears that the child might have; however, since this is early appendicitis, there is no urgency to pro-ceed with the operation right now. Therefore, at this stage, it would be over the top to try to push for surgery tonight.

6. Discharging the patient (Option B) is the least safe of all the available op-tions, and so Option B ranks last of those three options.

Scenario 94   ANSWER: BDACE

1. If the patient who is HIV positive refuses to have his status made known, doctors should respect his wishes unless the failure to disclose the status results in putting others at risk of infection. In cases where the sexual partners are not easily traceable then it is hard to do, but if the partners (e.g. his wife) can be found then they should be notified. Here we are told that he has unprotected sexual intercourse with his wife and she is therefore clearly at risk.

2. The emphasis should always be on trying to divulge the information with the patient's consent and, ideally, the patient should give the information himself. As such, the best option would be to allow the patient a reasonable amount of time to inform his wife, but to do it yourself if the patient does not comply (Option B). It can take time for the patient to come to terms with his HIV status. The patient would not be putting the wife at risk of infection whilst an inpatient (no sexual contact in the ward), and so some delay can be accepted (thus Option B ranks over Option D). Informing the patient that you will breach confidentiality is better than not telling him at all, so Option D ranks over Option A.

3. Options C and E both involve the risk that the husband may not tell his wife. Option C ranks higher than Option E because, at least you are attempting to remind the patient (who now has had time to think about his situation) of the necessity to tell his wife about his HIV status. This leaves Option C ranking fourth. Thus Option E should rank last, as it would leave the wife at risk.

Scenario 95   ANSWER: AECDB

1. Option B (keeping the patient on the medication) is the only option that continues the medication despite the potassium level being rather high already. High potassium is cardiotoxic, and Option B could result in the patient's death. Option B therefore ranks last.

2. When a clinical error has been made, even when no harm has come to the patient, the clinician should apologise and make the patient aware of what happened before any formal self-reflective practice can take place. Thus, Option A (stopping the medication and notifying the patient) ranks first.

3. Options C, D and E involve reflecting on the clinical issue.

- Completing a critical incident form (Option E) will ensure that the incident is properly investigated and that the right lessons are learnt. Several people were involved in the chain of events which led to the mistake being made. Completing an incident form will help improve clinical practice.

- Completing a yellow form for the MHRA (Option D) is not entirely suitable in this situation – it is for adverse drug effects (Sando-K has been prescribed to give the patient more potassium).

- Completing a reflective entry in your own e-portfolio (Option C) will allow you to acknowledge and learn from the error but will not ensure that lessons are learnt at team level, unlike Option E.

Thus Option E ranks second, Option C ranks next and Option D thereafter.

Scenario 96   ANSWER: AEBDC

1. As the person doing the procedure, you are responsible for your own actions (especially if it goes wrong). If you are unsure or inexperienced, you should ask for help from senior colleagues. This means that Options A, B and E rank higher than Options C and D. Since the need for the ascitic drain is urgent, you cannot delay action and therefore Option B ranks below Options A and E.

2. Asking the on-call consultant to come in (Option A) should be your first option. It may be more convenient to call another senior colleague on shift at the same time with the necessary experience, but the surgical registrar does not have the duty of care for that patient (Option E). It will therefore rank second.

3. Reading up on the procedure and attempting the procedure (Option D) is better than trying to work your way through it without any information or support at all (Option C).

Scenario 97 ANSWER: ACBED

1. When patients complain, it is in everyone's interest to be open and honest with them. In this particular scenario the patient is extremely angry and asked to talk to the consultant; making sure that he sees the consultant would ensure that the situation is not aggravated and will allow him to vent to someone who can deal with the problem swiftly and objectively. Option A is therefore the best way to proceed.

4. Apologising by proxy (Option B) is worse than Option A (asking the consultant to talk to the patient) or Option C (apologising yourself). It would not be fair on the registrar and would also most likely anger the patient further because he would not be seeing the consultant.

5. Options D and E are ranked lower down because PALS's job is to advise patients and not doctors. Avoiding further contact with the patient without attempting to apologise is unacceptable. Going to PALS proactively at least shows some insight into the situation. At least you are not avoiding the issue altogether, hoping that it might go away. Therefore Option E ranks before Option D.

Scenario 98 ANSWER: DEBAC

1. In providing assistance to the injured player, you have now assumed a duty of care. As such, the care of the patient should be your first concern until you are able to hand over to a suitably trained professional.

2. Option D (staying with him until the ambulance arrives) thus ranks first, and is followed by Option E (handing over to a first aider until the ambulance arrives).

3. Going back to the field is always a bad option; however, going over to check on the batter (Option B) is much more suitable than handing over to a non-trained professional to keep an eye on things (Option A).

4. Leaving the player by himself until the ambulance arrives with no one to keep an eye on things (Option C) is wholly inappropriate and should be ranked last.

Scenario 99 ANSWER: DACBE

1. This scenario tests your professionalism. Doctors should act with integrity at all times, be trustworthy and honest. The patient is your first concern and as such you should assess the patient fully and then carry out any necessary management. The coach's "advice" should not play a part in this.

2. As such, ignoring the coach's request (Options A and D) and dealing with the patient effectively is a priority. By telling the coach firmly that you disagree with his "advice" (Option D), you are dealing with the clinical matter, you are communicating appropriately and are not seen to be providing any unfair advantage to any teams. Therefore Option D ranks higher than Option A.

3. Option C (assessing the player and staying longer than necessary) would be slightly unprofessional but would ensure that the patient is safe. Calling the ambulance (Option B) regardless of your assessment would be inappropriate; but it would still be safer than simply leaving the pitch (Option E).

Scenario 100 ANSWER: AEDBC

1. The patient may be unfit to drive and therefore represents a danger to the public. In such cases, medical professionals should make attempts to tell the patient to stop driving, and ask him to inform the DVLA about his condition.

2. In this case the patient refuses to accept the fact that fits can impair his ability to drive, and is continuing to drive. As such, you are duty bound to contact the DVLA to report the patient (Option A), and you should notify the patient that you have done so. Thus Option A ranks above Option E.

3. If the patient disagrees, normally a second medical opinion should be sought (Option D); however, that is only applicable in cases where patients have agreed to stop driving in the meantime so as to minimise risk to others.

4. Options B and C rank last since you get neither a second medical opinion, nor a guarantee that the DVLA will be informed.

Scenario 101 ANSWER: CEABD

1. Patient confidentiality is paramount, and you have to be even more careful in situations where you deal with people who have been arguing. In situations where a known relative enquires about the well-being of a patient, you would reasonably be able to assume that the patient would consent to the relative to be updated in general terms, i.e. you could tell the mother that her son is "doing well" or "making progress", but you wouldn't be able to reveal any specifics without explicit consent. In this scenario, those options do not appear in the list, therefore before you say <u>anything</u>, it would be wise to speak to the son first to find out whether he wishes for you to disclose anything to the mother (Option C).

2. Asking the mother to speak to the son herself (Option E) is more constructive than refusing to speak to the mother outright (Option A).

3. Making the mother aware of any medical information (Option B) is wrong, and answering her questions (Option D) would be wholly inappropriate.

Scenario 102 ANSWER: CDEAB

1. You should obtain consent from the patient before she is anaesthetised. Although you may be under pressure to reach certain competencies, it is unacceptable to examine her when you have not obtained consent. Thus refusing the procedure (Option C) should be ranked first.

2. Option D also enables you to refuse to do the procedure and to do it at the next opportunity when you can get consent; however, it shows a degree of dishonesty. As such it ranks below Option C.

3. All other options involve examining the patient, all of them with no consent from the patient. The most "honest" of all is to do the procedure and then inform the patient (Option E). The husband cannot consent on the patient's behalf (Option A), but at least you are notifying a next of kin rather than just doing the PV examination. Consent Form 4 (for unconscious patients) (Option B) is not suitable in this scenario, since there is no medical reason for you to conduct a PV exam, and it is not in the patient's best interests. This is the worst option as nothing is communicated to anyone

and you are just trying to find a sneaky way not to have to mention it to anyone.

Scenario 103   ANSWER: EDABC

1. It would be inappropriate to assess the patient's acne and provide advice on treatment in such a public place and on a day off when there is no specific emergency. You wouldn't be able to prescribe anything if you needed to anyway. The best option would be to advise the patient to go to her local GP on a routine appointment for a check-up (Option E). Telling her that you are not a skin specialist and to see another doctor (Option D) is slightly more dismissive and non-specific, but it is an acceptable way of rejecting the patient's request.

2. Telling the patient to go to the out-of-hours service (Option A) is not the correct use of resources since the matter is not that urgent and can be left to the GP to deal with. It would be even more wrong to use A&E resources (Option B).

3. Ignoring the patient (Option C) despite the fact that she has recognised you is unprofessional and rude. In some circumstances, acknowledging a patient in the street may be seen as a breach of confidentiality but, in this case, she has approached you, and so she understands the context.

Scenario 104   ANSWER: CAEDB

1. The patient has capacity and clearly does not want further help. As such you would have to respect her wishes and maintain full confidentiality unless you believed that she was at risk of serious harm or death which, according to what she is telling you, does not seem to be the case. Therefore going to the husband (Option D) or the police (Option B) would rank low; going to the police is a greater escalation and should be ranked last.

2. The best that you can do for the time being is help her by giving her information and contacts she can use to gain practical advice and seek refuge if things get worse (Option C). This is the most productive of all remaining options. Making an outpatient appointment (Option A) will help you set up times where you can monitor the situation and identify any escalation but

won't help her deal with the problem. Giving contact details of a self-defence class (Option E) is likely to escalate things further and could incite retribution.

Important note:
In cases of domestic abuse when there are children around, in practice you may also need to contact social services so that the children are protected, even if the children are not physically being abused. This is not part of the options here and so it does not matter in the context of this question.

Scenario 105 ANSWER: DCEBA

You need to attend the arrest as soon as possible, but not at the expense of your own health and safety. It is tempting to rank Option C first but it causes you to neglect yourself. Running to an arrest is also not ideal. The best ranking is therefore as follows:

1. Option D: you need to attend the arrest situation straight away but should never put yourself in danger by running there. Taking your lunch with you should only take a second and will ensure that you have food for later.

2. Option C: in this option, you are neglecting yourself, as you need to eat. It is not ideal to run to an arrest call.

3. Option E: it is not ideal to run to an arrest and it is unsafe to run whilst eating.

4. Option B: by finishing your lunch you are delaying attending the arrest call. It is your responsibility to attend as "soon as you can".

5. Option A: by finishing your lunch and then buying water you are further delaying attending the arrest call. You need to attend as "soon as you can".

Scenario 106 ANSWER: ABEDC

1. You must find out from the patient whether it is truly an allergy and, if yes, what sort of penicillin allergy he has had. Perhaps the other FY1 is already

aware that the allergy results simply in a tummy upset but has not documented it in the discharge summary. Thus Options A and B rank first. Option A ranks over Option B because a potentially dangerous mistake was made and this needs to be properly recorded so that lessons can be drawn from the incident. Option B does include a reflective element but will only result in the FY1 (as opposed to the whole department) learning from the incident.

2. Unilaterally changing the antibiotic when you don't know the patient's history ranks lower (with Option E ranking over Option D because you notify the change to the other FY1). Ideally you should not be signing a discharge summary or a TTA that you did not prepare yourself.

3. Option C should rank last as there is a huge risk that the other FY1s would sign the TTA and discharge summary without reading it and noticing the penicillin mistake, particularly as you have not informed the ward sister of your colleague's error.

Scenario 107 ANSWER: BCAED

1. The patient consented to you doing the ABG and therefore you can't simply let the medical student perform it unless the patient has been duly informed and has consented to it too. Neither Option D nor Option E involves getting consent for the medical student to do the procedure and therefore those two options will rank bottom. Option E is more appropriate than Option D because you are supervising the student and are not leaving him to his own devices (he has never done one before).

2. In this instance, the medical student has not done an ABG before, and has only read the procedure in books; it would be more appropriate to let him observe it in the real setting (Option B) with you doing it first.

3. The next best option would be to allow the student to do the procedure under your supervision (Option C).

4. Option A (signing him off without doing the procedure) would be safe for the patient but would be unethical as you could not sign off on the procedure if the student has not actually done it. However, although Option A is dishonest and unethical (and should be avoided), it is better than letting the student perform the procedure without patient consent, which would

constitute an assault on the patient. In this case, dishonesty will rank higher than assault. You also know that, though you will have signed off on the procedure, the medical student will have many other opportunities to do some and learn from those opportunities. So the consequences are not as bad as doing a procedure on a patient who has not consented for it.

Scenario 108 ANSWER: DCBEA

1. As a junior doctor you are not entitled to speak on behalf of the Trust, however good your intentions. The press can easily misquote you or quote you out of context (even if you ask for reassurances) and you must ensure that the journalist contacts the right person. This means that Option A should come last. Similarly, Option E comes in fourth place as it implies that you yourself will be answering the journalist's questions; it is better than Option A though, because you are postponing speaking to the journalist.

2. Options B, C and D are all realistic options and the ranking can be determined as follows:

    *   Option B (telling her you can't speak to her and putting the phone down) is the rude option; such an attitude is not strictly necessary. It does not reflect well on the Trust and you may find a comment in the article about no one being available for comment except for rude doctors. Since the other two options are more helpful and polite, Option B should come in third place.

    *   Options C and D both boil down to sending the journalist to a more appropriate person; however, in Option D she must do the work herself to find the right person while in C you are doing the work for her. The latter is unquestionably the more helpful course of action *from the journalist's point of view.* However, in this situation, it is not your responsibility to do the journalist's job for her (surely, treating your patients should take priority) and therefore you should rank Option D over Option C.

Scenario 109 ANSWER: BCEAD

1. Option D is dishonest and would flaw the results. It will make your work entirely useless and, therefore, is the worst option.

2. Three of the options refer to the way in which you would handle the data:

   - Photocopy and anonymise (B)
   - Copy on paper (C)
   - Take notes home (A).

   Option A is the worst of the three. Removing the notes from the hospital not only risks a breach of confidentiality should they fall into somebody else's hands, but also leaves you open to losing these notes for good (not counting also that no one will be able to access them for the entire weekend). Option C would be acceptable in principle but rushing the exercise makes it more prone to error. Option B is definitely the best option as it provides you with a reliable record while maintaining patient confidentiality. Therefore B, C and A should appear in that order.

3. Option E (postponing the meeting) should appear in third position between options C and A: it is more appropriate to cancel a meeting with your supervisor about the audit than to get the data input done by taking the notes home.

Scenario 110 ANSWER: BAEDC

1. As a rule, you can only breach the confidentiality of an adult patient in a few circumstances, e.g. if there is a risk of serious harm or death to a third party or you are the recipient of a court order. Such exceptions are not relevant here and confidentiality must be maintained. Option C is the only option that clearly breaches confidentiality and therefore must be the least suitable option.

2. Option D is deliberately misleading since it falsely confuses competence with confidentiality. Competence dictates whether you can take consent from a patient. This option therefore ranks fourth.

3. Letting the ST5 take the call would be more appropriate than misleading the father, but would be a coward's approach; hence Option E ranks third.

4. Options A and B are suitable for the top two places. However, Option A is dismissive towards the father, while Option B is not only more compassionate but is also less likely to cause communication problems later on during this admission. In this scenario, we know that the father is aware that his daughter is in hospital because he brought her there and so it is suitable to reassure him that she is okay, provided you do not divulge any medical information. If the question had said "a father is on the phone saying that he thinks his daughter was admitted and he is asking how she is" then you would not be able to say that she is fine as, by doing so, you would then be confirming to the father that his daughter is receiving treatment, which he wasn't initially aware of.

Scenario 111 ANSWER: ABCDE

1. This is a very serious issue, which could lead to unsuitable students qualifying as doctors. The problem should therefore be addressed as soon as possible. The deanery staff will need to investigate the extent of the problem and, if necessary, write a new exam paper. In order to investigate, they will need to contact those who came into possession of the paper and therefore Option A (confiscating the paper and reporting the matter to the deanery) should rank as the most suitable option.

2. Option B (reporting without naming the student) would also be effective as it would raise the issue at the highest level where something can be done about it. Admittedly, by not naming the student, you are protecting him (which could be interpreted in many ways) but at least you are giving others in charge the power to sort the problem out. Note that there is no issue of confidentiality here. The student is not a patient. You must treat the incident sensitively but if need be you can name the culprit.

3. Option C (advising the student to throw away the papers without looking at them) is a feeble attempt at resolving the problem. It is almost guaranteed to fail, but at least you tried (which is not the case for the two remaining Options D and E).

4. Option D (ignoring the matter) is, of course, unethical, as there is an obvious cause for complaint here; but it is still *marginally* preferable to propa-

gating the fraud by encouraging the student to distribute the papers further (Option E). In SJTs, doing nothing is often the worst option because in most cases you are expected to be proactive in resolving problems. However, doing something that makes things worse is obviously less appropriate than remaining passive.

Scenario 112 ANSWER: DCABE

1. Option D: until you have all the information about the patient, you cannot judge how important the call is and how urgently you need to attend. You already know the patient is conscious and has low blood pressure but there are a number of causes of this (including a peri-arrest situation and wrong blood pressure measurement). You should always listen to a request from the nurses and, only then, decide the priority of that request.

2. Option C: if you are overwhelmed with work and are struggling to cope, or if there is likely to be a long delay in attending a sick patient because you are busy with other sicker patients, you should always call on your team for help. Ensuring that you have the contact number of a doctor who can help the nurses will ensure they can contact them quickly. You should only do this once you have all the information and know the patient is not at immediate risk (making it less suitable than Option D).

3. Option A: a patient on CCU is usually a "sick patient". A hypotensive patient on CCU could be in a peri-arrest situation and, if you cannot get any more information or there is no one else to help, you should attend as soon as you can. You must, however, ensure that the patients you are with are "safe" and ideally walk quickly, rather than run.

4. Option B: if you are busy and cannot attend a patient in a reasonable amount of time, the nurses who requested your attendance should be made aware of the potential delay. This will allow them to decide whether they need to call someone else, or if the patient can wait for you. In addition, be careful about "telling" nurses what to do. They are valued members of the multidisciplinary team and should be respected. A much better way is to explain why you are delayed, offering them an alternative doctor to help (as in Option C).

5. Option E: a crash call should only be used if a patient requires the crash team's input, not because you cannot attend.

Scenario 113 ANSWER: EABDC

1. Option E: when a patient doesn't take their medication, it is important for you to find out why. In this particular instance, if you ask her the relevant questions and give her all the information relating to her medication, you can then assess if she has the "capacity" to make an informed decision. If she has capacity, based on the ethical principle of autonomy, it is the patient's right to choose whether they take prescribed medication. You should always then offer the patient a follow-up appointment in case they change their mind.

2. Option A: in this option you have not assessed her capacity or asked about her medication (as in Option E). However, offering her a blood test in 3 months' time will allow her GP to assess her thyroid function at that time. It also ensures a follow-up appointment in case she changes her mind about her reliance on homeopathic remedies.

3. Option B: telling patients to take their medication often doesn't work; it is much better to listen and then negotiate with them. In this option you are referring her to her GP, who will ensure all the relevant follow-up is performed. Option B ranks lower than Option A because there is more telling than listening and there is no specific timescale for going back to the GP.

4. Option D: It is not ideal to do nothing. You should always try to engage with the patient (Options E and A) to gain their trust.

5. Option C (criticising homeopathy): this is the worst option. Even if you do not believe in homeopathic medicine, you should not impart your own beliefs onto the patient. If they have capacity, it is their decision. If you do judge patients' choices, you are likely to lose their trust and they are unlikely to return to see you.

Scenario 114 ANSWER: EDACB

1. Option E: calling Language Line is the best choice. It means you can see the patient knowing with certainty that the interpretation is correct and it will not delay the consultation too much. A 6-year-old child is too young to translate effectively.

2. Option D: wherever possible, it is better to offer your patient their choice of interpreter, although using a young child who is unlikely to understand the conversation, and who you cannot be certain will translate appropriately, is obviously far from ideal. By asking if anyone else can help, you are giving the patient a choice. However, it is likely to delay the consultation since we don't know if a relative is close by and how long it will take them to get to the hospital) and will be less independent than using Language Line.

3. Option A: rebooking the patient would be the next option. It is not ideal because you would be using two slots for that patient and she will have to come back, but the use of the interpreter will make the consultation safe.

4. Option C: by engaging with the child and grandmother, you can assess fully whether it is appropriate to use the child, although it would be better to try to find an alternative (as in Option D). It is highly unlikely that you will be able to use the 6-year-old, but at least you will not antagonise your patient. Telling her not to use the child again also ensures that you will not face the same problem a few weeks down the line.

5. Option B: simply refusing to use the child is not helpful. How are you then going to communicate with the patient?

Note on using family members as interpreters
The suitability of using family members will very much depend on the issues that are being discussed. So, for example, it would be acceptable to use an adult to translate for their mother in relation to a condition such as asthma or diabetes. However, using a husband to translate for his wife who is requesting a termination of pregnancy would be inappropriate as the husband may have a hidden agenda and you would not be able to determine whether he is actually translating what you are saying accurately or conveying the patient's words truthfully. Take the whole context into account.

Scenario 115 ANSWER: CBEDA

1. Option C: even though your shift is ending, there are times when, as a doctor, you will have to work late. We have a duty to all our patients, both alive and dead, and to their relatives. It is always essential to document fully any clinical contact with a patient and, before breaking bad news, you must ensure you are in a fit state to face the family. You are of no use to

them if you are upset, tired or in a rush and you may affect their grieving in the long term if you break the news badly.

2. Option B: it is important to inform the relatives as soon as you can but you must document the clinical episode and ensure you are "ready" to face the family as in Option C. Handing the task over to someone else (Options E and D) should only be done if you have no alternative.

3. Options E and D: it is never ideal to hand over a difficult situation to another colleague but, if you do decide to hand this task over, it should be to the person who will be responsible: in this case, the doctor taking over from you, i.e. Option E.

4. Option A: sending a cup of tea to the family is commendable, but here it has a very dishonest purpose, which is to delay the inevitable. In any case it would be better to offer a cup of tea to the family after the news has been broken rather than before. The main problem with this option, however, is that you are asking a nurse to ask someone else to do the work, when it is your responsibility to ensure that the task is handed over. This can cause confusion or delay and might even result in no one taking on the responsibility to get the job done. This approach is therefore less appropriate than Options E and D.

Scenario 116 ANSWER: CBAED

1. Options C and B: building a relationship of trust between the doctor and patient in a situation like this is crucial. Because the patient is at severe risk of harm (and in this case, death), you are allowed to breach confidentiality if, after trying to negotiate with the patient, she still refuses to tell the police herself, or refuses to allow you to tell the police. However, you should only breach confidentiality if there is no way you can convince her otherwise. Therefore, "telling" her you will go to the police (Option B) ranks after Option C, which states that you "ask" the patient to allow you to make the call.

2. Option A: the police need to be informed of the threats but it is better to engage with the patient and get her on board, as in Options C and B.

3. Option E: supporting the patient is imperative, but "wishing her luck" effectively ends your support. You need to let the police know one way or the other, ideally with her support (Options C, B, A).

4. Option D: there are many things you can do, as shown above.

Scenario 117 ANSWER: BCEDA

1. As an FY1 you should not be asked to consent patients for procedures unless you are very familiar with them. In this case, it is possible that the consultant wants you to have a go as part of your training and so the options that enable you to seek consent under supervision will rank top. Therefore Options D and A will rank bottom and Options B, C and E will rank top.

2. Option B: you should never request a patient's consent for a procedure that you do not fully understand. By asking your consultant for help, you will learn how to consent a patient for this procedure. In addition, rather than simply saying that you don't know, showing some initiative by using the internet to do some self-directed learning in preparation will be to your credit. This option is also safe because the consultant will be with you and will be able to evaluate your approach as the situation unfolds and will be ready to take over if he needs to.

3. Option C: you could of course ask your ST5 to help, but as the consultant asked YOU to perform the consent, it is better to approach the consultant directly (as in Option B) rather than ask an alternative team member. In addition, this option is more passive than Option B, as you are not showing any personal initiative to learn about the procedure, instead simply relying on a senior colleague.

4. Option E: this option does not address the problem that the consent needs completing although is much safer than Options D and A, which both state that you perform the consent yourself.

5. Option D: it is inappropriate to teach yourself from the internet about a complicated surgical procedure and then seek patient consent. You must ask a senior colleague, as in Options B and C

6. Option A: you must never consent someone for a procedure that you do not know about. Option A ranks lower than Option D because in Option D you have shown some degree of initiative and gained some knowledge.

Scenario 118 ANSWER: EBDCA

The bottom line is that assisting someone to die is illegal in the UK, whether you are doing it directly, or arranging for it to happen. As such, all options which suggest that you should do so should be ranked lower than others.

1. Option E: in this situation you first need to assess if the patient has capacity and can therefore make a sound judgement, and then always assess the patient for depression. It is very common for the elderly to have an element of depression.

2. Option B: although you do not need a psychiatrist to assess his capacity, you may wish to refer the patient to a psychogeriatrician if you are either unsure of how to assess capacity or if you are worried about the patient's suffering from depression. You should never assume a patient is depressed. Always assess them first (as in Option E).

3. Options D and C: it is important to assess the patient's capacity but it is illegal to assist a patient to die in the UK. This includes giving help and advice about assisted suicide clinics overseas (although since you assess their capacity, Option D is better than Option C).

4. Option A: this option is blatantly illegal. It is ranked last as it recommends your direct intervention as opposed to simply providing advice.

Scenario 119 ANSWER: CBADE

1. You should not prescribe antibiotics unless they are clinically indicated, and your consultant certainly did not feel that it was necessary. For that reason, Option E will rank last. Besides, despite the warning that she should only take them if her condition deteriorates, since she feels they are indicated, you can presume she may not wait that long to take them.

2. Option C: the best thing to do is to refuse to give the antibiotics but to give the patient a plan that will reassure her that the matter is in hand. Option C achieves that by advising her to see her GP in 48 hours; by doing that, you provide an easy way for her to be reviewed if she develops a chest infection as she fears. The patient did tell you that it is hard to get an appointment with the GP but this is an issue that she needs to take up with the GP himself. If she needs to be seen quickly, she will be seen. She also has the option to attend walk in-centres that can also prescribe antibiotics and, at worse, come back to A&E.

3. Options B provides the patient with a second medical opinion via the GP, and will provide reassurance to the patient that if she does deteriorate then antibiotics will be made available. It is better than a flat out refusal (Option A) but less ideal than Option C because we know that the GP is not easily accessible in this case and that there is some reluctance from the patient to go to her GP surgery.

4. Option A is justified and an explanation for the refusal is given. But there is nothing constructive about it and the patient is left with no real solution.

5. Option D can cause confusion by suggesting that the GP will prescribe the antibiotics for sure. Not only will that approach simply push the problem onto the GP, it will also raise the patient's expectations and make the GP's life harder.

Scenario 120 ANSWER: CDAEB

1. Option C: your priority is the patient in front of you. This man could have lung cancer and so you must investigate him.

2. Option D: this man may have an infection, although a cough present for 6 weeks will inevitably raise the suspicion of lung cancer. In an AMU situation, antibiotics would be an appropriate treatment if there were signs of infection, once you have done the relevant investigations. Prescribing antibiotics based on a strong suspicion is not appropriate but, by referring him back to his GP, you ensure follow-up. However, it is obviously better to investigate the man while he is in AMU in order to prevent any further delays (Option C).

3. Option A: this man may have lung cancer but, until you have investigated, you cannot be certain. You must investigate first (as in Option C). In any case, admission is unlikely to be a suitable solution for this man; indeed, he could be treated as an outpatient since the question states clearly that he is "otherwise well".

4. Options E and B: you cannot refer someone to Oncology without any investigation or a diagnosis, so Option E is not a good option. However, it is better than Option B (telling him he has been mistreated by his GP) which does not address the man's illness at all. By telling the patient that the GP's care is inadequate, you are undermining the trust that the patient has in his GP and you are putting them both on a collision course which may be detrimental to the patient.

Scenario 121   ANSWER: ACBDE

1. Options A and C: a nurse practitioner is trained to order investigations and to interpret those investigations. If she ordered the ECG, it is her right to be able to review it. If she does not know what it means or if she cannot then treat the patient, she can ask for help. The question states that the patient is stable; there is no indication that the nurse practitioner is otherwise detained, unwilling to interpret the ECG, or struggling with it. By offering to attend immediately if the nurse practitioner requests it, you ensure that the patient is not put at risk while respecting the nurse practitioner's role. Failing that, by asking for more information about the patient and the urgency of this review, you can determine how quickly you need to attend (Option C).

2. Option B: this could be a myocardial infarction but, unless you ask for more information about the patient (as in Option C), you will not be able to make that judgement. One of the most important tasks as a doctor is to prioritise your caseload.

3. Option D: placing a patient with chest pain at the bottom of your list of things to do without having more information (Option C) is poor prioritisation. It is far better to over-prioritise chest pain (Option B) than to under-prioritise it.

4. Option E: the nurses who called you did not request the ECG; it was the nurse practitioner; so this option is unhelpful and may result in no action

being taken by anyone, thereby potentially placing the patient at risk. It is also condescending.

Scenario 122 ANSWER: ECBDA

1. Option E: although the scenario indicates that this is likely to be a tooth abscess, without examination you cannot be sure that you are referring the man to the appropriate specialty. Always assess patients before making assumptions about diagnosis.

2. Option C and B: assuming it is a dental abscess, you should not be treating this as you are not trained in dental care. Always refer to a dentist for assessment, but giving an explanation as in Option C is preferable to simply sending him away.

3. Option D: by prescribing painkillers, you are delaying the patient getting to the dentist for definite treatment. By the time the patient has attended the hospital pharmacy and waited for a prescription, he could be at his dental surgery and the dentist can prescribe analgesia for him as required.

4. Option A: you should not prescribe antibiotics for a dental abscess without the patient being fully examined by a dentist. Antibiotics will mask the symptoms and this should be avoided if at all possible.

Scenario 123 ANSWER: EDBCA

1. Option A: doing nothing is not addressing the problem and potentially is putting your training at risk. This should therefore rank last.

2. Your first port of call should be your appointed senior. If you cannot resolve the problem directly with her, only then should you seek help elsewhere. By asking her rather then telling her (as in Option D) you are using better negotiation skills and are likely to achieve a better result.

3. If you cannot resolve the problem with your ST5 directly, then it is much better to ask another senior to help you (Option B), who may also then be able to talk to your ST5, rather than to go outside of the team. Discussing

the issue with the Clinical Director (Option C) should only be undertaken if you cannot resolve the problem within the team.

Scenario 124 — ANSWER: BEADC

1. Option B: treatment of anaphylaxis includes: A (airway), B (breathing), C (circulation) and treating with adrenaline.

2. Option E: after assessing ABC, if you are unsure about what to do you need to ask for more help. In this scenario, the most appropriate help will be from a senior colleague.

3. Option A: putting out an arrest call without any assessment is an over-zealous reaction. Anaphylaxis can progress quickly and, if the patient loses his airway, you may need help from the crash team; however, there is nothing in the question that suggests that you need this degree of help currently.

4. Option D: basic life support starts with the assessment of ABC, but Option D does not address the need for adrenaline. It also talks about mouth to mouth; you are in a hospital environment and no mouth to mouth should be given. You should have equipment (face mask, etc.) to hand.

5. Option C: this does not address the need for adrenaline either. Reassuring the patient when further medical management is needed is the worst option of them all.

Scenario 125 — ANSWER: EDCBA

If a patient is competent then he has the right to refuse treatment and you must respect his decision. It is good practice to make sure that everything has been understood properly so that there are no ambiguities but you should not coerce the patient into changing a decision that seems irrational to you.

1. Option E has all the right ingredients. It assesses capacity (a valid thing to do when a patient is elderly and recovering from a UTI), communicates appropriately with the patient, documents everything and also makes it clear to the patient that it is not necessarily a final commitment. This

leaves the door open for a possible change of mind without coercing the patient or making him feel guilty.

2. None of the remaining options include checking the patient's capacity and therefore the safest option will be that which involves calling the consultant, i.e. Option D. Thus it should be ranked second.

3. Option C is the most basic, i.e. simply accepting the patient's refusal. There is nothing wrong with it but Options E and D are safer as they leave the door open for an assessment of competence and offer better communication with the patient.

4. Option A ranks last, as you are not qualified to consent since you only have a sketchy knowledge of the procedure itself.

5. Option B is inappropriate because it is not true that the patient is still thinking about his decision; you would be twisting facts. Telling the patient that the surgery is important is fine but bordering on coercive when taken together with the fact that you are asking him to reconsider his position. However, this allows a period of time for the patient to reconsider, as opposed to Option A in which you consent the patient for the operation when you are not qualified to do so and write the patient's decision down as fact. Therefore Option B ranks just above Option A.

Scenario 126 ANSWER: DCBEA

1. Option D: even though the child is not your patient, as doctors we all have a duty towards the protection of children. If you have noticed something which you are worried about, you must act on it immediately. The child's GP will know if the child is on a child protection register and will be able to follow the child up for you, or inform the health visitor.

2. Option C: asking the mother about the state of the child is a possibility, but it is better to be armed with facts before doing this (as in Option D).

3. Option B: without information from the GP (Option D) or from the mother (Option C), it is difficult to know whether there is any need for admission. If there had been any bruising or you had witnessed abuse from the mother, it would be appropriate to admit the child for further investigation (in which case Option B would rank higher) but the text of the question does not re-

fer to any bruising and there may be a justifiable reason for the child to be in the state that she is.

4. Option E: referring this child to the medical team who will look after the mother is inappropriate as it will delay the matter and the team may not act on it (although better than doing nothing as in Option A). It is better to telephone the GP (Option D), confront the mother (Option C) or admit the child (Option B) than to leave the child at potential risk.

5. Option A: this is the worst option. If a child is at risk, it does not matter if she is not your patient; it is your duty to act.

Scenario 127 ANSWER: AECBD

1. Option A: the patient's safety is paramount. One lung has disease/fluid in it (the side you should have aspirated) and you have just compromised the other side by attempting the aspiration. Once you know the patient is stable, both he and your consultant need to be informed. In cases of large mistakes, especially if it is a potential medical negligence case such as this, seeking your consultant's help at the earliest opportunity is very important. He will be able to assist you in dealing with whatever clinical consequences have arisen and will also be able to offer advice on how to best communicate to the patient. That is why Option A is better than Option E.

2. Option E: it is better to seek your consultant's help as early as you can. Taking your consultant with you when you apologise to the patient may help fend off a complaint. Trying to do everything by yourself is not ideal.

3. Option C: there is no apology here, which is why this ranks below options A and E.

4. Option B: this option does not include any explanation (as in Options A, E and C) or apology to the patient (as in A and E).

5. Option D: you must acknowledge the mistake and inform your consultant. Proceeding to aspirate the other side before ensuring there is no pneumothorax is potentially dangerous and this is therefore the worst option.

Scenario 128 ANSWER: ABCDE

1. It is likely that this man is having another heart attack. He is not your patient and should be seen in A&E as soon as possible. Option A ensures he receives treatment immediately. The sister can arrange to get him transported to A&E.

2. Option B: by agreeing to review the man straight away and arranging for him to be transported to A&E, you are addressing the problem. However, you do not add much to the solution by dropping your own work and handling the matter yourself when it would be just as quick to get the nurse to send him to A&E (Option A). You knew, as soon as the nurse told you of the situation, that you could not do much yourself about it. Therefore delegating the responsibility to the nurse would be more appropriate on the basis that it achieves the same result but does not delay the care of your own patients. If, however, the patient was arresting, you would go and see him and start treatment with the crash team.

3. Option C: this man needs emergency treatment in A&E or a cardiac centre. Admitting him under the medical team is not addressing the urgency of his need. It is, however, better than to simply get him to take ineffective drugs (Option D) or sending him to his GP (Option E).

4. Option D: in 30 minutes, he may not be in a fit state to even talk to you. More urgent action is needed.

5. Option E: sending the man to his GP is essentially risking his death. He needs immediate attention.

Scenario 129 ANSWER: DCAEB

1. This scenario contains issues of confidentiality and duty of care. Although you are not officially on duty, you still have a duty of care to your patient. She will need to address the issue of her diet at some point but this will be best done with her GP and the diabetic team. It is essential to preserve confidentiality and you should therefore not discuss this with her in front of other people. Therefore Option B will rank last.

2. Option D: by calling the patient's GP and asking for her to come in for a review, you are dealing with the problem but you are not breaching confidentiality in front of her friends (you do not know if she has told them about her diabetes).

3. Option C: saying hello ensures that the patient sees you. She does not have to tell her friends who you are (and therefore you have not breached confidentiality) but this risks placing her in a slightly awkward position; so it is less ideal than Option D. By calling her GP and asking her to go in for review, you are addressing the problem.

4. Option A: writing a letter to the patient is not a good approach. Aside from the fact that she may think you are stalking her, she needs to build a relationship with the doctor looking after her diabetes, i.e. her GP or endocrinologist. It is always better to refer your concerns to them.

5. Calling the on-call diabetic team (Option E) would be totally inappropriate as there is no indication for that.

Scenario 130   ANSWER: DAEBC

1. Though the patient has indicated that he doesn't want his family to know that he has refused treatment, it would be beneficial if they were made aware of it so that they can accompany him during his dying days. That would also enable them to prepare themselves for his death which, although they are not your patients, is important. The ideal scenario would therefore be to encourage the patient gently and sensitively to speak to his family (Option D). Failing that you will simply need to keep the information from the family (Option A).

2. All the other options involve divulging some information to the family against the patient's wishes and are therefore ranked lower. Option E is probably the option that is likely to release the least amount of information, with just a general comment about the patient's state of mind. It does not release any information that the patient has asked you to keep quiet about. Note that, in general, it is acceptable to inform relatives of a situation in general terms (e.g. by telling them that a patient is "doing fine" or "recovering well"). But in this case the patient has explicitly asked you not to mention anything to his relatives and so releasing any information about

his wishes or information that is hinting at his state of mind would be inappropriate.

3. Option B is very likely to lead to the release of information and you should not bow to pressure from the relatives to breach the patient's confidentiality.

4. Option C is a blatant breach of confidentiality. No information should be released without the patient's consent.

Scenario 131 ANSWER: BDCAE

1. The reasons for asking to prescribe Orlistat are very obscure. Although the patient is slightly overweight, he is not that far off the norm. At this stage there would be many other ways to lose weight than by taking a weight-loss drug. You should not write a prescription simply because someone has asked you to, and even more so if it is not in accordance with NICE guidelines. You should satisfy yourself that this is the right thing to do for the patient. As such you should refuse to prescribe the drug (Option D).

2. However, before you get to that stage you may wish to query the reasons behind the request (Option B). It could be for example that, though the patient is not severely overweight, he has personal image problems or some other condition for which Orlistat could be prescribed on an off-licence basis. Though asking for clarification may not alter your refusal, the information you will get may give you an insight into the patient's thoughts, which could prove useful in helping manage him. So Option B ranks before Option D.

3. The next option would be to refer the patient to an NHS endocrinologist for a second opinion (Option C). You would do this reluctantly because there is no real clinical indication as the guidelines are clear. It can't hurt but it will use up NHS resources unnecessarily.

4. Prescribing Orlistat (Option A) would be less appropriate as it is not clinically indicated and, if there was ever a need to deviate from a guideline, as a junior doctor you would not do so without consulting senior colleagues first. In this particular scenario, you would be prescribing purely on someone else's say so; as such it is not an appropriate option.

5. Option E (referring the private consultant to the GMC) would, however, be totally out of order since there is no indication that he is doing anything wrong; indeed the facts have not been established.

Scenario 132 ANSWER: EDABC

1. The patient has the right to know about the mistake even if no harm was caused. The right thing for you to do would be to explain, apologise and reassure (Option E).

2. Informing the consultant (Option D) is a good thing to do but, because you have not told the patient, it will then be down to the consultant to do it. It is your mistake and you should be the one explaining and apologising. Therefore Option D ranks second.

3. Option A essentially dumps the responsibility onto the nurse. She was not involved in the mistake. Since she is not part of the doctors' team, she will be less appropriate than the consultant to break the news.

4. Lying to the patient and blaming someone else (Option C) is a devious approach and is in many ways more unprofessional than not informing the patient (Option B). Not telling the patient would be a lack of openness but lying would reflect badly on your probity and professionalism. So Option C ranks below Option B.

Scenario 133 ANSWER: ACDEB

1. In this protected teaching time, it is important for your career development to attend the teaching sessions. Ideally you should have handed your bleep to the Education Centre before the teaching session started so that they could triage the bleeps and either contact your team or hold the message for you depending on the urgency.

2. Out of the options given, it is best to contact your team's SHO to answer the bleep on your behalf (Option A) so that you can go back to teaching whilst ensuring that there is no risk to patient safety. Failing that, you should go to the ward to see what is happening as you have been bleeped

repeatedly, which shows that there may be an urgent situation developing (Option C).

3. Telling the ward that you will only come when your protected teaching time is over (Option D) should rank lower as there may be a clinical situation that cannot wait until the end of your session.

4. Ignoring the bleep (Option E) is bad enough, but switching off the bleep and ignoring the current bleep is even worse (Option B).

Scenario 134 ANSWER: CBEDA

1. Although smoking cessation would provide the best prognosis to the patient, if you feel that salbutamol nebuliser would benefit the patient then you should prescribe it. It would be best practice to inform the GP (Option C, followed by Option B).

2. It is inappropriate to make treatment depend on smoking cessation. Your role would be to encourage the patient to stop smoking by whatever means possible. Options D and E are therefore less appropriate but Option E ranks above Option D because you are at least starting treatment.

3. Option A (telling the patient that it is a waste of money because it is self-inflicted) is both insensitive and judgmental. As such it ranks last.

Scenario 135 ANSWER: BCEAD

1. Before you start increasing the dose or prescribing more drugs, it would be worth checking that the drug was administered to the patient and that he hasn't refused to take it. Reviewing the chart would be essential (Option B).

2. Pain can be a sign of a post-operative complication such as DVT, chest infection, PE or MI to name a few. It is essential that a patient be reviewed if they have severe post-operative pain (Option C). Always go armed with as much information as you can when you see a patient. That is why this ranks second; you should review the chart first.

3. Increasing the dose would be required once you have established that there are no issues with the patient: so Option E, followed by prescribing oral morphine (Option A), going up the pain ladder.

4. You should always document thoroughly in the patient notes (Option D), but attend to the patient first and document later.

Scenario 136 ANSWER: CBADE

1. The patient was placed on the emergency list; the order of that list will have been decided by the theatre team in view of specific criteria. It would be inappropriate for you to try to change the order of the list. In any case, the nurse is not deciding the order in which the patients are operated on; this is done by the surgeon and the anaesthetist. This tells us that Option A (asking the nurse to do you a favour) is less appropriate than Option B (accepting that you won't be able to observe the case). Bear in mind too that appendicectomy is a fairly common procedure so there will be plenty of other opportunities to observe one.

2. You could consider asking the nurse to bleep you (Option C) but the main issue here is that there is no certainty about when this is likely to take place. If you come back late to observe, there is a risk that you may be tired the next day. The option does allow for the possibility that you might then decline to come in, which makes it relatively safe. On that basis, Option C ranks top because you might achieve your objective in a safe manner.

3. Option D (asking some of the patients to swap with your patient) is a nice idea but is actually dangerous. The list will have been prioritised already and there is a real danger that some patients may accept to swap a slot to a position that is not in their best interest. In any case, it is not your job to rearrange the list and it is not up to patients to decide in which order they should be operated on. So, even if you managed to persuade them to swap, the consultant and anaesthetist would overrule you. The whole thing is very unprofessional.

4. Option E ranks last because it is a blatant lie and would likely be considered misconduct. Beyond the lie, you may force the team to reprioritise other patients down the list, who may actually need to be done earlier than your patient.

Scenario 137 ANSWER: ABCDE

1. The situation is delicate because the patient is clearly exasperated and has lost faith in your colleague. You will therefore need to deal with the situation effectively but also sensitively towards both the patient and your colleague. With Option A, you offer a solution to the problem by offering to assist and you are explaining to the patient the situation. The patient will then be more likely to understand and move on.

2. Option B: if you call your colleague out on a false pretence and then simply take over, the patient will be in your hands but this will not explain why your colleague made the simple error. The patient will be left with a bad impression of your colleague and therefore still a sense of mistrust. Therefore Option B ranks below Option A. Some candidates may think that it is preferable to extract the colleague from the consultation and talk to him outside to avoid embarrassment but, in truth, the patient is more likely to calm down if the handover is done in a more honest manner.

3. With Option C, you essentially address the patient directly and offer to take over without involving your colleague at all. This makes it worse than Options A and B as it could undermine him.

4. Calling the registrar (Option E) would be the most inappropriate option as we are told he is busy with a sick patient. That patient should take priority. The issue you are facing is fairly simple and benign; the registrar would expect you not to disturb him for something so petty when he has more pressing issues to deal with. Therefore, not interfering (Option D) would be better than asking the registrar to intervene (Option E). Hence Option D ranks fourth and Option E ranks fifth.

Scenario 138 ANSWER: BACED

1. When you make a mistake you need to be as upfront as possible. Option B clearly explains the mistake and does not make false promises.

2. Option A is of a similar nature in that you are not promising anything in terms of timescale but you are telling the team a white lie to avoid the blame. Though this is likely to be inconsequential, it is nevertheless considered unprofessional and therefore ranks below Option B.

3. Option C is blaming the GP, which is unprofessional, and raises the prospect of having to delay the discharge. At this stage you are not sure whether there is likely to be a delay and making such an announcement is premature. It is nevertheless better than Option E, which also blames the GP but does not inform the team about a possible delay.

4. Option D is the worst because it provides reassurance that you are not in a position to give. It may result in the patient being unsafely discharged or his expectations being raised too early.

Scenario 139 ANSWER: CAEBD

1. Option C: since the delay is at the pharmacy level, it would be reasonable to call them to ask them to expedite the dispensing. Although you would not seek to respond positively to every relative's request, it would be sensible to try to help, whilst minimising the inconvenience for everyone.

2. Option A: if you can't resolve the matter by talking to pharmacy, asking the relative to involve the ward sister would be a good option as the ward sister would have the power to put pressure on pharmacy and organise everything required.

3. Option E: discharging the patient home and taking the medication to their house in the evening is a possibility, though of course not something you would want to do for every single patient or before you have exhausted the obvious options.

4. Option B: delaying the discharge by one day would be a real inconvenience. It would stop another patient from being admitted and would also inconvenience both the patient and the daughter. Hence it ranks fourth.

5. Option D: arranging for the medications to be picked up the next afternoon would be unsafe as it would leave the patient without medication for one day and could place them in danger.

Scenario 140 ANSWER: CDEBA

1. Giving the locum free rein with your own login details when he works in a different ward (Option A) would be unsuitable. There may be a risk that you are locked out of your own account if he uses your details at the same time as you are attempting to use them; also, you would not be able to control what is requested under your name and whether he is accessing other parts of the system with your details. At worst, this could be unsafe, and, at best, not good practice; hence it ranks last.

2. The other options all involve other doctors being present when the tests are ordered, with varying degrees of flexibility and safety:

   • Option C: by asking everyone to help order the tests when the locum needs it, he will be able to get his tests ordered as soon as he needs them as he will have access to many resources in a timely fashion.

   • Option D: by asking him to bleep you when he needs to order tests, you are ensuring that his patients are safe; however, this option is not as safe as Option C, as there may be a delay if you are otherwise engaged. Involving the whole team would be preferable to taking on the burden yourself.

   • Options E and B: delaying the tests may be detrimental to patient safety. Option E (leaving it to the next opportunity) is safer than Option D (leaving it until you yourself need to order tests) as it will occur sooner.

Scenario 141 ANSWER: CABED

1. If you are going to write a reference about someone then it should be honest and balanced. Therefore Option C will rank first.

2. If you are going to write a reference then you should write it yourself. Asking her to write it will be equivalent to endorsing her as she will obviously be emphasising her positive traits. Hence Option D would be dishonest and will rank last.

3. We are now left with three options ranking in the middle:

- Option A: refusing to write the reference;
- Option B: writing a vague and non-committal reference;
- Option E: emphasising the positive traits only.

Writing nothing would be better than writing something that is inaccurate; therefore Option A will rank top of those three. Writing a vague reference would be more appropriate than writing a positive reference as it would minimise the support given and would be more representative of your opinion; therefore Option E ranks below Option B.

Scenario 142   ANSWER: ABCED

1. The fact that the daughter works as a consultant in your hospital does not grant her privileges over patient information. It would be appropriate to reassure the daughter that her father is okay without being much more specific as she already knows that he is in hospital (i.e. you are not revealing a secret here and you are not divulging any details of his condition). That would serve to reassure her without breaching confidentiality. Therefore Option A comes first.

2. Failing that, you could simply refuse to give any information without consent (Option C), but it would be less abrupt to send her to your consultant so that he can manage this delicate situation appropriately (Option B).

3. The remaining options all encourage the radiologist to gain information about her father and should be ranked last in the order that reveals less to more information. By attending the ward round (Option E) she may be able to gain information but you could keep this to a minimum and you could remain relatively vague in front of the radiologist. Also her father will obviously be there and can always object to her presence if he wishes to do so. However, by accessing the full notes (Option D), she will know everything. That would represent an inappropriate use of the system and she would get into serious trouble for doing that.

Scenario 143   ANSWER: CABED

1. The situation is urgent. You will therefore need to ensure that the drug is given to the patient as quickly as possible. However, you must also re-

spect the role of the nurses in administering drugs and should avoid interfering if you can. As such, your first step would be to make sure that the nurse has understood the urgency of the situation (Option C).

2. If she doesn't, then you should talk to the ward sister to make sure that she can find someone who can (Option A). That will also alert her to the nurse's refusal.

3. Failing this, the only remaining option that will ensure that the medication is given quickly is doing it yourself (Option B).

4. Asking the relatives to nag the nurse (Option E) is not ideal because they shouldn't have to do it and it isn't very professional. However, it might ensure quicker resolution of the problem than by simply waiting for the nurse to finish her round (Option D) and therefore ranks higher.

Scenario 144   ANSWER: ECBDA

1. The patient is competent and therefore has the right to make that decision. You would therefore be entitled to simply discharge the patient (Option B). However, it would be appropriate to review the patient a week later and give him that opportunity to raise the issue if he so wishes (Option E). Alternatively you could advise that he contacts his GP to discuss the matter further (Option C), but since you have already developed a rapport, you may be best as first port of call. Hence Option E ranks above Option C, and Option B ranks third.

2. Asking the patient to contact you whenever he wants to talk (Option D) is inappropriate. You are not their friend and allowing the patient to just walk in unannounced would not be productive. Offering a discussion as part of a planned follow-up is more appropriate.

3. Telling the patient that homeopathy will kill him is totally inappropriate. It is not true (since the main criticism against homeopathy is that it is likely to have no effect); it is the cancer that will kill him if left untreated. In any case, scaring the patient into submission is not a good strategy to engage with them.

Scenario 145 ANSWER: CDEAB

1. When breaking bad news, consideration should be given to keeping the bleeps outside the room to avoid any interruption. Giving the bleeps to your fellow FY1 to cross-cover temporarily is the best choice (Option C).

2. Keeping the bleeps and responding only to the cardiac arrest bleep would be appropriate in this situation (Option D). Failing that, the next most appropriate option would be to keep all the bleeps (Option E).

3. Giving the bleep to the nursing staff (Option A) is not a good choice as there is a risk that a doctor cannot be contacted following a cardiac arrest. This would delay the response and adversely affect patient safety. This options therefore ranks below Options C, D, and E.

4. Leaving the bleeps in the doctor's room is wholly inappropriate as you would miss all the calls.

Scenario 146 ANSWER: BCEAD

1. The scenario makes it clear that the workload is affecting your ability to cope and your attitude to life, with some early signs of depression. Rather than medicate and continue to be overworked, your first concern would be to address the situation with someone who can help you deal with the workload and is able to ensure that you are supported adequately. Addressing the matter with your consultant (Option B) should therefore be your priority.

2. Contacting your educational supervisor (Option E) may also be an idea as it will allow you to discuss workload issues. It would not, however, result in any quick action and, as such, it may be better to go to your GP (Option C) so that you can get something to help you sleep and you can talk the issues through.

3. Taking breaks, avoiding coffee and exercising will help you somewhat cope with the pressure but you are at a stage where you are now showing signs of depression and you need to take more serious action to address the underlying causes. This option therefore ranks fourth.

4. It would be inappropriate to let a colleague prescribe you antidepressants (Option D). Not only should you not be treated by doctors you know in a personal capacity, the issues here go slightly beyond a "quick prescription in the corridor" situation. You would need to be assessed properly before anything can be prescribed.

Scenario 147   ANSWER: CBEDA

1. The GMC clearly states that doctors should avoid treating themselves or those close to them and therefore you should avoid prescribing your colleague. Sending your colleague to his GP (Option C) is the most appropriate option so that a proper risk assessment can be carried out and the right medication prescribed. Failing that, sending him to Occupational Health (Option B) is also an option, though this is not strictly speaking an occupational issue. They may be able to help though by providing an independent assessment.

2. Refusing the request (Option E) would also be appropriate though not as helpful as suggesting alternatives to your colleague (GP or Occupational Health).

3. Encouraging your colleague to steal the medication from the A&E cabinets (Option A) would essentially be encouraging theft and will also mean that your colleague will self-medicate. It would therefore be more appropriate for you to prescribe him the medication (Option D). Hence Option D ranks above Option E.

Scenario 148   ANSWER: ABCDE

1. It is important that you trust and respect the experience of your colleagues, whilst at the same time feeling confident that you can share your concerns if you have any. If you are worried that the CT1 is performing the procedure wrongly and he explained that the registrar used the same process, then it would be most appropriate to call the registrar straight away (Option A) so that the matter can be settled quickly.

2. Reminding the CT1 that he is responsible and warning that you will report any incident (Option B) is not a particularly friendly way of approaching the

problem but may encourage the CT1 to think twice about what he is doing. It is actually his responsibility and you have already discharged your own by making sure that you raise your concerns with him.

3. Out of the remaining options, only one would make an immediate difference to the situation: Option E (explaining the problem to the patient and asking him to withdraw consent). This option causes several problems:

- You would be overruling a more experienced colleague. Perhaps you should consider the fact that you may actually be wrong (the question does say that two senior colleagues agree with the methodology and you are not comfortable with the procedure).
- You will lose the patient's trust.
- It is not the patient's job to decide what the best way to proceed is.
- The patient needs the LP soon so engineering a withdrawal of consent would not help.

As such, this option is the least appropriate.

4. Both remaining options (C and D) involve reporting the matter. Reporting to the consultant the next day (Option C) would have a more immediate impact than completing a critical incident form (Option D).

Scenario 149 ANSWER: BDECA

1. Although no reason was indicated for the prescription of amoxicillin, this would not have been done without a reason. It is your duty to find out why the drug was prescribed. The best way to establish the facts is to phone the discharging hospital and speak to the team involved in the patient's care (Option B).

2. Asking the patient why he takes amoxicillin (Option D) could give you the answers you need, but it is possible the patient simply won't know or won't be able to give the clinical details that you would otherwise obtain by speaking directly to the other hospital's medical team.

3. Prescribing the amoxicillin in accordance with the discharge summary (Option E) without finding out why is not the most appropriate option; however, it ensures that the patient gets his medication.

4. Phoning the GP would be pointless as he would only have access to the discharge summary (Option C) and would not be in a position to help you resolve the issue.

5. Ignoring the amoxicillin (Option A) is the worst option as it would deprive the patient of medication that other colleagues felt would be useful.

Scenario 150 ANSWER: EACDB

1. Although no harm is caused to the patient, you will still need to inform both a senior colleague and the patient. The lack of harm reduces the urgency of the need to report the problem but not the fact that you have to do it. Since you are doing nights, it would be inappropriate to call the consultant if the medical registrar is available. You can then inform the patient later on that night. There is no immediate need to inform the patient; it just needs to be done at some stage. Therefore Option E (informing the registrar and informing the patient later on during the night) should be the most appropriate option. Option A (phoning the consultant and informing the patient straight away) ranks next.

2. Taking no further action (Option B) is the worst option as it does not inform anyone about the mistake, and should therefore rank last.

3. A mistake has been made and, even if it has no impact on the patient, it should be reported via a critical incident form (Option C). This ranks after informing senior colleagues and the patient though because it won't have the same immediate impact on the situation.

4. Completing a reflective piece in your e-portfolio (Option D) is useful for your own purposes but is less useful to clinical practice than a critical incident form, which can help improve processes and procedures at departmental level and not just at personal level.

Scenario 151 ANSWER: ECBAD

1. There are many reasons why the registrar could be acting like this, ranging from stress to a flawed personality. Although the situation has been going on for some time and the registrar has a reputation, you should ad-

dress the problem with the registrar first if you feel that you can; the question states that you get on fairly well with him, which is a clue that Option E should rank first. If the question hinted that you were scared of the registrar then approaching him would rank below the options that involve approaching senior colleagues.

2. The next best option would be for your colleague to talk to his consultant (Option C). He may not feel that he can approach the registrar himself; the consultant, who is in charge of the registrar, has a natural line of authority to deal with it. The consultant could simply have a word with the registrar, or organise more support for trainees, or change the shift pattern so that this FY1 is not exposed so much to the registrar. Talking to the educational supervisor (Option A) would also be a possibility, though not as relevant as talking to the consultant in charge as it will not have the same immediate impact.

3. Options E, C and B ensure that the situation is dealt with informally to start with. If those options are not available or fail, then the FY1 will need to deal with the matter more formally and, in order to do so, he should keep a record of the incidents (Option B) so that it can be used as evidence.

4. Helping the FY1 make the theatre list may be helpful as a temporary measure if he needs to learn, but if that isn't the case, then all you will achieve is disguise the FY1's inadequacies without dealing at all with the bullying issue. This option therefore ranks last.

Scenario 152   ANSWER: DBCAE

1. When doctors are on call, they should be available. If the registrar is tired then he should decline to be on call, refuse to cover for someone else and deal with it by talking to his seniors. So, although you might want to go a little easy on him to show support, you should not shy away from seeking his help if you need it, even if it is to help insert a cannula. Putting it in a different way: if something goes wrong because you didn't want to disturb the registrar's sleep, you will be held directly responsible.

2. In this scenario, both the FY1 and SHO have tried to cannulate with no success. Trying again (Option A) will expose the patient to further unnecessary discomfort and will most likely still be unsuccessful. You now need

a senior colleague to attempt it, which, in this case, should be the registrar (Option D), regardless of whether he is asleep or not.

3. The anaesthetist should be contacted for help if required (Option B) as he will be on site and will have the expertise, but only after your registrar has tried to cannulate the patient. Bleeping the anaesthetist allows a senior colleague to try cannulating before calling in the consultant (Option C). The on-call consultant won't be in hospital at night time, and will take time to come to the hospital. If it is urgent (for IV antibiotics) then the line needs to be placed without delay.

4. Giving oral antibiotics (Option E) when the patient has been on IV antibiotics is potentially compromising patient care and should be ranked last.

Scenario 153 ANSWER: ADEBC

1. Reporting illegal activities would involve breaching the patient's confidentiality and would only be appropriate if there was a serious risk of harm or death. The patient is not harming others. Your primary role as a doctor is caring for the well-being of your patients and not acting as a substitute policeman/policewoman.

2. By reporting the matter to the police (Option C) or searching the patient's belongings (Option B), you would breach the trust that the patient has in you and the medical profession; this may cause the patient to disengage and consequently not receive the care that he needs. Therefore Options B and C rank bottom, with the most extreme option (Option C – calling the police) ranking last. In fact, in this case, doing nothing (Option E) would be more appropriate.

3. Before considering doing nothing about the situation, as a doctor there are actions you can take which may make a difference and would fall within your remit as a healthcare professional. Reminding the patient of the harmful effects of cannabis (Option A) would be useful. The patient mentioned his habit to you, which should indicate that he is receptive to talking about it. It would also be appropriate to write to the GP so that he can deal with the issue when he next sees the patient (Option D). However, since it is less immediate and there is no guarantee that the GP will actually see the patient, it ranks second.

Scenario 154 ANSWER: DABEC

1. The patient could be asking for more sick leave for several reasons. Perhaps they just fancy being off work, or perhaps they feel that they need a longer time to recover (a feeling which may be based on prior experiences of slow recovery, or being worse off by coming back to work too early). It would therefore be important that you consider the patient's request with respect, making sure also that you do not act against your best judgement; a sick note is a legal document about your evaluation of the clinical situation. In the first instance, it would therefore be appropriate to reconsider the facts (Option D) to make sure that you have taken everything into account. This may lead you to a different conclusion.

2. Failing that, the most appropriate options would be to grant the amount of sick leave that you believe to be appropriate, i.e. 1 week. Though Option B is appropriate because you explain to the patient that you are acting in accordance with your best judgement, Option A is better because it leaves the door open for the leave to be extended by the GP if the patient has not sufficiently recovered, without compromising your own judgement. Therefore Option A ranks second and Option B ranks third.

3. Options C and E both involve extending the sick leave. This would be unethical if your best judgement was that 1 week is sufficient. Those options rank last, with the "2 weeks" option (Option E) ranking higher than the "4 weeks" option (Option C) as it is less inconsistent with your own judgement.

Scenario 155 ANSWER: BDEAC

1. Before arguing with everyone, the patient should be your first priority and you will need to go down to A&E and review the patient (Option B). It may be for example that there could be grounds to admit the patient under the medical team. Reviewing the patient will also give you information that you can then use in your discussions with the other teams.

2. Discussing the case with the surgical SHO (Option D) would be the next appropriate option as he is the natural contact within the team and has knowledge of the situation. The next best option would be to arrange for your own registrar to contact his registrar (Option E).

3. Failing all that, it would be more appropriate to admit the patient under the medical team (Option A) than to simply refuse to accept the patient (Option C), which would delay care. Once the patient has been admitted you still have the option to transfer him across to a surgical ward if required.

Scenario 156   ANSWER: BAEDC

1. There is a risk that the patient's behaviour has compromised the doctor-patient relationship. It would therefore be safest for you not to examine the patient at all and to let another doctor examine the patient instead, preferably from the same gender (Option B).

2. If you need to examine the patient yourself, then doing a full examination with a chaperone (Option A) would be more appropriate than a brief clinical examination on your own (Option E).

3. Calling the patient's parents (Option D) would be inappropriate because (i) the patient is 19 and (ii) you would breach confidentiality. It would be marginally more appropriate than discharging the patient (Option C), which could be unsafe.

Scenario 157   ANSWER: DCAEB

1. The fact that your colleague is now watching TV does not mean that he wasn't busy at the time he was first called. In the first instance, you should avoid jumping to conclusions and should give him the benefit of the doubt. The best option would therefore be to request an explanation from him (Option D).

2. Doing nothing (Option C) about the issue would also be appropriate, particularly as this is the first time and there is no evidence that the colleague is actually unreliable. In the interest of good working relationships, you may want to let it go for this time.

3. If you are concerned about your colleague's reliability then you should first raise your concerns with the consultant (Option A); however, in this situation it would be a little premature since there was no risk to patients and

there is no evidence that your colleague behaved unprofessionally. If this became a pattern, then you may consider escalating the matter.

4. There is no indication that patient safety was compromised or nearly compromised and no mistakes were made; therefore there is no need to complete a critical incident form (Option E), unless you really want to be very picky. Here, the colleague is simply not showing support. If you had been in a situation where you had had to deal with two emergencies by yourself whilst your colleague was watching TV, then there would have been grounds to complete a critical incident form because your colleague's behaviour would have compromised patient care. This is not the case here, and your colleague's behaviour is best addressed by talking to the consultant or letting it go for the time being.

5. Asking the nurse to bleep your colleague first (Option B) would be unprofessional and vindictive.

Scenario 158   ANSWER: DAEBC

1. The registrar is behaving inappropriately and, in the first instance, you should raise the matter directly with him (Option D). Failing that, you should discuss this with the consultant (Option A), who will be able to have a word with the registrar.

2. Failing that, you will need to address this with the postgraduate tutor (Option E). He will not be able to address this directly with the registrar but will contact the consultant to emphasise the need to give you training opportunities.

3. Learning by watching the others (Option C) is not a bad thing, but it is rather passive. More importantly, it will not give you the opportunity to learn to perform essential procedures and you might find yourself in a difficult position if someone later on requests that you should do one by yourself. Therefore it would be more appropriate to let your feelings be known at the next ward round. It would be slightly unprofessional to force the issue in public at the next ward round (Option B), but it will be a lot more effective and, in the long term, safer than just standing back. Therefore Option B ranks higher than Option C.

Scenario 159 ANSWER: ACBDE

1. If the patient's behaviour seems at odds with the OT's assessment, then you should raise this with the OT herself (Option A). She will be able to discuss her assessment with you and, if needed, may then decide to do another assessment. Your discussion will also give you information that you will need to have if you ever needed to discuss the matter with the rest of the team.

2. It would not be your place to demand a new assessment from the OT (Option B). If you have concerns about the safety of the patient's discharge, you should share them with your consultant first (Option C) as he is ultimately responsible for the patient. Therefore Option C ranks second and Option B ranks third.

3. Sharing your concerns with social services (Option D) would achieve little since there is no real social or safeguarding issue here. However, it ranks higher than Option E (asking the relatives to purchase a safe cup holder and discharging the patient) because if the patient is not medically fit to be discharged, then it would be unsafe to do so. Purchasing a safe cup holder would also only resolve one problem but would ignore everything else.

Scenario 160 ANSWER: ABCDE

1. In this scenario, the patient's catheter will need to be removed, preferably by the nurse (Option B) or, failing that, by you (Option C). However, in this case, this is no emergency and it would be more appropriate to contact the ward sister so that she is made aware of how the staffing issue has affected the nurses' behaviour and she can then check that all unnecessary catheters are being removed (Option A). This would have a broader ranging effect than dealing with that one patient only.

2. It is important to inform the consultant (Option D), particularly if there is a risk that some patients may have an infection, but it is not as much as a priority as removing the catheters.

3. Similarly, a critical incident form (Option E) will be required because patient care was compromised by the failure to comply with instructions.

Scenario 161 ANSWER: A, E, F

1. The nurse has forgotten to insert the catheter, and it may well be an honest mistake. The most important thing is to make sure that:

   - The patient is safe by reviewing the patient's fluid balance to ensure that she is safe or to identify any harm (Option E)
   - The catheter is inserted.

2. Since it was the nurse's responsibility and mistake, and she has the capability to insert the catheter, it would be preferable if she did it herself (Option F). As ever, when mistakes are made, the consultant should be informed and you should apologise to the patient (Option A).

3. With regard to the other options:

   - Option B: you would only seek to insert the catheter yourself if there was an urgent need and the nurse was not in position to do so. Even then, it may be more appropriate to contact the ward sister to make sure that it gets done, rather than doing it yourself.

   - Option C: standing behind the nurse to make sure that she does it would be demeaning to her. She doesn't need a chaperone. If you want to make sure it has been done then you can simply come back a bit later to check.

   - Option D: it is clear here that a mistake was made (the nurse says that she simply forgot, which is different to prioritising the catheter down because there is no rush). You would therefore need to report it but, in this scenario, there are more appropriate options to select before you can select this one.

   - Option G: completing a reflective e-portfolio form would be good, but there are other more important options here.

   - Option H: speaking to the ward sister may be suitable since a mistake was made by a nurse. However, it may be more productive to encourage the nurse to raise her concerns about the workload at this stage. Though this option is good, there are more immediate concerns.

Scenario 162 ANSWER: A, C, F

1. The most important thing to do is to ensure that the patients are safe. The patient who is missing the insulin that had been prescribed should be reviewed using ABCDE and treatment should then commence (Option F). You should also make the consultant aware of the situation (Option A) and apologise to both patients (Option C).

2. With regard to the other options:

   • Option B: apologising to the patient who should have been on insulin is an appropriate option; however, since both patients are involved, you should apologise to both (Option C).

   • Option D: it will be essential to stop the insulin sliding scale for the patient who was mistakenly placed on it. However, there is no immediate rush because the infusion would be titrated based on the patient's hourly blood glucose, which would be normal in this case. So the only harm would be the frequent pinpricks from the lancet. The other options are more urgent and essential.

   • Option E: similarly the patient who was mistakenly placed on the sliding scale will not need reviewing.

   • Option G: completing a critical incident form will be essential but there are more immediate concerns.

   • Option H: asking the nurses to place the patients on different wards won't achieve much. The team will now be very much aware of the danger caused by those two patients having the same name and will therefore be more alert. Completing a critical incident form would be more useful than separating them because it would help address the key issues relating to labelling and checking patient identity.

Scenario 163 ANSWER: A, B, D

1. If the registrar is making decisions that you find questionable then you should raise the issue directly with him (Option D). It may be that he is indeed not acting correctly, but it may also be that he simply has his own

way of doing things and may not be unsafe. You are entitled, justifiably so, to contest his decisions and you should do so whenever you need to.

2. If you have concerns about the registrar's clinical skills and feel this may affect patient safety, then you should share your concerns with a senior colleague (Option B). This applies, even if no patient has been harmed. He may simply have been lucky so far.

3. In addition to those two options, which are designed to ensure that the root cause of the problem is addressed, you should not do anything that you feel is inappropriate (Option A). For example, some of the investigations may be invasive or expose patients to unnecessary radiation. If the registrar insists that you should do as he says, then you should refuse and let him take the risk himself. Your role is to try to stop him and report it to someone more senior.

4. With regard to the other options:

    *   Option C (do the investigations you think are right instead of those ordered by the registrar) is not appropriate because there may be legitimate reasons for him to make such decisions. You can argue if you want and you can refuse to do them if you want, but you can't override a senior colleague's decision just because you disagree with them.

    *   Option E (writing comments in his 360-degree assessment) would be a good idea but it is not addressing the immediate issue. Besides, it could be some time before the registrar sends you a 360-degree assessment form to complete, and you may well have left the unit by then.

    *   Option F: if you think that something is not the right thing to do then you should refuse to do it. You can't do something you disagree with and then simply cover your back by documenting it as you would not be acting in what you feel is the best interest of the patient.

    *   Option G (waiting until the patient has been harmed to act): you have the opportunity to prevent harm. If you have concerns, raise them before it is too late.

    *   Option H (refusing to work with the registrar) may help protect you, but this will leave other patients more exposed. At least by working with him you can check what is going on. In any case, there are more im-

mediate options available before you reach the stage where you simply walk away.

Scenario 164 ANSWER: B, C, E

1. Exam revision is a daily reality for junior doctors and there is no reason why special allowances should be made for someone who failed to plan appropriately. However, the stress incurred by the CT1 and the fatigue that ensues will inevitably have an impact on her ability to perform her duties safely. In addition, the fact that there is no need to make special allowances does not mean that you should not be supportive.

2. In this scenario, your colleague's exams are obviously affecting your own workload, and the work involved is causing her to make mistakes. It would therefore be fair to discuss the matter with the CT1 (Option B). This may help you come to an agreement about the manner in which you can help (rather than just having the bleep imposed onto you).

3. Your colleague's tiredness and the impact it has on your own workload may be cause for concern and will leave you and your colleague more exposed to making mistakes. This concern needs to be addressed with the consultant (Option C), who may then be able to arrange for a different allocation of work or more senior support. Discussing with managers and the rota coordinator the possibility to recruit locums (Option E) to take some of the work burden would also be useful. It would enable the work to get done safely.

4. With regard to the other options:

   - Option A: it is absolutely true that patients should be her main concern, but that doesn't necessarily mean that she has to sacrifice her own exams because of it. It means that she must ensure that her revision doesn't impact on patient safety and, as such, she has already taken steps by handing over her bleep to you. Options B, C and E will help introduce further safety measures. In any case, forcing the CT1 to stay at work will only make her worry more about her exams and will likely impact on her ability to care for her patients; so that could prove counterproductive.

- Option D: asking the nurses to call the CT1 first will only put more pressure on her and will confuse the hierarchy. The staffing situation should be discussed properly and any such decision will need to be taken by a registrar or a consultant, not by you.

- Option F: asking the nurses to leave you alone may compromise patient safety. If nurses need to contact you, they should be able to do so. If you feel you can't cope with the workload then you should address the matter with senior colleagues.

- Option G: refusing to take the bleep won't help matters.

- Option H: telling your colleague that she should take time off is not appropriate as this will place further burden on you and the rest of the team. It is something that she may wish to discuss with her seniors, but is not for you to suggest.

Scenario 165 ANSWER: D, E, G

1. The issue here is essentially a moan by relatives who want to vent their frustration about an issue that has pretty much already been resolved and which is fairly mundane in the scale of things. The emphasis will be therefore on making sure that you are treating the relatives' comments with respect, but at the same time, not making a mountain out of it. Encouraging the relatives to discuss the issue with Dr Smith (Option D) and encouraging Dr Smith to talk to the relatives (Option E) would be a start as this will ensure that the issue is discussed, an apology is issued and the matter is put to rest. It would also be appropriate to enquire about the rest of the care received by the patient (Option G) so that the problem can be placed in the context of the overall positive experience of the patient, and so that any further issues can be identified.

2. With regard to the other options:

- Option A: offering to re-examine the patient's foot will achieve nothing. The athlete's foot has already been diagnosed and there is no need to fuss further over the patient.

- Option B: explaining that athlete's foot is not a cardiology matter would seriously undermine your and your colleague's credibility. The patient and his relatives probably know a lot about it as it is a common condition. In any case, the expectation from the patient and relatives is that you should be able to handle pretty much anything yourself or know someone who can. Trying to find an excuse for the delay would sound bad and suggesting that your colleague has no knowledge of basic conditions would sound worse.

- Option C: completing a critical incident form is a remote possibility (there was only a delay in diagnosing something with no consequence and nothing critical about it), but it is a possible consideration. However there are much better options to consider before you can get to that stage.

- Option F: the relatives are complaining about something that they are already aware of, so there is no real confidentiality issue here. Even if you considered that there was one, telling them you can only discuss the complaint with the patient would be a very abrupt way of handling a fairly simple matter. It is much better to encourage a dialogue between them and Dr Smith.

- Option H: there is no need to involve the consultant at this stage over such a small issue. See if it can be resolved directly and simply first. This option would be appropriate but, considering the other choices, it is slightly over the top.

Scenario 166 | ANSWER: A, C, H

1. Just in case you were wondering: Devmatizimab is a name we made up to make sure no one had heard of it!

2. If the registrar has prescribed a drug then there will usually be a good reason and, as such, there is no immediate need to do anything about it unless the patient experiences side effects or becomes unstable, which is not the case here. Your main role will therefore be to communicate appropriately so that she can get back to the patient with something and a constructive approach can be followed. It would therefore be appropriate to be honest with the nurse about the fact that you don't know and make it clear that you are in a hurry (Option A).

3. You will also need to help the nurse out by reassuring her that she can tell the patient you are onto it but need a little bit of time because you are currently occupied (Option H).

4. Finally you will be able to get the information you need from the BNF when you can find a moment (Option C), at least as a first port of call for the information.

5. With regard to the other options:

   - Option B (asking the nurse to stop the drug) could be potentially dangerous, especially if you don't know what the drug does. If your registrar has prescribed it then he should be trusted. If you have an issue with it then you should look it up or talk to him but not act unilaterally.

   - Option D (asking the nurse to contact the registrar) will result in the registrar being disturbed by the nurse when he is busy dealing with patients in A&E. This will also result in the information being passed on to the patient via the nurse, i.e. second hand and therefore not ideal.

   - Option E (contacting the registrar yourself) would be better than asking the nurse to do it, if you had the time. However, it would be appropriate for you to show some independence and make some effort to look it up in the BNF first (Option C) or to look in the patient's notes to determine why it was prescribed.

   - Option F (asking the nurse to look it up on the internet and inform the patient) is not appropriate. The information she will gather may be erroneous and she may totally misinform the patient. The patient may also ask further questions that she won't be able to answer, leading to more frustration. As such the answer should come from a doctor rather than a newly qualified nurse.

   - Option G is actually true but it doesn't explain that you are in a rush and has a slightly dismissive tone to it. The option is not bad but others such as Options A and H are better.

Scenario 167 ANSWER: B, C, F

1. If the patient has a fracture, then he needs to be recalled and an apology issued (Option B). Because the incident and the discharge happened whilst on your ward, the consultant will also need to be informed (Option F). Because of the fall and the fact that the fracture was missed, a critical incident form will need to be completed (Option C).

2. With regard to the other options:

   - Option A: bringing the patient back via A&E under a false pretence would be inappropriate. Lying to a patient is unacceptable for two reasons: (i) it shows a lack of personal integrity and (ii) if the patient found out, this may affect his trust in you, the team, and in some cases his trust in the medical profession.

   - Option D: if the patient has a fracture he should be recalled even if he is asymptomatic.

   - Option E: blaming another doctor, even if he remains unnamed, is dishonest. Indeed, the patient may well find out that you are the doctor who missed the fracture and this may affect his trust in you.

   - Option G: taking painkillers won't resolve the problem of the fracture. And if the patient is in pain it may actually be best if he came in without taking painkillers so that the pain is not masked before examination.

   - Option H (not recalling the patient) would be negligent.

Scenario 168 ANSWER: A, B, D

1. There are two issues here: your colleague's slightly rude behaviour and the nurse's inappropriate reaction to it. You are in a position to do something about both but, though you would need to make sure that something is done about it, you would also want to minimise disruption and avoid getting drawn into the argument. It would be a good idea to encourage your colleague to apologise to the nurse (Option A); he was a bit rude to her and apologising may help avoid the risk of a formal and unfair complaint

being raised against your colleague. In doing so it would be important that your colleague is made aware of the nurse's feelings towards him so that he approached the discussion with her in the right way (Option B).

2. Telling him that the nurse wants to report him for making racist remarks (Option C) at that stage won't help much. It may worsen their relationship and may therefore affect patient care. Instead it may be appropriate to share your concerns with the consultant (Option D) so that he can address the issue with the other FY1 and perhaps the ward sister at an appropriate moment.

3. The nurse has made inappropriate remarks and, for the moment, they have not been followed by actions. You may consider going to see the sister but you have no real proof of anything and, at this stage, it is unlikely to lead to anything since the nurse would simply deny it. You can't accuse the nurse of bullying (Option G) because all she has done so far is remind your colleague of the drug charts; and you can't ask the sister to discuss the matter with the consultant (Option H) because she would only be repeating what you have told her, and the nurse has not done anything yet. If you want the consultant to be involved, you might as well involve him yourself (Option D) as he may then decide to approach the sister himself. Indeed he may already be familiar with the nurse's attitude and may be able to use other incidents to put together a case against her if action needs taking. There is no need to use the sister as an intermediary.

4. Going to Occupational Health (Option E) will achieve nothing. They won't deal with personality issues.

5. Option F (asking the other nurse to mediate) is unfair. She is not really involved and you would embarrass her. This needs to be addressed either directly by the protagonists or at senior level.

Scenario 169 ANSWER: A, C, D

1. It is clear that the patient cannot go to theatre for the time being and you will need to inform theatres as soon as possible (Option A) so that they can start with another patient. They will also be able to determine whether the patient can be placed towards the end of the list instead (it is a hernia operation and so can wait a little). Taking the patient back to the ward and

placing him on nil by mouth again will contribute towards that. You should also reiterate the meaning of "nil by mouth" to the patient (Option C).

2. The patient was already on his way to theatre, having drunk a milkshake not long before. The incident is therefore a near miss and will need to be reported (Option D).

3. With regard to the other options:

    - Option B: calling the consultant immediately is not necessary because you will have already called theatres and he will therefore have already been informed in that way.

    - Option E: the patient could get reflux which could place him in danger.

    - Option F: this has nothing to do with the catering manager.

    - Option G: the nurses can't watch every patient every minute. The problem is mostly that the patient lacked awareness about the meaning of "nil by mouth". Checking and reviewing the information given to patients would be more helpful in tightening up the protocols. That will hopefully be achieved as a result of the critical incident reporting.

    - Option H: this shouldn't be done until all options have been considered by the theatre team. It may be that this will only result in a delay rather than a cancellation.

Scenario 170 ANSWER: A, B, E

1. In this scenario, there is no real emergency but your first step should be to make sure that the tube is properly inserted. Asking the nurse to place a new tube would therefore be appropriate (Option B).

2. The scenario points to the fact that the other FY1 has made a false entry; however, it is important not to jump to conclusions. It is possible that the entry on the radiology system is incorrect. It is also possible that, if the FY1 did see an X-ray at 3pm, he wrongly interpreted it because the path is difficult to make out. In that case, it would be an unfortunate error but nothing worth reporting to his supervisor (if possible, he would need to talk to

his supervisor himself). Before taking any drastic action, it would therefore be appropriate to check the story with the FY1 (Option E).

3. Regardless of the circumstances, this is a mistake which compromised the patient's safety: a doctor has approved a tube that was incorrectly positioned. You will therefore need to complete an incident form (Option A).

4. With regard to the other options:

   • Option C (discussing with the FY1 supervisor your suspicion of a false entry): this may be appropriate but there is no guarantee that this was a false entry. Since you need to do a critical incident form anyway, the truth will come out one way or another as the incident is investigated.

   • Option D (getting an immediate report by the radiologist): there is no need to do that if the nurse has placed a new nasogastric tube (Option B)

   • Option F: discussing the matter with your own consultant won't help much. There are better options.

   • Option G: the nurse did nothing wrong. In fact, it is because she followed protocol that the issue was identified and raised.

   • Option H: if the FY1 has indeed made a false entry, his superiors may well report the FY1 to the GMC. However, at this stage it is premature.

Scenario 171 ANSWER: B, E, F

1. The situation is an emergency and therefore you don't want to take risks or mess about. It would be important to let the nurse know that you believe the sample is a venous sample and that you explain why (Option B).

2. It is also crucial that you repeat the sample. Because of the urgency of the situation it would be safer if you did it yourself, in which case it would be professional to let the nurse watch you (Option E). He could check what you are doing and might also learn from it. That makes Option C and Option D irrelevant.

3. Calling the registrar to review the results (Option F) would be a good thing to do in view of the seniority of the nurse; he will also be able to remove some uncertainly in the result.

4. With regard to the other options:

   - Option A: the seniority of the nurse has nothing to do with it here. You, the doctor, are in charge of the patient and you need to be sure that your decisions are made on the basis of facts that you can trust. If you have doubts about the results, you need to repeat the sample.

   - Option G: there is no need to complete a critical incident form in this instance.

     i. The nurse is perfectly entitled to take ABG samples.
     ii. Taking a venous sample instead of an arterial sample is a common occurrence (i.e. not a mistake – it's just one of those things that can sometimes happen).
     iii. The nurse did not act on the sample and asked for advice.
     iv. The problem was picked up as part of the normal routine, showing that the system worked as it should.

     There would have been a need for a critical incident form if the nurse had taken the ABG without training, or had taken it upon himself to send the patient for intubation; or if you had wrongly interpreted the results and sent the patient for intubation yourself. In this instance the nurse simply made recommendations to you based on the wrong type of sample.

   - Option H: transferring the patient to HDU is not required here.

Scenario 172 ANSWER: D, G, H

1. With the father present, you will find it hard to identify any potential issues. You will therefore need to find an opportunity to try to raise the issue with the girl when her father is not around (Option H). If you can, it would also be a good idea to see if the father is aware of any problems, though, in order to avoid breaching confidentiality, you would need to keep the conversation at a fairly general level. Therefore Option D will be appropriate, but Option C will not.

2. There is a lot of fact finding to do before decisions can be made, particularly with regard to the circumstance surrounding the self-harming. Before any actions can be taken or envisaged, it would be wise to consult your registrar (Option G) to discuss any possible issues of safeguarding. He may be able to advise on possible action that needs taking.

3. With regard to the other options:

- Option A: it would be essential to discuss the marks with the girl at some stage, if only to determine if there are risks of suicide or abuse for example.

- Option B: you should not mention anything when the father is in the room. The patient has made it clear in her own way that she does not want the father to know.

- Option E: more information would be required before getting her reviewed by a psychiatrist. Doing so in A&E could, in fact, make things worse for her if the father is around, and might put her off contacting doctors in future about the issue.

- Option F: making a social services referral today is inappropriate. There are no grounds because the patient is not in immediate danger and you need more information before doing anything of the sort.

Scenario 173 ANSWER: B, D, F

1. If the patient is getting distressed and his breathing is deteriorating, you will need to stop what you are doing and reassess the patient from an ABC point of view (Options B and D). The safest thing to do then would be to ask an experienced colleague to take over from you (Option F) since you have already failed twice and the patient is showing signs of distress.

2. With regard to the other options:

- Options A and C: you should not pursue the procedure if the patient is in distress; it would not be safe.

- Option E: given that the patient is in distress, it would be safer for an experienced colleague to do it himself rather than supervise you. You obviously need to learn, but not at the expense of patient safety.

- Option G: venous gas is not the investigation that is required here.

- Option H: leaving the room would be abandoning a patient in distress.

Scenario 174   ANSWER: A, B, C

1. Your consultant wanted the patient reviewed today. So, if there is a problem with the timescale, you should inform him, explain the reasons for the delay and seek advice on how to proceed (Options A and C). Since you have worked in Psychiatry before, you will have the skills to assess the patient's mental capacity and as such you don't actually need the ST3 to review the patient; you could suggest that you should assess the patient yourself (Option B).

2. With regard to the other options:

- Option D: you don't know what else the ST3 has to do; he may be dealing with patients who are far more urgent or complex than your pre-discharge assessment. You cannot simply demand that he does the assessment because your consultant asked for it.

- Option E: trying to use your connections to force someone's hand is not very professional unless you have serious concerns about patient safety, in which case you would be entitled to act in such a manner. We are told here that the assessment is needed to inform discharge planning. The delay will merely inconvenience you and the patient, but is not unsafe.

- Option F: lying to get what you need would be unprofessional.

- Option G: there are alternatives to accepting the ST3's decision, such as doing the assessment yourself (Option B).

- Option H: the nurses should have no part to play in the referral.

Scenario 175 ANSWER: A, D, H

1. When you make a mistake you should be honest about it and you should aim to resolve the problem as effectively as you can. In this case, calling your consultant (Option A) will be required so that he is aware of the problem; he may be able to liaise with the radiology department and get an urgent scan organised. Alternatively, he may be willing to alter the theatre list to allow you more time to sort out the ultrasound.

2. Being honest with the radiology department and talking to the on-call consultant (Option D) will also be a good option; they may appreciate the honesty and will cooperate if the scan is required for the patient with that degree of urgency. However, before you consider doing so, you may want to enquire about the workload that the ultrasound department is currently facing because that will inform you as to how much pressure will be required to get the urgent ultrasound organised (Option H).

3. With regard to the other options:

    *   Options B and C: asking for an urgent ultrasound to be done immediately is not the right way to go about it, whether it is on the phone or face to face. You should present your case and explain the situation but the ultimate solution will need to be negotiated with the radiology department.

    *   Option E: an intra-operative ultrasound scan would not be appropriate and, in any case, this is a decision that would need to be taken by the consultant rather than you.

    *   Option F (delaying the surgery): the decision to delay the operation should be made by the consultant, not by you. Your role is to keep the consultant and the theatre team informed of the situation so that the right decisions can be made.

    *   Option G, however tempting, is dishonest.

Scenario 176 ANSWER: A, C, E

1. If the gel causes your eczema to flare up, you should not be using it (Option C). Since the infection control nurse is available right now, you should discuss your personal circumstances with her so that she can advise you on suitable alternatives (Option A). It would also be a good idea to arrange a meeting with Occupational Health to see whether they can help you deal with the problem or can identify specific areas which may cause you trouble at work (Option E).

2. With regard to the other options:

   • Option B (using the gel as normal) would be ill-advised if it has such an effect on you.

   • Option D (using your own emollient) would only help moisturise your hands, but would not kill all the germs that the alcohol gel would. From an infection control this could prove disastrous. The same applies to Option F.

   • Option G would go some way towards infection control, but since you would still be touching the gloves with your hands at some stage this would not be appropriate. It does not guarantee as strong a level of protection as using the gel or an alternative.

   • Option H (only using the gel half the time to minimise exposure) would not address infection risks appropriately.

Scenario 177 ANSWER: A, E, G

1. In this scenario it would be tempting to jump to conclusions and think that the nurse is being bullied when it could be that she is finding it difficult to cope because she has personal issues outside of work. We simply don't know. You will obviously need to show some support towards the nurse but you will also need to make sure that you deal with the situation in a constructive manner. Asking her how things are outside of work (Option A) and offering her your support (Option G) will help you identify any side issues and will provide her with some reassurance. It would also be wise to encourage the nurse to talk things through with her line manager so that

they can discuss the issues that concern her and she can get proper support beyond your own personal support (Option E).

2. With regard to the other options:

- Option B (reassuring her that she is doing the right thing and offering a reference) sounds like it is supportive but it is failing to address the fact that there may be other issues. This is the type of thing you would say when someone has already found a new job and is actually leaving, because at that stage there is nothing more you can do. In this situation, there are concerns that need to be explored in relation to relationships at work and the nurse's own state of mind.

- Option C (suggesting she simply does not fit in the team) is not a very nice thing to say but, beyond that, it makes an assumption that it has something to do with personalities. Some fact finding and proactive action would be better than making such judgemental comments.

- Option D (go off sick for stress and use the time to look for a job) is not necessarily a bad idea if she is really stressed. However, it would not be her decision. She would need to be signed off work by her GP or by Occupational Health. If the option had been worded "Advise her to see her GP so that he can give time off for stress, and tell her she can use that time to look for a job", it would be a strong contender.

- Option F (suggesting she needs a thicker skin) is as judgemental as Option C. If she is oversensitive because of other problems outside of work then you would actually make her feel worse.

- Option H: this would offer support but if she has a problem with other nurses, she may not feel this is the most appropriate. It would be best for her to talk to her manager, who could then determine the type of support she may need. This option also makes the assumption that she will be leaving soon, when the most appropriate option may simply be to help her cope with the situation better.

Scenario 178 ANSWER: B, E, D

1. The situation poses a real danger to patient safety and, being so understaffed, the consultant needs to be informed (Option B). This will most

likely prompt him to come in and offer some help. You will then need to deal with patients, prioritising in accordance to clinical need (Option E) and not order of arrival (Options F and G).

2. Because of the seriousness of the situation and the real danger to patient safety, you should complete a critical incident form (Option D) even if you manage to cope. The point is that no help was available to you if you needed to discuss a clinical issue and you may well have got bogged down with dealing with some complex patients, forcing you to neglect others. Filling in a critical incident form may result in implementation of another method of locating a locum doctor to fill in the gaps for example.

3. With regard to the other options:

   • Option A: NNPs are not trained to clerk in patients and having to supervise the process will hinder you more than help you.

   • Option C: asking a sick doctor with diarrhoea and vomitting to deal with patients is not appropriate.

   • Option H: there is no point in emailing the FY2. He is off sick and therefore not working. There are handovers and patient notes to keep people informed.

Scenario 179   ANSWER: A, D, G

1. The most honest and cleanest way to handle the matter is to document the change in the notes using the date and time at which you make the entry (i.e. Option A), inform the patient of your mistake (Option G) and write a critical incident form so that lessons can be learnt (Option D) (perhaps there are issues with legibility of handwriting, checking protocols, etc.).

2. Removing any trace of your original entry (Options B and E) would destroy the trail of events. There needs to be a clear audit trail, not least because if there is a complaint the team will need to establish what happened.

3. Backdating the note (Option C) or altering the note (Option H) will just confuse matters and is dishonest.

4. Blaming the nurses (Option F) is hypocritical.

Scenario 180 ANSWER: C, D, E

1. If you have information that could alter the clinical decisions made by the team, you must share it. You should do so at a time which is relevant. In this situation, there is no point in allowing the team to discuss a case on the basis of information that you know is incomplete. You should therefore interrupt the discussion and let the team know about the hysterectomy (Option D).

2. It would also be important to verify that information both by consulting the notes and talking to the patient in order to avoid any ambiguities (Options C and E).

3. With regard to the other options:

   - Options A and B: talking to your consultant or the radiologist after the meeting is just wasting everyone's time (though it's better late than never) and would waste the opportunity to affect the clinical management of the patient at the earliest opportunity.

   - Option F: telling the patient that her uterus is still intact is inappropriate. We do not know if this is a mass they are seeing or whether they are simply looking at the wrong patient's notes. There is no point in upsetting the patient or causing distress until further discussions and/or investigations are completed.

   - Option G (calling her husband) is inappropriate on grounds of confidentiality.

   - Option H (critical incident reporting) is not entirely inappropriate. It would be applicable if the wrong patient's notes were being used to make clinical decisions. However, as it stands, we are not sure whether this is the case. Therefore completing a critical incident form is a little premature.

Scenario 181 ANSWER: C, F, H

1. We are at the initial stage of an issue raised by a patient. The patient is making some generic comments about the coffee and the therapy, which

warrant exploring. In reality, there is little you will be able to do about the coffee but there is no harm in mentioning it to someone in charge. With regard to the speech therapy, you would need to ensure that you understand what the patient has been told, how it was explained to them and what their expectations were. Therefore reassuring the patient that you will look into the coffee issue and discussing their speech therapy expectations (Option C) is essential.

2. Asking the Speech and Language Therapy team to talk to the patient (Option H) will be of benefit. They will have decided the number of sessions that the patient requires and will be able to explain their management plan to the patient. They will also be in a position to answer his questions. It is best to involve the team directly. If you act as the messenger between the two (Option G), there is a risk of misunderstanding and you won't be in a position to answer specific questions from the patient; this may decrease their level of confidence further.

3. Documenting your discussions with the patient (Option F) will be essential to inform the team of the patient's expectations.

4. With regard to the other options:

- Option A: buying the patient a coffee is a nice thing to do but you are not a catering assistant. Also, it would be inappropriate to single out a patient for favours as it would then lead to complaints from the others. If there is an issue with the coffee, it should be raised with someone in charge of it.

- Option B: cutbacks won't necessarily affect the coffee. They may affect some decisions relating to the amount of therapy but clinicians and therapists won't simply cut back on sessions because of NHS budgetary issues; clinical need will also be an important consideration. The problem here is that you are just speculating and basically making an off-the-cuff comment which is probably incorrect and will leave the patient feeling short-changed. This won't help them regain confidence in the care that they are receiving.

- Option D: the decision to review the number of sessions given to the patient will rest with the Speech and Language Therapy team, not you.

- Option E: a formal complaint is a very premature step when it has not been identified yet whether there is actually an issue. It is best to nip a possible complaint in the bud by taking proactive steps and communicating appropriately with the patient first.

Scenario 182 ANSWER: A, D, E

1. In the absence of a phlebotomist you will need to take the bloods yourself. Patient care should be your focus. You should ensure that you prioritise the tasks appropriately and seek relevant help if needed. By asking the nursing staff to help you take the bloods (Option D) and prioritising the samples, doing as many as you can (Option E), you will ensure that the most urgent cases are dealt with quickly and that the others are done as soon as you can.

2. It will also be important to bring the matter to the attention of someone who can deal with it, particularly as it is not the first time. Informing the phlebotomist's manager at the first opportunity (Option A) will ensure that the matter is addressed, whether this is a behavioural issue or a simple misunderstanding.

3. With regard to the other options:

- Option B (critical incident form): there may be grounds for a critical incident form if patient care is at risk. There is no suggestion of that here; the text mostly indicates that you are just very busy (no mention of sick patients having had their care compromised or nearly compromised). However, in the first instance, it would be more appropriate to raise the issue verbally with his manager. The decision to write a critical incident form can come later.

- Option C (postponing the less urgent bloods until Monday): dealing with the most urgent bloods is of course the right thing to do, but systematically leaving the non-urgent samples until Monday will delay the care of those patients. It is entirely appropriate to prioritise them down the list, but you should ensure that the samples are taken as soon as you can (that could be Monday morning, but that could be earlier if you have the opportunity). Your role is to look after patients, not just the urgent ones. Option E would be more appropriate.

- Option F (stopping reviewing your patients to take the bloods): you have to prioritise your tasks by looking at your whole list of jobs. Stopping the review of your patients to take the bloods would be in appro-priate if some of your patients needed urgent review.

- Option G: by not taking the bloods that day (especially the urgent ones) you would not be acting in the best interest of your patients. You cannot wait for the phlebotomists to come to work on Monday and hope that they will read your email.

- Option H: the consultant on call won't be able to do much. Unless all your bloods have to be taken urgently, he is unlikely to tell you much more than "Prioritise your tasks and call me if you are finding it hard to cope".

Scenario 183 ANSWER: C, D, F

1. If a patient makes an allegation against nursing staff then the matter should really be handled by a senior nurse, i.e. the ward sister. She would therefore need to be informed (Option C). At the same time, it would be appropriate to ensure that there has indeed been a theft and that the pa-tient has not simply left her purse in her bag at her bedside. So offering to look for it would also be sensible (Option D). If the patient has mentioned that she has lost trust in the nursing staff then it may be sensible to move her to a different ward (Option F). In practice you would need to think twice about doing so because you can't just give in to every patient's whim, but there is some rationale for it and the other options are less appropriate.

2. With regard to the other options:

- Option A: the fact that nurses are bound by a code of conduct does not mean that they adhere to it. Mentioning this to a patient would be tantamount to telling the patient that you don't really believe that what she says is true.

- Option B: reporting the theft to the police is a possibility but that would really be down to the patient. There are some less extreme options to try first.

- Options E and G: searching people would be extreme and inappropri-ate.

- Option H: reassuring the patient that you were not involved in the theft will achieve nothing. She never accused you anyway. This is a slightly sly way of getting the patient to trust you and distancing yourself from the problem.

Scenario 184 ANSWER: A, B, H

1. There is a difference between making the odd mistake as a result of being tired, being distracted or misinterpreting information; and repeat mistakes which are left unchecked. In this scenario, the colleague is consistently sloppy (either because he is inadequate or because of other reasons such as stress – we are not told), and this is posing a significant risk to patient safety. The answer to the scenario will therefore need to include an element of honesty towards the colleague, an element of reporting your concerns to someone senior and an element of offering support to the colleague concerned.

2. Option B ensures that the colleague is made aware of the problem and that action is taken to correct the mistakes. Because the mistakes are his, it should be his job to ensure that they are corrected. That is why Option E (in which you check all his jobs) is unsuitable; you have your own patients to worry about and you can't do his job as well as yours.

3. Because the volume of mistakes made is high and some of them are cause for concern with regard to patient safety, it would be sensible to inform the registrar of your concerns (Option A). He will then be able to take charge of the situation and provide closer supervision to your colleague. If he is concerned about the colleague's behaviour, he will also be able to escalate the matter to the consultant or other appropriate individuals for further action. Informing your educational supervisor (Option C) is not appropriate; it would be more useful to inform the trainee's own supervisor instead.

4. If you have some spare time, you could offer to help your colleague out (Option H). This would minimise the number of patients that he sees without affecting your own work too much; it would also relieve pressure off him in the event that he found it hard to cope with his workload.

5. Options D (emailing the other doctors) would be insensitive. If other doctors need to be informed, this should be done by a more senior figure within the department, and certainly not by email.

6. Option F (reporting each incident) would give you quite a lot of work. In theory, this should be done but there is no urgency to it. Indeed the main problem is your colleague's behaviour rather than each individual mistake. The priority should be in minimising the impact on patient safety and addressing the colleague's underperformance. It would also not be your job to complete every critical incident form if you have not been involved in the mistake or in dealing with it.

7. Warning nurses (Option G) is not a long-term solution and does not offer a systematic approach as it relies on judgement by the nurses.

Scenario 185 ANSWER: B, F, G

1. The main problem here is that you simply can't tell what is going on. It may be that your colleague is simply not coping, or it may be that there is indeed an issue of support. The fact that you coped when you worked in that firm before is no indication that the colleague should cope too. Perhaps he just doesn't get on with the ST3; perhaps the ST3 has other things on his mind; and it might not even be the same ST3 at all. On the whole, it should really be down to your colleague to sort things out, but by solidarity and because there is a potential risk to patients, you should offer some degree of support.

2. You will allow him the freedom to sort it out by himself by encouraging him to discuss the matter with his ST3 and his clinical supervisor (Options F and G). You will offer appropriate support by listening to him (Option F) and offering to meet with the night ward sister with him (Option B). The night ward sister may provide a good insight into some of the issues and may provide clues that would be vital to determine how to best handle the matter.

3. With regard to the other options:

   • Option A: your colleague is clearly having problems. Reassuring him that it will settle when there are possible patient safety issues is not the most appropriate thing to do as it encourages a wait-and-see approach.

- Option C: the Medical Director is far too high up for that. This is a matter to be discussed with the ST3 and the clinical supervisor in the first instance.

- Option D: you don't know that your colleague is not coping. Contacting the FY1 course director would undermine your colleague at a very premature stage. It would be best to encourage him to take local action first. If there were concerns about your colleagues, there may be a need to discuss the situation with the FY1 programme director, but that would be down to his own seniors unless you had serious concerns that you felt were not being addressed.

- Option E: by talking to the ST3 yourself, you would be interfering too much. It is better to encourage your colleague to approach the ST3 himself.

- Option H: the defence union would only be able to offer very limited advice here. This is either a team issue or a personal coping issue. It needs to be sorted out at a personal level.

Scenario 186   ANSWER: D, E, F

1. It is indeed unfair that you should be covering all those dates yourself; however, it is important that you adopt a constructive approach in dealing with the problem. It is likely that the rota was not intentionally designed to ruin your seasonal period and so having a word with the ST3 in charge of the rota will be a good start (Option D).

2. Instead of lumbering him with the task of rewriting the rota in a more suitable manner, it would be useful if you could make an effort to come to a consensus with all your colleagues (Options E and F) so that it saves time for everyone and the new rota does not end up being something which suits you better but is detrimental to someone else.

3. With regard to the other options:

- Option A (extreme emergencies only): if you work the rota then you should be fully available as and when you are needed. Working reduced duties would be unacceptable.

- Option B (calling in sick on the last night) would be dishonest and would leave the department in serious trouble as there would be less cover available at a time when most colleagues would be away and locums hard to find. This would affect patient safety.

- Option C: you have no authority to cover the medical ward if you are not a medical FY1. At least it would need to be cleared by both respective consultants. In any case, this would place an unacceptable burden on you and the other FY1 and could compromise patient care.

- Option G (approaching the consultant): this is not appropriate until you have approached the ST3. He is in charge of the rota and so you must give him a chance to get it right before you escalate the matter.

- Option H: offering to cover part of the period is a noble thing to do, but this option imposes conditions on the group. As such it is less constructive than some of the other options available.

Scenario 187   ANSWER: E, G, H

1. Your main concern and focus will be the patient's clinical situation. As a competent adult she is perfectly entitled to self-discharge, but since it is detrimental to her health it is important that you do what you can to re-engage with her, using sensible methods. In that regard, talking to the girl about the DKA episodes (Option E) and exploring her reasons for non-compliance will allow you to explore why her diabetic control is so bad (perhaps she has been badly taught how to use her insulin pens and is thus non-compliant with her medications).

2. If you are concerned about her compliance (which would be the case since it is the seventh episode), writing to the GP would ensure that she is adequately followed up in the community (Option G). Since you are trying to re-engage with her personally to help her change her behaviour, it would also be useful for you to follow her up, at least at the start of the

process (Option H). This will allow you to see the girl in the outpatient setting to monitor progress and to discuss with her any issues that may have arisen.

3. With regard to the other options:

- Option A: calling the family would breach confidentiality; but even if she agreed to it, using threats will achieve little. This may in fact prompt her to lose faith in the system altogether and disengage.

- Options B and C: using shock tactics would be unreasonable and unprofessional; it may well result in the desired outcome but there are nicer ways of going about it. There is also a risk that you scare the patient so much that she totally disengages or starts becoming depressed; you could potentially cause more harm than good.

- Option D: writing in the discharge summary that she is not to be admitted again is essentially condemning the girl to a poor prognosis. She will either go somewhere else or disengage altogether. Until you have tried all the options open to you, you won't have satisfied your duty of care towards the patient.

- Option F: telling her that you can't help because it is her decision is not helpful. There are things that you can do to help, and you can't give up until you have tried them.

Scenario 188   ANSWER: A, C, G

1. The codeine is clearly affecting your ability to function fully and you should recognise that. You also need to be open about it with your colleagues. Therefore informing your consultant (Option A) would be important as he has ultimate responsibility for the care of the patients admitted under his name. Other than simply being aware of the problem, he may actually be able to suggest a solution to deal with the matter. For that reason, Option D (not mentioning the matter to anyone) is inappropriate.

2. If you can, you ought to come off the codeine, but you need to do that in the proper way: by going back to your GP for an alternative (Option G). Taking drugs from the trolley or asking nurses to do it (Option B) would be inappropriate (basically theft). It would be equally inappropriate to write

your own prescription (Option H) – indeed as an FY1 you would not be able to write a private prescription anyway; even if you were able to, it would be unethical to self-prescribe.

3. Because you tend to get tired towards the end of your shift, it would make sense to swap the ward cover with someone else (Option C).

4. Option E (sticking to sedentary work) would be unfair to the others. In addition, the problem is not so much the leg pain here but the side effects of the codeine. It could be equally unsafe to do sedentary work when you are tired as you may not be able to concentrate enough to remain alert.

5. Option F (sleeping more) is unlikely to help much.

Scenario 189   ANSWER: A, B, G

In stressful situations (e.g. night time), staff members are at high levels of stress. Maintaining good communication and working relationships between staff is vital for patient care.

1. Whatever argument you are having with the nurse, your first priority should be the care of the patient. Rather than arguing back, if the nurse is not willing to prepare the cannula then simply do it yourself (Option G). She might feel a sense of victory over you but it isn't about scoring points so don't argue back and get on with the job.

2. The question says that it is the first time that the nurse reacts aggressively. She may be stressed, tired or frustrated. It would be a good idea to discuss the incident with the nurse after some time has passed, when emotions are cooler (Option B). Taking the time to talk to your line manager (Option A) would also be appropriate. He may be able to advise you on how to handle your relationship with the nursing staff, and, if he is aware of other issues relating to this particular nurse or other nurses, may be able to discuss them with the ward sister.

3. Regarding the other options:

    •   Option C: in the same way that it was inappropriate for the nurse to have a go at you in front of one of her colleagues, it would be inappropriate for you to reply back in public. Keep your cool.

- Option D is just tit for tat and totally ignores the patient's interests. The cannula will have to be put in regardless of whether the nurse apologies.

- Option E: informing the ward sister may be premature if this is only the first time it has happened. It would be preferable to discuss the matter with your own senior first to get advice on how to handle it, and to discuss the matter directly with the nurse. If the behaviour becomes a pattern or the consultant feels that it warrants escalation then the sister may need to get involved. Such an approach would be better coming from the consultant.

- Option F: informing HR would need to be done by the nurse's superior, i.e. the ward sister, if there was real cause for concern in relation to her behaviour. It is a little premature and not your role anyway.

- Option H would be detrimental to patient care and would get you into trouble.

Scenario 190 | ANSWER: B, F, H

1. Misspelling or miscalculating a drug prescription is dangerous, and can severely affect patient safety. You will therefore need to take appropriate action to ensure that patients are protected. At the same time, this should be done in a manner that is sensitive and supportive towards your colleague. Option F (helping your colleague and offering to check his prescriptions in your spare time) offers that support, without making you neglect your own duties and patients (since you would only be providing the support in your spare time).

2. Telling the AAU consultant (Option H) will allow the issue to be formally acknowledged and dealt with, and will ensure that the consultant is aware of the potential issue of patient safety. Your colleague poses a potential danger to patient safety and it is therefore right that you should alert the consultant (albeit informally to start with). It will then be down to the consultant to take the most appropriate course of action. It would be even better if the colleague could inform the consultant himself.

3. All drug charts should be vetted by ward pharmacists anyway for accuracy and safety but it would be worth bringing the matter to the pharmacist's at-

tention so that he can be extra vigilant. He may also be able to support specifically the FY1's needs directly. Therefore Option B is also appropriate.

4. With regard to the other options:

    *   Option A: reporting the colleague to the GMC would only be appropriate if nothing was being done locally to protect patients. And if nothing was being done, you would most likely also need to report the consultant for failing to act.

    *   Options C and E: it is not the nurses' or the ward sister's job to check prescriptions. They may be able to spot issues using their experience but it is down to the doctors to ensure that the prescriptions are accurate.

    *   Option D: you have other things to do than checking all his prescriptions. This job should be down to his seniors, not you. You can offer some help temporarily if you have some spare time (Option F) but that is as far as you can go.

    *   Option G: you would essentially be stalking him. In any case, although you need to remain alert, it is not your job to check his work or instruct him to do his job properly. This should be left to the registrar or the consultant.

Scenario 191 ANSWER: A, B, C

1. If you are certain of the diagnosis (as stated in the question) of benign epididymal cyst then you do not need to refer the patient for further tests or for any treatment. Informing him of the diagnosis and reassuring him is essential (Option A). Suggesting that he should see his GP if he is concerned ensures that he has the opportunity for follow-up if he chooses (Option B). Sending him home is the correct management (Option C).

2. With regard to the other options:

    *   Option D: sending him to his GP for follow-up is a good suggestion and it may be that an ultrasound is warranted if clinical examination has not eased the man's worries or if the clinical findings change. Be

careful about prompting patients to "request" an investigation. The GP will decide if an investigation is warranted and request it if necessary.

- Option E: if you are certain of the diagnosis, an ultrasound is not required.

- Option F: to the patient, the situation is serious and you should respect that. By telling him off for coming into hospital for a benign issue, you are assuming he is able to assess the seriousness of his own condition, you are not acknowledging his fears or resolving them, and you are potentially putting his life in danger if, in the future, he decides to wait for a GP appointment first when his condition in fact warrants immediate attention.

- Option G: benign epididymal cysts do not need referral to urology if small and causing no symptoms.

- Option H: it is inappropriate to send this man to Oncology before a diagnosis is made. If you are certain (as the question states) that this is a benign cyst, Oncology will never be involved.

Scenario 192   ANSWER: C, E, F

1. The clinical picture presented to you is highly suggestive of metastatic breast cancer. The patient needs admission so that she can be assessed and treatment can start (Option C). Before you admit her, however, you should perform basic tests to include liver function (Option E).

2. Option F: the patient needs to know that there is something wrong with her liver as this is proven by the jaundice and hard craggy liver. At that point, you do not know for certain that this is metastatic breast cancer (although this is highly likely).

   If a patient asks you directly about the connection with her breast cancer, you have to be honest because the likelihood is strong; however, you shouldn't worry the patient unduly by volunteering information which may prove incorrect once all the tests have been performed.

3. With regard to the other answers:

- Options A and B: the patient will be referred to palliative care in time. However, given that the diagnosis has not been confirmed, this is a little premature.

- Option D: the patient does need urgent tests, but a liver MRI and mammogram are not indicated at this time.

- Option G: there is no need to worry the patient unduly about the likelihood that her cancer has spread until you have confirmation through the relevant tests. At this stage, you should stick to the facts and only address the issue of the cancer if she asks, at which point you will need to be honest about it (Option F).

- Option H: the fact that the cancer has spread is not proven so far and it would therefore be wrong to confirm it to the patient.

Scenario 193 ANSWER: D, E, H

A suspected subarachnoid haemorrhage is a medical emergency. If you are concerned enough to want a patient seen by the medical team for review, that team should never refuse to see him.

1. Option D: if you are a junior doctor and come across a difficulty in referring for admission, you must first seek help and advice from your senior, i.e. your ST1. He is your natural line of reporting and informing him should be your first step. The responsibility will then be on him to make sure the patient gets seen quickly.

2. Option E: the ST5's refusal could endanger the patient's life and there may be a cause for a complaint. The reasons behind the refusal will need to be investigated. The possible complaint will need to be first discussed with your own seniors as it will likely be made by your consultant to the medical ST5's consultant.

3. Option H: documenting every step is crucial so the reasons for the delay are clearly explained. This may then form the basis for the complaint.

4. Regarding the other answers:

- Option A: discharging a patient when the situation is an emergency would be very unwise. If the headaches get worse, he will be unlikely to be functioning well, let alone get to A&E.

- Options B and C: contacting the on-call medical consultant or a relevant subspecialty may be a good idea, but your first port of call should be your own senior, i.e. the ST1.

- Option F: this would be lying to get your own way and is not an acceptable way to proceed.

- Option G: the matter needs addressing more urgently. You can't simply get a nurse to observe the patient and let him deteriorate.

Scenario 194 — ANSWER: A, B, E

You need the bed for another patient, but that is no reason for discharging an existing patient to an unsafe home. The Occupational Therapists are professionals and are present in our hospitals for a reason. They are an essential part of the multidisciplinary team and should be respected.

1. It would be very unwise to discharge the patient if the home visit has not been done. If something happens to the patient at home, you could be accused of negligence. You will therefore need to ascertain from the OT when is the earliest that she can do the home visit (Option E). You will then be in a better position to approach the consultant and ask for his opinion as to how the matter should be handled (Option B). Armed with the facts, he may be able to think of alternative solutions. The ward manager will also need to be advised as she will be responsible for bed allocation and movement of patients (Option A).

2. Regarding the other options:

- Option C: asking the patient to put pressure on the OT would be totally inappropriate. You would be seriously undermining the OT's credibility and you would destroy any team spirit. It is your job to sort the problem out, not the patient's job.

- Option D: by telling the OT that the patient will be discharged without a home visit, you are flagrantly disregarding her clinical decision written in the notes. You are also not acting in the patient's best interests.

- Option F: OTs are busy professionals and will not unduly delay a discharge. Even if the home visit takes place today, the patient will still not be discharged in time enough to help your consultant. It would be appropriate to apply some gentle pressure, but it is not appropriate to leave the OT with no choice. In any case, this could prove a dangerous move.

- Option G: by discharging the patient, you are not respecting the Occupational Therapist's clinical decision written in the notes and are potentially acting against the patient's best interest.

- Option H: no mistake has been made and no patient has been endangered so far. The priority should be to find a solution.

Scenario 195   ANSWER: B, D, E

1. A one-off blood pressure recording of 190/100 without symptoms in an otherwise well patient should not be immediately treated. Only sustained hypertension needs treatment. There is a strong possibility here that the patient suffers from "White-coat hypertension" and your main task here will be to ensure that you ascertain whether this is a one-off reading or something recurrent and therefore more serious.

2. Option B: reviewing the patient's notes and medication fully to assess previous blood pressure readings, blood results, medication and investigations will help you ascertain whether this blood pressure reading is an isolated one.

3. Option E: asking the patient to sit outside and then get her blood pressure taken by a nurse later on may help you ascertain whether you were in fact the one causing the problem.

4. Option D: by performing serial blood pressure readings at home (as long as the machine is correctly calibrated) you can determine whether she suffers from hypertension. By then sending the patient to her GP with these results you will help inform the GP so that he can deal with it accordingly.

She will also likely feel more comfortable seeing a GP she knows well, i.e. her own.

5. With regard to the other answers.

- Option A: this will only ensure that she is not so stressed when she has her blood taken at the GP's surgery. However, it will not help resolve the matter.

- Option C: there is no indication for admission here.

- Options F and G: without reviewing her notes or performing serial blood pressure measurements, you cannot decide whether she requires medication for her blood pressure. It is better to send the patient to her GP.

- Option H: getting the patient reviewed by the consultant might actually stress her more and risks exacerbating the problem.

Scenario 196   ANSWER: B, C, G

1. There are many reasons why a patient may miss appointments and you should not write the patient off too quickly. It may be for example that they have concerns about a possible diagnosis and are reluctant to confront their illness. It may be that they don't trust healthcare professionals or are scared of the hospital environment. Perhaps they are scared of a potential surgical intervention. As such, before any firm action can be taken against the patient, you will need to satisfy yourself that you have investigated the situation enough to make the right decision.

2. At the same time, since it is the fifth time the patient has missed an appointment, he will also need reminding that he has some obligations.

3. Following on from that, Option C (asking the patient what he is up to and checking he is okay) is appropriate as it will ensure that any immediate issues are identified. Option B (Informing the clinic manager so that she can explain the clinic's policy) will also be important. The patient should be made aware of the fact that he has been missing so many appointments and of the possible consequences of missing more. Just because you

have to be nice does not meant that you can't be a little bit firm; you just need to make sure that this is handled sensitively.

4. Since the patient's GP will have made the referral and will be expecting some kind of report back, it would be important to advise him that patient care is being delayed by his non-attendances. Contacting the GP may also prompt him to contact the patient to make sure that he is okay (Option G).

5. Regarding the other options:

- Option A: documenting the non-attendance will be mildly useful, but since it is the fifth time it is not as effective as the other options.

- Option D: confronting the patient may actually put him off attending even more. You may get a reason out of him, but it won't actually do much more than just satisfy your curiosity. Your priority should be to re-engage with the patient.

- Options E and F: it may well be that it will come to a stage where the patient will no longer be accepted in your clinic, but that is not a decision for you to make. It will be taken by consultants in conjunction with managers.

- Option H: caring about the patient is a nice thing to do. Unfortunately, contacting his wife would be a breach of confidentiality.

Scenario 197 ANSWER: B, E, F

If someone is attending for her fourth termination of pregnancy at the age of 21, then she needs some degree of sex education and a form of long-term contraception such as the coil or a contraceptive implant.

1. Option B: offering to insert a coil at the time of TOP means the patient will have a long-term (five- to ten-year) reversible contraception and will not have to worry about the procedure of inserting it, as she will be under general anaesthetic.

2. Option E: it is important that the patient is told that repeat surgical TOP is potentially dangerous and she knows that it is not a form of contraception.

3. Option F: counselling may help address some of the issues underlying her behaviour and the risks that she is taking. This may help uncover issues of misinformation or even abuse and will at least result in some basic education.

4. With regard to the other options:

    •   Option A: there is no indication that a psychiatrist is needed. A chat with a suitable doctor, a councillor or a health adviser would be sufficient to start with (Option F).

    •   Option C: the combined oral contraceptive pill is less protective than a coil or implant and is not long term.

    •   Option D: condoms are important to protect her from sexually-transmitted diseases, but are less reliable than a coil from a contraceptive perspective.

    •   Option G: you should never "tell" a patient to have a procedure. This patient is only 21 and the question does not say whether she has any children yet.

    •   Option H is not a solution and would not discourage her from getting pregnant with babies she doesn't want in the first place.

Scenario 198 · ANSWER: C, F, G

1. Option C: it is essential to be aware of child protection issues and to safeguard the well-being of all children in your care. You must always listen to a child and document everything he or she says.

2. Option G: once the child has explained everything, your asking if this has ever happened before gives them the opportunity to talk about other abuse.

3. Option F: having a nurse with you gives the child extra support and provides you with a witness to what the child is saying.

4. With regard to the other answers:

- Option A: you need to give the child time to talk and, if he has chosen you to open up to, you should listen to him. Admitting him immediately and informing the child protection doctor may breach that trust and the child may not say anymore. It may become necessary to admit the child but you should talk to him first. As such, although it would be an appropriate action to consider, it does not feature in the top three here. Be aware, however, that you are a very junior doctor and should not take sole responsibility in this case. You must seek senior help as soon as is practical.

- Option B: always believe a child when they talk about abuse. NEVER tell them or imply that they may be lying. A full investigation will follow any allegation of abuse.

- Option D: always document every allegation a child makes. It may never be repeated again. By ignoring the first allegation, you may send the child back into an unsafe environment.

- Option E: you do not need to wait for the mother to return to talk to this child. He has obviously waited for his mother to leave before opening up to you. Respect that and act on it.

- Option H: the mother will not be the most reliable witness. In addition, bringing the issue to her attention may actually result in a worse situation if she denies it and then tells the father about the allegations. You would need to be careful about approaching either parent. The most appropriate course of action is to gather as much information as you can and then either contact social services or admit the child.

Scenario 199 ANSWER: B, C, G

1. The situation is sensitive. Your ST5 has made a mistake that could have had serious consequences on a patient. He needs to be made aware of the problem so that the matter can be sorted out and he also needs to ensure that the right lessons are learnt. In such circumstances it will be important that you make the ST5 aware of the mistake he has made (Option B), that the patient is referred to a rheumatologist (Option G) and that a

critical incident form is completed (Option C). The case can also be used as a teaching tool (which is also addressed in Option B).

2. Regarding the other options:

- Option A: not telling the ST5 is inappropriate. He has made a mistake and should be informed of it so that he can deal with it and learn from it.

- Option D (telling the consultant) would be a possible candidate but it would be more appropriate if the ST5 contacted the consultant himself. If you did so yourself, the ST5 would get the feeling that you are going behind his back. You should consider telling the consultant if you saw that the ST5 had not done so. In any case, if a critical incident form is completed then the consultant will be made aware of the problem soon enough.

- Option E: the mistake has nothing to do with the ST3. If anyone is informed, it should be the consultant.

- Option F (informing the GMC) is not appropriate at this stage. That would only apply if you had serious concerns about the ST5 which the Trust was not addressing appropriately.

- Option H: contacting the patient is not your role here. This should be done by the ST5 who has made the mistake or by the consultant.

Scenario 200   ANSWER: C, D, E

1. Options C, D and E: it is important in medicine to admit your mistakes and to always ensure you act in the best interests of the patient. You must document your clinical findings, always explain to the patient and inform your consultant of the problem.

2. With regard to the other options:

- Option A: you should never ignore a clinical finding; it must always be documented.

- Option B is marginally preferable to Option A, since it involves leaving the clinical findings in the hands of the anaesthetist. However, there is no way of knowing if the murmur will ever be detected by another clinician pre-operatively. Although the anaesthetist does (usually) listen to the patient's heart, you are essentially "passing the buck". Having discovered an issue, it is your responsibility to deal with it.

- Option F: it is unlikely that the echo lab will be able to perform an echo at such short notice; even if it could, your consultant and the patient should still be informed as in Options D and E, and the murmur documented (Option C).

- Option G: completing a critical incident form may be appropriate at some stage down the line as a mistake was made. However, this is not a priority right now and other options are more appropriate.

- Option H: telling the consultant that the patient is ready for surgery would only be possible if it was preceded by tests. Some of the options are more immediate than this one and therefore Option H does not feature in the final three options.

Scenario 201 ANSWER: A, B, D

1. There are many reasons why a patient may want to die. This may be as a result of depression or loneliness, a recent event, the death of a friends, etc. It is also possible that the patient may not have capacity and as such it would be important to assess them for capacity (Option A) and offer support (Option B). If the patient has capacity, then it will be his decision to stop the medication under the principle of autonomy (Option D).

2. Options C and E: this would be illegal as it would constitute assisted suicide. There are many better ways of dealing with the matter, including helping the patient understand why he may be feeling this way.

3. Option F: a DNR order would be the responsibility of the doctor in view of the clinical situation. To issue a DNR order you would need to be confident that it would not be in the patient's best interest to be resuscitated. There is no clinical indication for that here; he only has high cholesterol. In any case, you would need to consult a senior colleague before a DNR order can be issued.

4. Option G: involving the relatives may be a good idea but you would be breaching confidentiality if you simply informed them. You would need to obtain the patient's consent before you can do so.

5. Option H: the fact that someone makes a decision that you do not think is rational does not mean that they are not competent. The patient would need to be properly assessed by you, another doctor from your team, or a psychiatrist.

Scenario 202 ANSWER: B, C, D

1. Agreeing to make the change (Option A) could lead you into great trouble (possibly being struck off). You are responsible for your own decisions and therefore the only option open to you is to refuse to make the entry (Option B). The fact that the consultant is about to write a reference for you does not alter your responsibility to do the right thing.

2. Your next step would be to contact your defence union (Option C) and to make sure that you keep a note of the conversation that you had with your consultant as you may need to testify in future. They will be able to advise you on the legal aspect of the case and your duties as a doctor. Since you are involved in the care of the patient, you will need to do everything possible to protect yourself and do everything by the book.

3. Since it is linked to a fitness to practise issue for the consultant, you will need to report the matter to a senior colleague as soon as possible. Your Clinical Director is the obvious candidate for this (Option D). When you see the Clinical Director, you should raise with him the issue of the reference so that he can make sure you are not being victimised.

4. Informing the GMC (Option F) is a little premature. If there is cause for concern, the Clinical Director may well do that but later in the process. As for informing the police (Option G), this is also a possible course of action but not one that you will need to take by yourself. If need be, the police will be called following a decision made at Trust level (e.g. by managers, the Medical Director, the Chief Executive) but not by you.

5. Informing the patient that a mistake has been made is a good idea and should be done. However, Option E also says that you should tell the patient about the consultant's attempt to modify the notes. If a decision is

made to tell the patient about the consultant's request then it will be made in consultation with the Trust's management (as there is a legal risk). You should stick to the clinical aspect of the work and let the managers handle any situation that has possible legal implications. This makes Option E inappropriate.

6. A critical incident form (Option H) should be completed for the mistake which was made in the first place, but not for the attempt to cover up. The cover-up should be dealt with through a formal approach of the relevant authority (e.g. Clinical Director) and not by sharing the whole event with the team for reflection purposes.

Scenario 203 ANSWER: A, B, E

1. There are two issues to consider in this scenario: your consultant's integrity and the fact that two doctors have potentially fake CVs and therefore pose a possible danger to patients by misrepresenting themselves to future employers. The issue is further complicated by the fact that you still need to work with your consultant and therefore need to be careful in your handling of the matter.

2. Talking to your consultant privately would be a good start, which makes Option E a good candidate. During the meeting you should ensure that you do not become an accessory to the fraudulent activity that is taking place and you will need to refuse to add the names to the publication unless these individuals have had some input into the process (Option A). It would be tempting to go ahead with the publication with the inclusion of the extra names for the sake of an easy life (Option C) but you must think about the consequences of your own actions and also the consequences of helping two doctors to represent themselves fraudulently. Whether we are dealing with a case report or a more important publication is irrelevant. The issues at stake are your personal integrity and your broader ethical duty towards your patients and society generally.

3. Reporting your consultant to the GMC (Option F) will achieve little. Although his approach is unprofessional, you would need to discuss the matter with the Clinical Director (Option B) first as he is your consultant's line manager. The Clinical Director is best placed to handle the matter by himself without involving the GMC. It may be that he then decides to involve the GMC himself, particularly if this is a recurrent problem.

4. You may, however, want to contact the GMC about the two other doctors (also in Option B) as their fraud is a potential risk to patients. Indeed, they will be able to list the publication on their CV as their own. They may have lied about other things too and therefore obtained jobs under false pretences. In an ideal world, it may be appropriate to contact their Clinical Directors, but since you have no direct dealings with them, the GMC is your next best option.

5. Checking with others (Option D) sounds like a good idea but it would only serve to spread rumours and gossip. In any case, if the consultant had been trying the same trick with other colleagues, the next step would be to contact the Clinical Director and not the GMC. So, Option D is not suitable.

6. Warning the paper (Option G) will achieve little in the long term. The paper will most certainly reject your case report as they wouldn't want to take the risk that the names may be fraudulent and so you might as well not submit it.

7. Informing the registrar (Option H) will not help much. At best he may give you some advice but that will be fairly limited. All you will do is undermine your consultant's credibility with another colleague for not much benefit in return.

Scenario 204 ANSWER: C, D, E

1. In such a situation, it would be important to stop the conversation if you can. Option A allows you to do that in a rather abrupt manner and would also embarrass the ward clerk. Option E is slightly dishonest but with no consequences; it will, however, be effective in stopping the conversation.

2. This behaviour is unacceptable and several patients will have heard the conversation. They may be left thinking that similar comments are being made about them, and witnessing such a scenario will seriously undermine their trust in the whole medical team. It would therefore be right to involve the clinic manager so that they can take appropriate action. You must make sure it does not happen again (Option C). You will also need to reassure the patients that something will be done about the problem (Option D).

3. Regarding the other options:

- Option B (waiting for the next occurrence to discuss with the clinical manager) is not appropriate as this will essentially allow the ward clerk the chance to behave in such a manner again. There may also be several instances where they behave like this but which you won't be witnessing. The patient's trust in the team is at risk and you must ensure it is acted upon swiftly.

- Option F (discussing with your consultant) is less appropriate than discussing with the clinic manager. The consultant is not in the reporting line of the ward clerk and therefore will have little responsibility. He will likely simply report the matter in turn to the clinic manager. Going to the consultant would be the most appropriate thing to do if the person mocking the patient was another doctor.

- Option G: documenting the matter won't achieve anything and has no relevance to the care of the patient or the handling of the patient involved in the conversation.

- Completing a critical incident (Option H) is too formal a step. There are more direct ways of handling the situation in the short term.

Scenario 205 ANSWER: A, B, F

This is a relatively small issue which can have serious repercussions, e.g. patients not feeling they want to engage much with this doctor and the rest of the team trying to steer clear of him. It is therefore important that the situation is resolved as soon as possible. At the same time it has to be done sensitively so as not to embarrass your colleague.

1. Option F is appropriate as it would be sensible to deal with the matter directly with the colleague again. Since it is a recurrent issue, it may be wise to inform a senior colleague so that they can intervene if needed. Hence options A and B are also appropriate.

2. With regard to the other options:
   - Option C: you don't need a survey to decide if someone has strong body odour. This would not be a sensitive or useful way of handling the matter.

- Options D and E: whether the colleague is present or not, having a team meeting on the matter won't help. There is no specific behaviour that the team can adopt to make things better. The colleague simply needs to be talked to by one person. The fewer people you involve, the better.

- Option G (anonymous note) is unprofessional.

- Option H is not required at this stage. This may be required if all other options have failed. It would most likely come from the consultant.

Scenario 206 ANSWER: A, D, F

1. Option D (talking to the ST3) is an appropriate course of action as it attempts resolution of the matter in the most direct manner. However, since it has been going on for some time, you will need to bring it to the consultant's attention (Option A) because he is responsible for patient care and will need to influence the situation so that patients are safe.

2. Option F (critical incident form) is appropriate because the ST3 has failed to review a very sick patient and therefore patient safety has been compromised. There are clearly lessons to be learnt; completing a critical incident form will assist the learning process.

3. Options B and C both advocate that the problem should be ignored. This should be avoided. This problem needs resolution.

4. Option E simply invites colleagues to gossip and introduces an element of mistrust. This is not a good team playing attitude; you should be more open in your dealings with others.

5. Option G is inappropriate because a senior nurse has no direct hierarchical responsibility over the ST3.

6. Option H may be something that happens at some stage in the future but not before a local resolution has been found. Reporting the colleague to the GMC will be something that the senior clinicians or the Trust should do, rather than you.

Scenario 207 ANSWER: C, D, E

1. Option C: your consultant is in charge of the patient and has asked for these results. He will need to know.

2. Option D: once the consultant has been informed, the CNS will need to go and see the patient for support and to discuss the next steps.

3. Option E: it is essential that any results you get are clearly documented in the patient notes.

4. Regarding the other options:

   - Option A: although the patient is anxious, it is essential that a senior member of the team who can answer all questions informs the patient of the result. Therefore Option D would be more appropriate.

   - Option B: the oncologist may not be the next best step as this will depend on the type of tumour. You should always wait until your consultant or CNS advises you before referring to Oncology. The patient should also be informed of his diagnosis before he is referred to another team.

   - Option F: the ward nurses will need to know and should ideally be present when the diagnosis is made, but Options C, D and E are of more immediate concern in this situation.

   - Option G: this would be breaching patient confidentiality and is inappropriate.

   - Option H: asking her sister to put her complaint in writing is not appropriate when (i) she didn't complain to you and (ii) the results are back and there are some greater priorities to deal with.

Scenario 208 ANSWER: B, C, E

1. You must always check the patient for signs of life (Option C), even if a nurse has told you they have died. You will be certifying the death and therefore you need to be 100% certain that this is accurate. That automat-

ically discounts Option H.

2. Clear and precise patient notes (Option E) are essential during life and after death.

3. The death certificate (Option B) is very important and should be done as soon as practically possible to ensure that you do not inconvenience the relatives of the deceased patient.

4. With regard to the other options:

- Option A. the patients sharing the bay have no right to be informed of the death. You still owe your patient confidentiality even in death.

- Option D: you need to check for signs of a pacemaker only if the patient is to be cremated. In any case, this would be done by the person completing the cremation form. There is no indication that the patient's wishes are known.

- Option F: since this was an expected death and it happened in hospital, there is no need to discuss the case with the coroner.

- Option G: the ALS algorithm is for an arrest situation. It has no place when certifying a death.

Scenario 209   ANSWER: C, D, G

1. The key factors to consider here are as follows:

- You have finished all your jobs and clinical; there doesn't seem to be much more for you to do.

- The text says that you are tired. It is also important that you look after yourself and have breaks when you can have them.

- You are paid until 6pm so you should stay until 6pm. Once you have taken care of your patients, there are other things you can do and the audit is one of those.

- It would be nice to help your colleagues but you don't have the obligation to do this if they are coping with their own work, you are tired, and you have other responsibilities to fulfil (e.g. your audit, which is equally important).

This points to Options C, D and G being the most appropriate.

2. Looking at the other options:

- Options A and H: hanging around won't help unless you help your colleagues. You have other priorities and would need to remain available if they needed you, but that doesn't mean that you have to do their job for them. You would likely consider those options if you didn't have the audit to do.

- Option B (going home) would go against your contract. You may still be needed at a later stage and your colleagues will assume you are still on-site. You would only consider doing that if you could not function anymore; this would require approval from a senior colleague (consultant or manager).

- Options D and E (keeping the bleep vs. handing over the bleep): you are on duty and therefore the bleep should stay with you.

- Option F: relaxing would be fine but you have 2.5 hours to kill and your employer would be expecting you to do something productive. Relaxing is therefore less appropriate than doing the audit.

Scenario 210 ANSWER: B, F, H

1. The patient is 16 and so is the boyfriend; the sexual relationship is therefore legal. Since there is no indication that she is being coerced or in any particular danger, there is no need to inform social services. Therefore Option E is inappropriate.

2. Informing the mother (Option D) is equally inappropriate as this would be breaching the patient's confidentiality when there is no real reason to.

3. You can actually prescribe anything on the formulary (thus making Option G inappropriate), but it would be much better if the patient's situation was

assessed properly in an environment where her specific circumstances could be discussed adequately. A GP appointment or an appointment at the local sexual health clinic would be a more suitable option (especially if the risk of having unprotected sex is limited by the fact that the boyfriend is on holiday). Therefore, since there is time, it would best for you not to prescribe the pill (Option F) and instead to let those who can spend more time with the patient and have more specialist knowledge take the matter over (Option B). This automatically makes Option A less appropriate.

4. Option C is essentially blackmailing the patient and is inappropriate.

5. Option H would ensure that the patient has information which can make her safer and, in view of the fact that she is having unprotected sex, is entirely useful and in her best interest.

Scenario 211 ANSWER: C, D, G

1. The colleague poses a risk to patient safety. His judgement will be impaired by the alcohol and he is therefore not fit to see patients and should be sent home (Option D). Option H (telling him he should see patients with a chaperone) is not appropriate; he smells of alcohol and patients will therefore be able to see that there is a problem. This could affect their trust in the team negatively.

2. Your colleague has shown a serious lack of insight by not recognising that he was not fit to work. For that reason, you should report the matter to a senior colleague, e.g. the consultant (Option C). Waiting for the next occurrence (Option F) is not appropriate as you are allowing the situation to worsen and therefore you are potentially endangering patients (there is no guarantee you will be there when it next happens).

3. Your colleague is clearly having problems and it would be nice to show some support. Therefore Option G would also be appropriate.

4. Option A (giving him chewing gum) would only assist your colleague in hiding the problem and is therefore inappropriate.

5. Option B (CAGE questionnaire) is way over the top. The colleague is not your patient and there are more pressing issues to deal with.

6. Option E (critical incident form) is pointless. There has been no mistake made. You would consider completing a critical incident form if he had been allowed to see patients without anyone noticing or daring to say something; or obviously if a mistake or near-miss had taken place. As it currently stands the situation is of a personal nature.

Scenario 212 ANSWER: B, D, G

1. The text tells you that the patient is not overweight, and thus he would not be eligible for any sort of weight losing treatment. Therefore Options A and C would be inappropriate.

2. Asking the patient why he wishes to lose weight (Option D) and referring him to a psychiatrist (Option G) to explore the issues that surround his behaviour may help approach the problem from a different angle and may entice the patient to stop taking the ephedrine.

3. Regardless, the patient has come to you so that you may monitor his blood pressure and heart rate, and you should comply with this request because it is a sensible thing to do in circumstances where he is taking medication which may be damaging to the heart. Reminding the patient of the danger of the drug would also be good practice. Hence Option B is suitable.

4. Option E is unsafe and inappropriate. The fact that the patient is using the wrong medication is actually the reason why you should be supporting him and not giving up on him. Patients are entitled to make their own decision and blackmailing them is not the way to engage with them. For that reason, Option F is also unsuitable.

5. Advising the patient to keep taking ephedrine (Option H) is unsafe and, in any case, illegal if the drug is banned.

Scenario 213 ANSWER: A, G, H

1. In general, it is better to address issues directly with patients and their families; however, an exception is usually made when you strongly suspect child abuse. In situations where you have a suspicion of child

abuse, no matter what the parents say, reporting is mandatory, even based on suspicion alone. As much as possible, any such reports should be done with the advice of senior colleagues. As such, Options A and H are two of the most appropriate options. You do not have the authority to remove the child from the custody of the parents. Only social services or a court can do that.

2. Calling the police (Option D) would be appropriate if you felt that a crime had been committed against the child, or if a child was thought to be in imminent danger. At this stage there is only a suspicion and social services are a more appropriate channel. Social services may enact protection orders to protect the child and, depending on their investigations, may refer to the police for criminal investigations.

3. Admitting the boy into the hospital (Option G) may remove him from the harmful environment and also allows the opportunity for senior colleagues to carefully re-examine the boy again for further signs and manage his well-being.

4. With regard to the other options:

- Option B: reassuring the father would be inappropriate. The injury needs to be treated but that will be done when the child has been admitted.

- Option C (discharge) would be inappropriate as the child is in danger.

- Option E (asking the mother about the abuse) would not be helpful. This would infuriate the father further, she is likely to deny it and you don't need the information to act.

- Option F: a lawsuit would not be the responsibility of the hospital. Your priority is the child and social services' involvement.

Scenario 214 ANSWER: A, C, F

1. You have made a mistake, which is a combination of unfortunate circumstances, resulting in a patient being discharged without the medications that the consultant wanted to prescribe. The patient was given her old medications without the newly required heart failure medications. This

could mean that the patient could have another episode of decompen-sated heart failure and be admitted to hospital again if nothing further is done.

2. Since the patient has already being discharged, it is important that you contact the consultant and are open about your mistake (Option A).

3. Calling the patient, apologising and asking her to come back for the new set of medications (Option C) is essential in this case, as it enables you to personally inform the patient of the mistake you have made and to ensure that the patient is on the right medications. Once you have done that, the patient will be safe and all that needs doing is completing a critical incident form so that the problem can be recorded and the right lessons learnt (Option F).

4. Option D is not appropriate as her old medications may not be suitable for her anymore and will not result in the patient being safe. You need to en-sure that she gets the heart failure medication soon.

5. Option E will not be fast enough.

6. Option G: making the GP aware of the mistake is pointless if you have dealt with it and he has no role to play.

7. Option H is a possibility but it would be safer to recall the patient straight away.

Scenario 215 ANSWER: C, D, F

1. Nursing staff often raise issues, and you should not order any nurses into doing anything that they may feel uncomfortable about. The SJTs will give you all the information that you need – in this case we are told that the speed and amount of magnesium to be infused is reasonable for this clini-cal scenario.

2. It would be important to establish fully why the nurse feels uncomfortable that the infusion is going in too quick (Option C) and, if necessary, to edu-cate her on the correct infusion speed. More importantly, since you cannot force the nurse to do something that she does not want to do, then chang-ing the speed of infusion (Option D) might be an option that the nurse is

happy with. Speaking to your seniors for advice at this stage (Option F) is also useful, since they may advise that there are other preparations of magnesium available, or that dietary changes will be fine, or perhaps that the patient does not need the magnesium at all.

3. Administering the magnesium yourself (Option A) would not resolve the issue of the nurse being uncomfortable with the infusion and may make her feel that her thoughts are being ignored, which may harm future working relationships with that nurse. Option D is a much better option because it is perfectly safe and would solve the issue of the nurse's discomfort.

4. Ordering the nurse to administer it despite her protests (Option H) is inappropriate.

5. Options E means that the patient will not get the magnesium he needs.

6. Option G: her refusal would need to be documented but there are better options available.

7. Option B (completing a critical incident form) may be appropriate but there are more immediate options.

Scenario 216   ANSWER: A, C, G

1. When a clinical mistake has been made, you need to inform the consultant looking after the patient as a priority, especially if the patient has already been discharged (Option A). You will then need to speak and apologise to the patient themselves (Option G). You will also need to correct the mistake as soon as you can (Option C).

2. Looking at the other options:

- Option B (doing nothing) is not appropriate.

- Option D: whilst filling in a critical incident form and reflecting on your own mistake is important and will need to happen at some stage in the process, it still does not make the patient get his final dose of IV iron. Speaking to the GP (Option C) and arranging for a community appointment for the final infusion is the most appropriate option. Basically the critical incident form is not as much of a priority in this situation as some of the other options.

- Option E: the nurse bears some responsibility and therefore will need to be informed at some stage. But there are some more immediate concerns.

- Option F: documenting will be important but not as much of a priority here.

- Option H: simply inappropriate and over the top.

Scenario 217 ANSWER: A, D, F

1. The situation is embarrassing and will severely affect the trust that patients and relatives have in the team. Your first move will be to communicate appropriately with the relative and the patient. You will need to apologise and provide reassurance (Option A). Recognising that the behaviour is not acceptable is also an appropriate response as it will convey that you are serious about their complaint.

2. It will also be important that the nurses and medical student are told that their behaviour has been witnessed and that it is unprofessional/unacceptable (Option D). This will ensure they do not perpetuate it. Ideally you should also warn them that you will be reporting the matter.

3. You are not best placed to deal with the matter but you will need to ensure someone in authority does. Hence, reporting the issue to the consultant (in charge of the medical student) and the ward sister (in charge of the junior nurses) will be essential (Option F).

4. Regarding the other options:

   - Option B (contacting HR) will be something that may well be done, but that will need to be actioned by the consultant and the ward sister. Your role is to go to senior colleagues who are directly responsible for the individuals concerned and who can handle the matter.

   - Option C (completing a critical incident form) would be extreme in this situation.

- Option E (telling the patient and the relative that they can make a complaint) is actually a very appropriate option. However, this is not as much of a priority as ensuring that the matter is being dealt with by talking to all interested parties.

- Option G is actually telling the patient that you knew of the problem before. This will not reassure the patient that the matter is in hand. If they ask you a question about prior incidents, you will have to be honest, but you don't have to volunteer the information.

- Option H (sending the nurses and medical student home) is not your responsibility. It might be a useful thing to do so that the patient is not aggravated by their presence, but that is not a top priority.

Scenario 218 ANSWER: B, C, H

1. If you are confident that the student knows what he is supposed to do and has some experience already then you can allow him to carry out the procedure under your supervision (Option H). Before that you will need to ask the patient's consent, making it clear that a medical student will be performing the procedure (Option C). The consent given previously by the patient was given on the premise that a qualified doctor would be performing it. You will also need to document the whole thing in the notes (Option B).

2. Regarding the other options:

- Option A: the medical student should not do any procedure unsupervised.

- Option D: it would be nice if you could allow the medical student the opportunity to learn. Nothing in the text suggests that you are in a hurry or that the catheterisation is a difficult one.

- Option E: asking for the registrar's or consultant's approval is not necessary. If you are happy that the student is capable of doing the procedure under your supervision then you can go ahead.

- Option F: very few nurses would do male catheterisation. The procedure needs to be supervised by someone who is competent in doing the procedure themselves. A nurse would not be a suitable supervisor.

- Option G: the previous consent was given on the basis that a doctor would be doing the procedure. You should not just tell the patient that it will now be done by a medical student; you really ought to get consent again (i.e. Option C is more appropriate).

Scenario 219 ANSWER: A, B, F

1. Option A: it is essential that you inform the patient that a mistake has been made. Aside from the fact that you need to be open and upfront, the patient will need to be told why you are changing the antibiotics, which may in fact result in a delay in discharge. This allows for professional trust to be maintained with the patient. The registrar will also need to be informed. This makes Option D inappropriate.

2. Cancelling the prescription and writing the new one (Option F) is equally important. The mistake has to be rectified as soon as possible. Leaving the old less effective antibiotic in place until the course is finished (Option G), or continuing with the less effective antibiotic (Option H) are not appropriate choices. Option C is not sufficient; you need to prescribe a new antibiotic.

3. Option B (recording the event in your reflective portfolio) will be useful as it will enable you to think about and learn from the incident.

4. Option E is actually wrong. A mistake was made and so, in theory, a critical incident form should be completed. Indeed there may be lessons to be learnt from that incident.

Scenario 220 ANSWER: C, D, H

1. Option A: it is right that you should continue to answer the bleep. However, reporting to the ward sister every occurrence when there was no emergency will get on her nerves as much as the situation is getting on yours. This will swamp the sister with a huge volume of information and is more likely to make her think that you are the one who is causing a problem.

2. Option B: ignoring the bleep is not a safe thing to do. If something is urgent, it won't wait 30 minutes.

3. Option C: discussing the matter with the other FY1s will help you ascertain whether this is a general problem or something linked to that particular ward. It will enable you to get your colleagues' perspective on the situation. You will then be in a better position to present a full picture to the ward sister when you meet with her.

4. Option D: if the bleeps are causing an issue, it needs to be addressed. The best person to address it is the ward sister as she will be able to liaise with the nurses and make sure that there is a consistent approach to the problem.

5. Options E and F: try to sort it out by yourself first. The matter could be resolved through simple consultation. Show some initiative first and escalate the matter to your seniors only if you are unable to find a way forward. You may wish to discuss the matter with your seniors for advice before you take any action. But the wording of the two options makes them inappropriate. Option E talks about "informing" the registrar, which won't help much. Option F actually gets the consultant to do the work.

6. Options G and H: getting one of the nurses you know to place a note at the nurses' station is not a bad idea, but that assumes they will see it and that they will actually take it into account. There are also probably nurses who think that something is urgent when it isn't. As such it would be more appropriate to simply discuss the issue with one of the nurses you know so that you can get her perspective on the situation (Option H). This may give you a better idea of how to approach your discussions with the other FY1s and the ward sister.

Scenario 221 ANSWER: A, D, F

1. The patient will feel distraught and will need to be supported. At the same time, it would be ideal if this could be achieved without impacting too much on the other patients who are due to be seen as part of the ward round. As such, excusing yourself temporarily from the ward round to contact the cancer nurse (Option A) will ensure that the patient has support without slowing down the ward round too much. It would also be good practice for you to go back to the patient once you have finished the ward round to

make sure she is okay (Option F). Finally, the consultant's behaviour is not acceptable and you should try to raise the matter sensitively with him (Option D).

2. Looking at the other options:

- Option B is not appropriate as the nurse is needed for the ward round and asking her to leave would achieve nothing.

- Option C would deprive other patients of care. The ward round should continue regardless of the communication mistake that has been made.

- Option E will achieve nothing other than informing the ST5. He won't be able to do much about it and it is best if you mention the matter to the consultant yourself in an appropriate manner. If you can't get through to the consultant and he continues to behave like this, you may need to escalate the matter to the Clinical Director.

- Option G (critical incident form) is a remote possibility. The problem is just with one person's communication skills and there are more immediate things that need to be done in this instance. Completing a critical incident form on a named consultant is not as appropriate as trying to deal with the problem directly. The incident form would be best coming from them.

- Option H: leaving the ward round would not be appropriate. It would be better to ensure someone stays with the patient, finish the ward round and then get back to the patient.

Scenario 222 ANSWER: C, G, H

1. Calling or writing to the patient once he has been discharged and asking him to get involved is not appropriate. You would need to retrieve the patient's contact details from the hospital's system to handle a matter that is mostly a personal matter, in a context where the patient is not even directly involved since the thief is one of his relatives. Therefore both Options A and B are inappropriate because they would constitute an inappropriate use of patient details and would unfairly involve the patient.

2. Since this is a criminal matter, the police should be involved. With Option D, you are revealing the name of the patient and his contact details to the police. Technically, revealing the patient's name would be a breach of confidentiality. It would be more appropriate to let them talk to the patient whilst he is still in hospital (Option C) so that you don't have to reveal his name. When they talk to him, they can ask him for his relative's contact details. Option C also allows for the police to talk to Mr Jones away from the ward, which will ensure that it does not cause distress to the other patients in the ward.

3. Option E is not appropriate because the patient is not the guilty party here. Even if the patient was the guilty party, careful consideration would need to be given as to how banning the patient from the hospital would impact on his future care before he is banned.

4. Option F is also inappropriate because it has nothing to do with the patient.

5. Option G (talking to the patients whose notes were seen by the relative) would be useful and appropriate. We are told that Mr Jones's relative was filmed looking at patient notes. The confidentiality of those patients has been breached and they should be duly informed of that fact. They should also be reassured that measures will be taken to make sure notes are better protected.

6. Option H: all your colleagues need to be made aware of the issue so that they can be more on their guard. Raising it at a team meeting will help. Completing a critical incident form will also ensure the event is documented, reflected upon and further measures are introduced to ensure it doesn't happen again.

Scenario 223 ANSWER: A, B, F

1. This situation is potentially tricky as there has clearly been a breakdown in communication somewhere along the line, and it has led to a situation where the nurses are blaming doctors and doctors blaming nurses when everyone is probably at fault. The sister has taken the trouble to do something about the matter, albeit very much in a one-sided manner by placing the blame on you. You should use the opportunity to make sure the whole matter is handled effectively and sensitively.

2. There is a hint of frustration in the sister's approach and you should avoid anything which is unnecessarily confrontational or defensive before you have had a chance to consider the comments from a more objective perspective. So for example:

- Option C is asking the sister to name her sources but does not really address the actual issue of what they think is wrong. It is a fairly defensive move.

- Option D is also defensive as it is telling the sister that, if there is a problem, the nurses are equally to blame for it. This may be true but won't really help resolve the matter. You are just deflecting the blame in a way that may be inflammatory.

- Option E is essentially refusing to deal with it yourself. This would be a fairly rude thing to do. The sister could have gone to your consultant first but she approached you instead.

- Option G will be confronting the nurses who complained against you. This will place them in an embarrassing situation and may cause resentment.

- Option H: similarly to Option G, this will put people on the spot.

3. Option A (reassuring the sister that you feel you are working hard) will briefly set out your position on the matter without prejudging what she has to say.

4. Option B: the statement made by the sister is pretty vague. You cannot reflect on the situation and deal with it unless you have specific examples that will enable you to determine how you could have handled the situation differently. You can't simply accept a general feeling that people may have about you.

5. Option F: talking to your consultant will have two effects. You will get support from him and he will be able to get additional help for you on the ward if indeed the nurse is right and you need additional support. The consultant will also be able to provide advice on how to handle the comments made and may in fact take responsibility to deal with it by himself. It is also possible that similar comments were made about other doctors and the consultant will need to be made aware that there are some specific issues relating to doctor-nurse relationships.

Scenario 224 ANSWER: C, D, G

1. Options A and D: in many Trusts, the ward pharmacists can prescribe and change TTOs such as this. However, though this is convenient, it is not necessarily a clean way of doing things. It is your mistake and you should therefore ensure that you correct it. The best way to achieve that would be for you to represcribe the TTO in order to prevent patient discharge delays. Therefore Option D would be preferable to Option A.

2. Option B: explaining the mistake and apologising to the patient is not appropriate. It would only be necessary to do so if some medication had actually been given to the patient already (even if he hadn't reacted to it).

3. Options C and G: any mistake that you make as a doctor in training should be reflected upon to prevent it recurring in the future. A reflective journal is a good tool for it. Since you have made a mistake, which could potentially have affected patient care (you were lucky that the pharmacist spotted the problem), you will also need to complete a critical incident form. This will encourage the team to think about why the mistake was made and valuable lessons might be learnt from it. For example, the investigation may help identify the fact that allergies are not recorded prominently enough in the notes.

4. Options E and F: informing your seniors, though commendable, would not serve any purpose. The mistake has already been made so there is nothing they can do about it. You would only need to inform them if the drug had already been dispensed to the patient.

5. Option H: documenting the mistake in the patient notes will serve no purpose. A critical incident form will be a more effective way of recording the mistake.

Scenario 225 ANSWER: B, D, E

1. There is nothing illegal or unprofessional about relationships at work; the only criterion is that you must make sure that it doesn't impact on patient care (that could be the case if you keep arguing with each other or if you spend time together when you should be dealing with patients). In this scenario, you are told that he/she comes to help you once he/has com-

pleted his/her work so there is nothing to be concerned about. This rules out Option C (ending the relationship).

2. Options A, F, G and H are over the top unless patient care is affected, which is not suggested here.

3. This leaves Options B (accepting his/her help), E (helping him/her back) and D (Sitting down with him/her to agree how to manage the relationship within the work environment) as this will ensure that patient care is not affected in any way.

Scenario 226 ANSWER: B, D, H

1. One key point to bear in mind in such situation is that patient safety is only compromised if you comply with the ST6. As such:

- Option A is unsafe.

- Option F is pointless because it does not apply to the ST6's behaviour; you would only need to complete a critical incident form if YOU made a mistake because YOU had taken on a task that wasn't appropriate for your level of aptitude. There is no indication that you have done so.

- Option G is not quite correct, i.e. he is not directly compromising patient care; that would require compliance to his requests by you. You would be directly responsible for any mistakes made, though of course he would play a role in it by putting pressure on you. That is a heavy-handed approach and there are better options available.

2. The best thing to do would be to approach the ST6 again. The text mentions that you have already approached him once and he dismissed your concerns with some patronising comments. You might have caught him at a wrong time and it would be sensible to give him a chance to put things right (Option B). You would only consider involving the consultant (Option C) if you failed to address the matter directly with the ST6. You would also only consider raising the matter with medical personnel to initiate the bullying procedure (Option E) once your own attempts to resolve the problem directly with the ST6 have failed and once you have raised the issue with the consultant.

3. Sharing your concerns with the ST3 and asking for his guidance (Option D) is also appropriate. Indeed the ST3 will have a bit more knowledge and understanding of the problem than you. He may also be able to address the issue with the ST6. Perhaps he is also experiencing the same problem and you could meet with the ST6 together.

4. Discussing the matter with your medical defence organisation (Option H) is also appropriate. It does not tie you down to any particular approach but will ensure that you get external advice on a sensitive matter.

Scenario 227   ANSWER: B, D, E

1. Option A: the GMC states that, wherever possible, you should avoid treating yourself. Even though you are looking at headache medication here, that principle applies. In any case, stealing from the drugs trolley would not be very ethical. Based on the same principle, Option H is inappropriate too.

2. Options B and C: going to the local pharmacy to obtain some analgesia would be a viable option. Since your headache is just starting, you may be better off going yourself to have access to the medication as early as you can. Sending another doctor would not only delay the remedy, it would also deprive your unit of another doctor, with possible impact on patient care. Therefore Option B would be preferable to Option C.

3. Option D (faxing a request for a repeat prescription) would be a good idea to ensure that the situation does not recur.

4. Option E (asking someone to hold your bleep until your migraine settles) would be appropriate as it would enable the team to maintain patient safety and would enable you to recover before you can start seeing patients again.

5. Option F would take too long and A&E would not look on you kindly for wasting their time for analgesia.

6. Option G is the easy way out. You would only consider that if your headache was already in full bloom and you were unable to care for patients.

Scenario 228   ANSWER: C, D, E

1. You have a duty of care to this patient and, if she is at risk, then you can break patient confidentiality to protect her. In order to fracture a femur, a huge amount of force is required and, if her partner really has done this, she is potentially in great danger and would be classed as a "vulnerable adult". In an ideal world you would talk to the patient, gain her confidence and get her to agree to you talking to your senior colleague to enable both you and the patient to get support.

2. In this scenario, the patient is telling you that she doesn't want you to mention it to anyone else. In most cases, by "no one else", patients mean their family or institutions such as social services or the police. Since you are a junior doctor, you would be entitled to talk about the case with a senior member of the team. If, by chance, the patient said that she didn't want you to mention the abuse to anyone, including your team, then you would have a strong case for mentioning it to your team anyway on the basis that it is essential to her care. Therefore Options C and E are appropriate.

3. It will be important that the conversation is documented properly. The notes are a legal document and may be used in a court of law of evidence where required. Documenting the abuse would also be beneficial to the patient should she be admitted at a later date with other symptoms. As such it would benefit her care. You should only leave out of the notes anything which is totally irrelevant. However, it would be good practice to make sure the patient understands why you are documenting the information and, in this case, reassuring the patient that no one else will see the notes without her consent is crucial. Therefore Option D is appropriate.

4. Option A: you cannot agree to keep the secret when the patient is at such risk of harm. It is possible that you may end up not breaching her confidentiality, but it would not be wise to promise that you won't.

5. Option F is not appropriate. You should not leave anything out of the notes. Option G is even worse. Calling the police (Option B) may happen eventually but there are more suitable answers.

6. Option H is problematic. The GP may be able to keep an eye on the patient's well-being but that would pretty much rely on the patient actually visiting the GP on a regular basis. If the patient is being abused, the GP should be able to spot it without your help, particularly if there is a large

degree of violence. A bigger problem with this option though is that you are telling the patient that you will share the information with the GP straight after she has told you that you must tell no one else. It is one thing sharing the information with your consultant (part of the same team) and quite another to share the information with an external colleague. By itself, this is not a stupid idea at all but if you wanted to do that you really ought to put the idea past the patient first so that she agrees to it, instead of imposing it onto her in such difficult circumstances.

Scenario 229 ANSWER: A, C, G

1. The bottom line is that you should try your utmost to avoid placing yourself in situations where you are or are perceived to be in breach of duty. In principle, it may be acceptable in some circumstances for a doctor to be-friend a patient once the patient is no longer under their care (for example if you met that patient in a bar by chance 5 years after they had been dis-charged and you had never seen them since). But in many cases if there was a complaint made to the GMC about the friendship or relationship, it would be hard to prove that there was nothing untoward. Some could ar-gue that your friendship developed whilst they were under your care, that you abused their trust or their vulnerability, etc. As such, you should be as transparent as possible and be strict with yourself. Therefore, refusing the patient's number (Option A) and reporting the approach to your consultant (Option C) will be appropriate in the circumstances. Reporting the issue to someone else is particularly important to cover yourself. Indeed one might envisage situations where the patient, angry that you refused their ap-proach, starts spreading rumours that you were inappropriate towards them, etc.

2. In such situations it would be important not to play along with the patient and to nip the problem in the bud at an early stage. Being nice but firm to-wards the patient will be essential (Option G).

3. Option B (taking the number) is not by itself unethical but it gives the wrong impression to the patient and potentially to your colleagues too. It would be best to refuse the number, but if you felt that the patient would be very distraught by your refusal, you may consider in some circum-stances taking the number, being non-committal towards the patient and then throwing the number away as soon as the patient has left the room.

In this scenario, there is no indication that the patient would be greatly harmed by your refusal and so there are better options to consider

4. Option D (meeting the patient once they are discharged): you would find it hard to prove that their care was not affected by your friendship and so this is an inappropriate answer.

5. Option E (telling the patient their approach is unethical): it is not their approach that is unethical – the patient is not bound by any code of ethics. It would be your acceptance that would be unethical.

6. Option F: telling the patient that you can't but that you were tempted is inappropriate because you are declaring your feelings for the patient and are only encouraging them.

7. Option H: documenting that the patient has mental health issues is not appropriate for several reasons: (i) the fact they like you doesn't mean that they have a mental illness, (ii) the patient could potentially request access to their notes under the Data Protection Act and they would be very angry to see such remarks about them in the notes, (iii) if you thought they had mental health issues, you should do something about it and not just document it. What you should document are the facts but not your judgements. Documenting the conversation would be appropriate, but not much more.

Scenario 230 ANSWER: A, C, E

1. You have a duty of care even when you are not at work and the medical defence organisations do cover you medico legally for "Good Samaritan" acts. As with any collapse situation, you should follow BLS/ALS guidelines.

SAFE approach

Shout for help (Option A)

Approach with care (Option C)

Free from danger (also covered by Option C)

Evaluate the patient (Option E)

2. Option B is not appropriate as you have a duty of care even outside of work.

3. Option D would be a possible option but only if you didn't have a phone with you. Option A would lead to a faster response from the emergency services.

4. Option F would seriously delay the care the man is receiving as he would receive no care during transportation. Moving the man may also harm him. Calling the emergency services would be more effective and safer.

5. Option G is a luxury but would achieve little with regard to caring for the man.

6. Option H would place you in dereliction of duty. As a doctor you have a duty of care.

Scenario 231 ANSWER: A, E, F

This is a situation where the registrar is cutting corners and you have a duty to challenge him if necessary, though of course you should do this in a sensitive but effective manner.

1. Option A (telling the registrar that all options should be tried) is the right thing to do. All that is needed is to make sure you can find someone who can translate properly. This option does not say that you won't help; it just says that you won't help until all options have been exhausted.

2. Options E and F will ensure that the registrar is aware of your position and that he has a proactive proposal to remedy the situation quickly. Those two options together are better than Option D (contacting the translators and seeking the consent yourself) because (i) the consent is best taken by the person who performs the procedure and knows the procedure best (as such, your own attempt at seeking consent may be insufficient too) and (ii) you want to try your best not to undermine your colleague. Therefore encouraging him to do the right thing is better in the short term than overriding the situation.

3. Option B will not achieve much since the consultant won't be able to do much more than putting pressure on the registrar over the phone. It is not

necessarily a bad idea but the combination of A, E and F will be more effective. In particular your own refusal to assist unless consent is sought may be enough to prompt the registrar to do the right thing.

4. Option C: there would be legal implications in intervening without consent.

5. Option G (completing a critical incident form) is not the most immediate or appropriate action to take. It may be a suitable action to take if the registrar persists in being stubborn, but there are more important things to worry about first. In any case, calling the consultant would be more appropriate than completing a critical incident form.

6. Option H (asking the nurse to find a replacement) is pretty much pointless. She is not going to walk around the hospital to find someone else who speaks the same language. There is an easier and faster option: talking to the official translators.

Scenario 232 ANSWER: A, C, E

1. Option D is not acceptable. The fact that the mistake has had no impact on the final outcome does not mean that you do not have to act.

2. In such a situation, the consultant (who is ultimately responsible for the patient) should be informed. A critical incident form should also be completed, as it is a mistake that could have been avoided with better processes in place. An investigation into the process will be required to determine where it went wrong and how future occurrences can be prevented. Option A is therefore the most suitable option. Option B can be dismissed because you should not wait until mistakes have been made several times to raise the issue and/or take corrective action.

3. Informing senior Trust managers (Option G) is not strictly relevant unless there is a serious risk of the Trust's being sued as a result of the mistake (in which case it would be important for the Trust's lawyers to be informed as soon as possible). If the relatives threaten to sue, for example, then you would need to go to your Clinical Director as soon as possible so that he can involve the relevant managers. In the context of this particular scenario we are not told of any particular threat and the relevant Trust authorities will be informed via the critical incident form, which should be enough given the circumstances. In any case, there are more suitable options to consider.

4. Informing the rest of the team (Option C) is an important factor because they will need to learn as individuals from the situation. It will not have any impact on the patient who died but the team will become a lot more aware of the type of issues that can arise. They can then play an important role in implementing changes within the team to make sure that such a mistake does not recur.

5. Options E and F both raise the issue of talking to the relatives. The options imply that the consultant was not present at the time of the incident and the scenario states explicitly that the relatives are upset (though we are not sure whether they are upset only because of the death of the patient or because they became aware that a mistake was made). Waiting until the consultant comes back could take a while and it would be careless to let the relatives wait around for any length of time. If there are sensitive issues to discuss, you could always let them know that you would like to talk to your consultant before going into detail but, in the absence of the consultant, you will need to meet with the relatives sooner rather than later (unless, of course, there is an ST5 around, say, but this is not an option here). Option E is therefore more appropriate than Option F.

6. Option H (throwing the DNR order in the bin) would most likely get you struck off.

Scenario 233 ANSWER: C, F, H

1. Option A would only be an option if you felt that you were being bullied (in which case hospital procedures may indicate that you should complain either to a senior colleague or to Human Resources). However, there are many routes that you can take before making a formal complaint. The question suggests that this perceived overly severe tone of the consultant is a one-off incident or a first occurrence. If it had suggested that it happened frequently then A would be a possible appropriate action; but in the absence of more details, we can leave it out.

2. Option B is inappropriate because this is a matter between the consultant and you. By complaining to a senior nurse you are seeking support from someone who will not want to interfere in this hierarchy and who really has nothing to do with the problem. At best she can have a word with the consultant but the consultant will feel aggrieved that you have involved people who are unrelated to the incident.

3. Option C encourages you to think properly about your actions before going ahead. This should certainly feature in the list of appropriate actions. Generally, in conflict situations, it is best to step out and think with a clear head.

4. Option D is the "tit-for-tat" response and will only inflame the situation. Your consultant probably does not realise that he has been out of order and therefore any attempt to respond in a similar manner will achieve nothing. Besides, sorting out the problem in front of the patient is not the best solution. Your consultant will never forgive you for embarrassing him.

5. Option E not only involves the patient in a conflict, which is really none of their concern, but you are also undermining the consultant's credibility. This is one of the worst actions that you can take in the circumstances. If you need to involve a third party, make sure it is someone who can actually help resolve the problem. The patient is not one of them.

6. Option F is a sensible course of action. If you have a problem with someone, talk to him or her. It may not be a nice meeting but at least they will know how you feel and they may even learn something about themselves in the process. This is the best approach to regaining a sensible working relationship with the consultant and you may find that he respects you for this.

7. Option G is fundamentally inappropriate. To complete a critical incident form, there needs to be a critical incident, i.e. an incident that had or could have had an impact on patient care. The team must be able to learn from the incident so that a concrete solution can be implemented to prevent future occurrences. Critical incident forms do not deal with personality issues unless they lead to behaviours which compromise patient care.

8. Involving your education supervisor (Option H) is one of your preferred options, for three reasons: (i) he is responsible for your education and the incident was part of the educational process; (ii) he is a consultant and part of your hierarchy; (iii) he is in a position to intervene or provide advice at a relevant level.

Scenario 234 ANSWER: B, C, D

1. Option B: if a patient is refusing to listen to the facts then you should establish why that is the case. You would then be able to find a way to communicate the information that suits the patient's needs. Without being able to provide the patient with sufficient information, her consent will not be valid so your first step will be to ensure you can get to a point where you can give her some information. Asking the patient if it would be okay to involve her relatives is a good idea. It may be that she is scared and needs someone she can trust at her side in order to make her decision. Since you are asking for her consent to involve the relatives, there is no issue of breach of confidentiality. Therefore Option B is appropriate.

2. Option C: every important conversation with patients should be recorded in the notes, and even more so if there are legal implications. Therefore Option C will be appropriate.

3. Option D is key to the whole scenario. She will need to be given relevant and sufficient information by someone who knows about the procedure in order for her consent to be valid.

4. With regard to the other options:

   - Option A: the fact that the operation was deemed to be in the patient's best interest is no reason for imposing it onto her (you would only consider that if the patient was not competent). She has given verbal consent but the consent is not informed and therefore you are not in a position to establish whether she fully understands the situation. As such, the consent is not valid.

   - Option E: the consent is not valid as she is not in full possession of the facts.

   - Option F is not appropriate because the consent she has given is not valid and so recording that she has given verbal consent will be misleading as your colleagues will assume she has done so with the full knowledge of the facts. You will need to record the whole context and not just the consent.

   - Option G goes directly against the patient's wishes. What might sound inoffensive to you may sound differently to the patient.

- Option H (encouraging the patient to lie and thereafter doing a procedure on a competent patient without consent) is highly unethical.

Scenario 235   ANSWER: E, F, G

The husband seems to be frustrated by the secretary's behaviour more than the fact that his wife is not around. Your role in this situation is to ensure that you are constructive and sensitive in the way you handle the situation.

1. The department has a zero tolerance policy; however, it doesn't necessarily mean that you have to apply it strictly if some key boundaries haven't been breached. At the end of the day, if you ban him from visiting his wife, this will most certainly have an impact on her too and therefore you won't have acted in her best interest. Options A and B are at the more extreme end of the scale. It would be much better to calm him down and keep him occupied. A combination of Option E (telling him that his wife won't be long and asking him to wait patiently) and Option G (asking another secretary to give him a cup of tea) would do that well.

2. Option D is actually giving the husband some information about his wife's care, i.e. that she is having a scan done, and so is breaching confidentiality. So that option is out.

3. Option C (informing him of previous complaints) is not appropriate. First of all, it's none of his business and, secondly, it further undermines the secretary at a time when she probably needs support. This will leave the husband with a worse feeling towards the secretary and the team, and would make him question why she hasn't been sacked. It would actually fuel his anger. Option F is more appropriate because it acknowledges his comments and therefore reassures him that he has been listened to. But at the same time, you are providing a rebuke of his behaviour, in a softer way than would have been achieved through Options A and B.

4. Option H (telling the secretary to get her act together) is a tempting proposition and it may well be what needs to be done at some stage, albeit in a more sensitive manner and a more appropriate setting. In any case, it is not your role to tell her off or discipline her. It would be more appropriate for you to report your concerns to the person who is hierarchically in charge of the secretary.

Scenario 236 ANSWER: A, C, F

1. As part of a team, it is important that you show some flexibility in your relationship with your colleagues, particularly if they have requests that are not unreasonable. Do to others, as you would want others to do for you! However, this is of course dependent on ensuring that patient safety is not compromised. Option D (insisting that he stays) seems harsh in a context where all the jobs have been done and this is a special occasion, particularly if:

   - he has checked that everything has indeed been done (Option F);
   - a senior has cleared it (Option A);
   - you take his bleep (Option C).

2. Option E (contacting Medical Staffing) is pointless since it will take time and they will only tell you to clear the matter with a senior colleague (which is Option A).

3. Option B (letting him slip away) shows the greatest flexibility on your part, but it is not very safe. What if the ST5 needs to get hold of him urgently? Also, one of your seniors may have had plans for him, thinking that he would be around; therefore it would be best practice to let someone senior know.

4. Option G (redirecting his bleep to the on-call doctor) is unsafe, as the on call hasn't even started. In any case, if you take the responsibility to let your colleague go then you should take the problems that come with it, i.e. you should take the bleep yourself.

5. Option H is a bit far-fetched. Technically speaking it is correct that there will be a lower level of cover. However, the team should be able to deal with the unexpected in the absence of a junior colleague. This is just an attempt to make the colleague feel guilty.

6. In this context, options A, C and F seem the most logical options to choose.

Scenario 237 ANSWER: B, D, E

1. Adult pornography is not illegal. However, it would certainly be seen by both patients and staff as very unprofessional to watch it in any workplace environment, particularly a hospital, where patients can become exposed to it. Your colleague is acting unprofessionally by watching it in an inappropriate place. He is going against hospital policy, but in many ways that is his problem more than yours. However, it is likely to become a real problem if it starts to offend others, particularly patients.

2. Because watching adult pornography is not actually illegal, the simplest thing to do would be to give the ST3 a gentle warning. Hence Option B is one of the most suitable options. The issue of patient safety also cannot be ignored and therefore Option E is appropriate too.

3. Option G (contacting the police) is irrelevant since what your colleague is doing is not illegal. Option C (confronting him as a group) is just an unnecessary act of public humiliation. If possible, you should take a tactful approach.

4. Options A and F might become appropriate actions at a later stage, but in any case they would need to be initiated by a senior colleague rather than you. It is not for you to make such decisions.

5. Option H is not only ridiculous and a waste of your and his time, it will also ensure he never has a rest and so could affect patient safety. The situation calls for a more long-term solution.

6. This leaves us with Option D (talking to the consultant if it happens too often), which seems a sensible thing to do. If you have real concerns about someone's professionalism because of the way they act then you should feel free to approach a senior colleague about it. The consultant may act or not, but at least you have raised the issue. Working your way through the hierarchy, of course, you would tactfully raise the problem with the ST3 first before going to the consultant.

Scenario 238   ANSWER: A, C, D

The simplest approach is to proceed by elimination:

1. Option G (filling out the critical incident form) is not an immediate answer to dealing with someone who is washed out. You should complete a form whenever a critical incident occurs (not just the next time), regardless of how tired the doctor is. In any case, by the time you complete the form and it gets processed, he will have had plenty of time to make other mistakes. As such this would only be an appropriate answer if there were no other suitable options. Option H is even less appropriate since completing a critical incident form should take place whenever an incident has occurred, regardless of whether it caused patient harm. Near misses also qualify.

2. Option F (contacting Occupational Health) is also ineffective. Firstly, if you are going to contact someone about it, it should be one of your seniors. Secondly, Occupational Health is not responsible for that FY2 so they would not be able to do much. It would be more appropriate to advise the FY2 to go to Occupational Health of his own free will so that they can discuss how he may be able to deal with stress and fatigue; but it is really not your place to inform them.

3. Option E (finding a locum through Medical Staffing) should not be your decision. If a locum is required to relieve the pressure on the FY2 then finding one should be done through the proper channels, as a result of a discussion between your FY2 and his seniors. You are interfering.

4. You are now left with A, B, C and D. They are all possible candidates for selection, but you need to eliminate one of them. Option B stands out because it's comparatively harsh and unsupportive. If the FY2 ends up actually placing patient safety at risk then you may resort to discussing the situation with the consultant, but you should aim to achieve this without resorting to threats and by showing that you are available to support him.

5. The best way to deal with the situation is to express your concerns to the FY2 (Option A), provide support by discussing with him the possibility of taking on some of his work (Option C) and encouraging him to talk to the consultant (Option D).

Scenario 239 ANSWER: A, B, G

1. This question tests your integrity. If you have made a mistake then you must own up to it, whether it has any consequences or not. Option A is the most honest answer. You will just have to bite the bullet. Option B ensures that a senior colleague is informed and that the right course of action is being followed. Option G ensures that the team can learn from the incident.

2. Option C is not safe, as you simply cannot wait until the patient has a reaction to the drug in order to take any action.

3. Option D shows that you are being honest with your team but you must also tell the patient if you have injected them with the wrong product, even if this means taking the consequences (hence why Option A is the highest-ranking option).

4. Option E attempts to minimise the stress on the patient; but it is dishonest. It is NOT a procedure that is sometimes carried out; it is just a mistake that sometimes happens.

5. Option F blames the nurse. Whoever brought the wrong product, you are the one who injected it so you must take responsibility for your mistake. If there is a problem with the nurse then you can sort it out later with her but do not involve the patient in such interpersonal staff matters. This will look unprofessional and can reduce the patient's confidence in the medical team.

6. Option H is not appropriate because if you have made a mistake you should admit to it whether the patient asks or not.

Scenario 240 ANSWER: A, B, D

1. Your role is to support the secretary in getting the issue resolved but not necessarily to resolve it <u>for</u> her. Hence, encouraging the secretary to check the staff manual (Option A) and encouraging her to report the matter to her seniors (Option B) would be appropriate.

2. Alternatively, she could also approach the HR department about it; it would not be your place to do it for her. Therefore Option F is not the most suitable.

3. There will be little value in confronting the consultant directly about the issue, as it is openly antagonistic, so Option C is not the most appropriate course of action here. Such message should come from someone higher up than him and your role is to try to get the system to deal with it, as it is an ongoing problem.

4. Option G essentially publicly humiliates the consultant in question and is also unlikely to lead to any substantial result. Approaching another senior colleague (Option D) would be more constructive as it enables the senior team to become aware of the problem and to find a suitable, less hostile, way of approaching the consultant.

5. Contacting the GMC (Option E) should be resisted unless the situation has reached such proportions that the local procedures cannot handle it. (Were that to be the case, of course, the decision to refer to the GMC would not be yours to take in any case.) It would thus not feature as one of the "most appropriate" options in such a situation.

6. Option H (asking another secretary to offer support), by itself, it not a bad option. However, all it does is spread the information around and involve another party when the secretary who is being harassed may prefer to keep things confidential. In this option you are imposing on someone else to become involved (thereby putting the other secretary in a difficult position too). It would be more judicious to simply ask the secretary who is being harassed if there is someone in the team she could confide in rather than impose it onto her.

Scenario 241 ANSWER: D, F, G

Hepatitis C is only an issue if he is performing procedures that expose his patients to risk. This makes D one of the appropriate actions.

1. Option A is not appropriate because, even if you notice that your colleague is performing high-risk procedures, you should report the matter to one of your senior colleagues and not to Personnel/Medical Staffing.

2. Option B is impossible, as a vaccine against Hepatitis C virus does not currently exist.

3. Option C is not appropriate because you would not report to a senior unless your colleague has been performing high-risk procedures (D).

4. Option E is not appropriate because it is not the role of the senior sister to spy on your colleague. She is not responsible for his actions.

5. F and G are both appropriate because they encourage your colleague to take responsibility for the situation, to seek advice from appropriate sources and to raise the matter himself with senior colleagues so the team can identify how to deal with the issue.

6. Option H: it is possible that Occupational Health may need to be involved, but it would not be your responsibility to inform them. It is more likely that your colleague will need to go and see them of his own accord once he has discussed the situation with his senior colleagues.

Scenario 242 ANSWER: A, B, D

This situation is tricky because on one hand you can see that the nurse is clearly painful to work with, and on the other hand you are new enough in the department to see the problem without prejudice and maybe make a difference by handling properly.

1. Option A: asking the nurse to discuss the matter with the ward sister would be an appropriate thing to do as the ward sister would be responsible for that nurse and she should therefore really be dealing with it. It is likely that the nurse either sees the ward sister as part of the problem or has not dared approach her in the past. But nevertheless, making her aware that this is the right course of action might prompt her to do something about it.

2. Option B: an informal but private discussion with two individuals who have the power to deal with it would be appropriate. They may well be aware that the nurse is painful to work with, but they may not have the insight into how she feels and into the animosity that has developed towards the nurse within the team.

3. Option D: the nurse trusts you with her problem so it would be appropriate to at least give her an opportunity to tell her story, but 5 minutes clearly won't be enough for it. Option D is a good option for that as she will be getting some immediate attention, whilst allowing you not to neglect your duties towards your patients.

4. With regard to the other options:

- Option C: emailing all doctors might make you look a bit naïve. They are well aware of the issue, as the question suggests, so your email would feel patronising. If you were to address the problem with other doctors, you would need to do this face to face so that you can relate to them the emotions of the situation. Sending an email would also most likely just fuel more gossip and prejudices. Option B would be better.

- Option E: it would be inappropriate to prioritise the nurse's problems over the care of your patients and to make one of your colleagues pay for it; so Option E (asking a colleague to cover for you) would not feature in the final list. That option would be more appropriate if the issue was urgent or serious but, in this case, there is no major rush and you will serve the nurse's interests better by making her wait for a suitable time when you give her your full attention – like after work.

- Option F is not a bad option but it is a bit defeatist. In a way, Option A achieves the same thing but has a more proactive feel to it.

- Option G: though it is entirely correct that she should complete incident forms if doctors' actions delay patient care and patients suffer, you don't actually need to remind her of it and this is slightly over the top. This is encouraging the nurse to take her revenge on doctors instead of dealing with the more complex problem of interpersonal relationships. It will actually make her look more painful in everyone's eyes and may aggravate the problem.

- Option H is playing right into her hands, allowing her to add one more complaint to her list and blaming you for being just as bad as the others. Though you may have a perfectly valid point, from a communication perspective this wouldn't be the most judicious approach as you would probably worsen the problem.

Scenario 243 ANSWER: A, B, F

1. There are two issues to deal with here: the mother's fears and the son's possible HIV status. In this situation your patient will be the son, not the mother. Your actions should therefore reflect that, whilst obviously trying to deal with the mother's situation at the same time.

2. We are told she believes her son to be gay, though he denies it. He could be denying it because it isn't true or because, at the age of 15, he doesn't feel that it is something that he can readily confess to his mother, especially if she demonstrates the sort of prejudice that she has shown when entering your clinic room. As such it would be most appropriate to talk to the son alone; so Option F is appropriate.

3. Your main concern will be to ascertain whether there is anything to worry about and therefore taking a sexual history from the boy will help you understand if he has been exposed to a risk. Therefore Option A will also be very appropriate.

4. Option B (giving the mother some leaflets on HIV) would be a good idea as it will allow the mother to educate herself on the topic and possibly realise she has overreacted. Option D (performing the test) is also a valid option but would only be done if there had been exposure to risk. It does not have to be done straight away, particularly if the visit was prompted by the mother's fears rather than the son's free will.

Since there is no strong clinical case for HIV testing other than the mother's fears and that, so far, none of the options selected addressed her concerns, offering her some leaflets on HIV would go some way towards educating her; and making yourself available for more questions would be a nice thing to do.

If, following the sexual history, you felt an HIV test was appropriate you could either do the test at the practice if it is available there or refer the patient to a GUM clinic. Unless the patient had been put at risk very recently, there would be no major urgency to do the test (meaning it could wait a few more days – and certainly it may be best to do the test when the mother is not around if you want to avoid any hysterics). Therefore Option B would be more appropriate than Option D.

5. Looking at the other options:

- Option C (telling the mother the son is unlikely to have HIV) is simply wrong. HIV is a possibility at any age and younger people are in fact more likely to engage in risky behaviours.

- Option E (telling the mother she is overreacting) would be patronising and insensitive. Maybe her instincts are correct. You just don't know.

- Option G breaches the son's confidentiality and is therefore out of the running on that basis.

- Option H is very judgemental. You have no right to impose your values onto patients. Whether the mother thinks that being gay is a problem or not is not so much the issue here. She is clearly worried about something and your job is to explore her concerns and deal with them, not to lecture her.

Scenario 244 ANSWER: C, D, F

1. It is not appropriate for the nurse to issue prescriptions pre-signed by another doctor. It is in fact not appropriate either for the registrar to pre-sign prescriptions for patients he hasn't seen. Such practice poses a risk to patient safety (and even more so if the nurse has not yet achieved her prescription status) and as such you should refuse to sign the pad. Hence Option C would be more suitable than Options A and B.

2. The registrar is most likely in breach of duty and therefore you would have reason to suspect that there are fitness issues. It may be appropriate to talk to the registrar about it and, had he been around, you might have wanted to have a word with him on the matter (this would make Option E suitable). However, regardless of whether you talk to him or not, the GMC's *Good Medical Practice* imposes that you should raise your concerns with a senior colleague; you will therefore need to report the matter to a senior colleague. Option D should therefore be in the list.

3. In this situation, we know that many patients have received prescriptions which may not be totally appropriate. It may be over the top to recall each patient (Option G) but, in the interest of patient safety, all patients seen by the nurse would need to have their notes reviewed so that you can identify

whether any need to be seen again. As an FY1, asking her to provide the list of patients would help you show some proactivity in addressing patient safety issues. So Option F is also suitable.

4. Option H (praising the nurse and offering support) is inappropriate in this context. Something wrong is going on and the situation should be dealt with. You will in fact need to explain to her that remedial action needs to be taken. Option H is either providing false reassurance to the nurse or is misguided. Either way, it is inappropriate.

5. We are therefore left with a shortlist of four options: C, D, E, F. Out of those, Option E (addressing the matter with the registrar when he comes back) is the least useful in the short term. Although it would be good practice, it does not address the issue at all, whereas the other three options are essential ingredients to make sure the problem is fully addressed and corrected immediately. The consultants can then have a word with the registrar when he gets back from holiday.

Scenario 245   ANSWER: A, E, C

1. In such a situation, despite the fact that no harm has come to the patient, you will need to be honest. Part of your communication with the patient will involve reassuring him that no harm was done and that you will make sure the team learns from the incident. Therefore Option A should feature in the answer.

2. There is, however, a more immediate need to ensure that no other patient is being given out-of-date antibiotics; so checking the drug cupboard straight away would be an appropriate thing to do (Option E).

3. All other options refer to different means of reflecting and learning from the incident:

   - Because the mistake was made by the nurse, it would make sense if she was involved in completing the critical incident form and so Option C (getting the nurse to do it) would be better than Option F (doing it yourself).

   - Getting the nurse to complete an incident form (Option C) would also be better than reporting the incident to the ward sister (Options B and D). The incident form will raise the matter to the attention of the relevant team members anyway, and overall it is better if the steps are taken by the nurse herself rather than for you to report the matter behind her back.

- Option G: sending an email to other doctors won't deal with other members of the team, e.g. nurses. It would be more effective to do an incident form so that proper procedures are implemented for everyone.

- Option H is inappropriate as the trigger for a critical incident form will be the fact that a mistake was made, and not the fact that a patient was harmed. Critical incident forms are designed to ensure that lessons are learnt from mistakes. In this case, you just happened to be lucky that no harm was caused to the patient. There are still lessons to be learnt.

Scenario 246 ANSWER: A, B, C

1. Potentially, the patient is asking you to help her to commit insurance fraud, so there is absolutely no way you would delete the information from the notes. In addition, erasing all mentions of drug taking from the note may compromise any future care given to the patient and is potentially harmful. That means that D and E are not suitable and that C is suitable. If you ever received a court order asking to see the notes, your integrity would be questioned if it was revealed that you had deleted important information.

2. Option A is appropriate because, unless the patient has consented, you will not be able to give any information to the insurance company. The insurance company may subsequently refuse to give the patient any cover but this will be the patient's problem for refusing to give consent in the first place.

3. Option B is appropriate as, although you may never get consent from the patient to reveal information, you should always notify her whenever you are considering breaching confidentiality. Making this clear will reassure the patient without compromising your integrity. In reality, you would not seek to breach the patient's confidentiality voluntarily in this case. But you can envisage a scenario whereby the insurance company seeks a court

order to obtain medical information (e.g. to check on a claim), in which case you would be forced to reveal any information the court order is asking for. Saying otherwise would mislead the patient.

4. Option F is not correct. Unless you have the patient's consent, you cannot reveal the information. Saying the opposite to the patient would just be telling a lie and would be unethical.

5. Option G would be suitable only if you contacted the insurance company without naming the patient, i.e. as a general enquiry on a no-name basis.

6. Option H is not appropriate. The full patient history is essential to the notes and the patient care. The fact she stopped taking drugs would not make her past history of drug-abuse less relevant. Generally speaking, it is highly inappropriate to delete anything from patient notes.

7. The three most suitable options are therefore A, B and C.

Scenario 247   ANSWER: C, D, F

1. Option A (informing the GMC) is not wrong but it is a little premature (it will not be immediate or in the short term). Calling the GMC may come at a much later stage if the colleague presents a real danger to patients. For the time being, all we know is that a bag of marijuana has fallen out of his bag.

2. Option B (calling the police) is just as bad as Option A. If the police need to be called, it will be by a hospital manager or someone in charge after initial investigation (also not immediate). You are hardly going to get on the phone to the police as soon as you see the bag.

3. Option E (keep quiet if he flushes the drugs away) is a bit naïve. Of course he will give you his reassurance. He might even tell you it was planted there by a vindictive love rival. Telling him that you will keep quiet if he gets rid of the evidence is unacceptable anyway. The problem needs to be looked into because there is a possibility that it may impact on patient safety; so you cannot ignore it.

4. Option G (critical incident form) is pointless here since there has not been a critical incident. This would not address the safety aspect or the need to

resolve your colleague's drug problems. It would only serve to raise awareness of the problem to senior colleagues, something which can be done in a more sensitive, more effective and less public manner via Option F, i.e. informing the ST3.

5. Option H (reporting the issue to the Clinical Director) is a bit strong, though not entirely inappropriate; however, there are other people between you and the Clinical Director and you should use them, particularly if they are present in other options – for example, a consultant (Option F).

6. This leaves us with the three correct options, which are also the most sensible ones. Option D (discussing the issue with your colleague) should really be your starting point. Because of the possible impact on patient safety you ought to discuss the matter with a senior colleague whom you can trust (Option F – the consultant) and, as both friend and doctor, you would be wise to advise your colleague to seek help before his drug problem escalates (Option C).

Scenario 248   ANSWER: B, C, G

1. Option G (asking the consultant to go home and paying for a taxi) will ensure that he does not see patients that day and that he gets back home safely.

2. Option C: the consultant shows little insight into the fact that he is drunk and that he is not fit to see patients (otherwise he wouldn't have turned up for work) and you would need to raise the issue with a senior colleague. In this situation, you would need to go to a colleague who can actually do something about the problem. Going to another consultant (Option C) would therefore be more appropriate than going to a registrar (Option E) who would only pass the message on to a consultant anyway or would ignore the matter.

3. Option B: since the consultant is "obviously" drunk there is a chance that the clinic may need to be cancelled. At the very least, some of the appointments will need to be cancelled while others will be honoured by other doctors. The wording here is quite vague ("Discuss cancelling the clinic session"), which makes it appropriate. If the wording had been stronger (such as "Tell the manager to cancel the clinic") then it may not

have been appropriate as you might have needed to consider alternatives first.

4. With regard to the other options:

- Option A: going to the GMC will be a little premature without any kind of preliminary investigation and without giving the consultant an opportunity to change. The matter should be first handled at local level and only escalated to GMC level by your seniors if the consultant continues to present a danger to patients despite efforts to resolve the situation. At your level, your concern should be to ensure that someone senior to you whom you can trust is aware of the situation (hence why C is appropriate). You would only ever consider going to the GMC yourself if none of your seniors acted appropriately in relation to the matter at hand.

- Options D and F are all unacceptable. If the consultant is "obviously" drunk, there is no way that you would allow him to see patients, whether you are with him or he is with a chaperone; and certainly not on his own. Not only is it likely to attract complaints from patients, it may also make them lose faith in the Trust. You could get sacked for letting this happen.

- Option H is involving patients in the problem for no reason. To be fair, it may result in a safer situation for the patients as, at least, they won't be exposed to the risk of being seen by someone drunk. But it will seriously affect the trust they have in the doctors in your service and will seriously undermine your consultant's credibility. It would be a very unprofessional approach.

Scenario 249 ANSWER: C, D, F

1. The situation has been going on for a week but it doesn't mean that it will become a permanent problem. It may be for example linked to train problems or temporary childcare issues. The first thing to do will therefore be to discuss the issue directly with your colleague (Option C).

2. Because her delay is affecting your workload and therefore has a potential impact on patient care, you would also need to ensure that a senior colleague is informed. He may be able to deal with the matter more effec-

tively than you will (Option F). In the meantime it will be essential that you compensate for your colleague's absence by working harder to ensure that patients are safe and their care is not neglected (Option D).

3. With regard to the other options:

- Option A: she may have personal problems but talking to her husband would be inappropriate. You should talk to her personally (Option C).

-
- Option B is more like a dressing-down ("express your discontent"), which could potentially result in conflict.

- Option E: if there is a problem to discuss, you should discuss first with other junior colleagues or a senior colleague but not with the nurses. Your colleague is not reporting to the nurses and there is little they will be in a position to do about the issue.

- Option G: doing nothing is never an option unless it is really none of your business or unless the other options are obviously worse than doing nothing (e.g. unsafe). In this particular option, you decide to do nothing because you think someone else will notice the issue. This means that you prefer to keep quiet, hoping that it will become some-one else's problem. Imagine the consequences if your colleague's lateness contributed one day to the death of a patient. In a situation where patient care is potentially affected by the delay, you simply cannot afford to ignore the matter

- Option H: you would only complete a critical incident form if patient care had been compromised because of her absence. There is no indication of that for the moment.

Scenario 250 ANSWER: A, B, E

1. Option A: you are using the skills and expertise of another team member appropriately; the nurse is already with the relatives and it makes sense that you may want to know more about the relatives' request in order to ensure that you can have the relevant information ready when you do eventually meet with them.

2. Option B: although this may inconvenience the relatives, as they would obviously prefer to get answers straight away, you are nonetheless being honest with them and demonstrating that you want to get their queries resolved, even if it is only by phone.

3. Option E: talking to your ST3 may help you identify a good way around the problem. Also, if you need to go and see the relatives, then pursuing this option will make your superior aware of the situation and your team will be better able to deal with your temporary absence.

4. With regard to the other options:

   • Option C: while a possibility, this is potentially placing your colleague in a difficult situation; it also looks like you are trying to pass the buck.

   • Option D: this places the nurse in a difficult position.

   • Option F: this may seem like a good tactic in the short term but is actually unhelpful: PALS won't be able to deal with the relatives' queries, and will merely encourage the relatives to contact you again, thus prolonging the problem. In any case, you should consider it part of your duty to deal with the relatives, particularly if you have been dealing with the patient before his death.

   • Option G: this is rude both to the relatives and to the nurse, whom you will place in a difficult position.

   • Option H: asking the relatives to contact the consultant is not a very proactive and supportive thing to do. First of all, it is placing the onus on the relatives to contact the consultant when you should make sure the consultant contacts them. Secondly it is ignoring their feelings and, thirdly, it is making the nurse take the blame by imposing that she should be the messenger. Overall one of the worst answers for team playing.